D0626860

# GLOBALIZATION
# AND AMERICAN
# POPULAR CULTURE

# GLOBALIZATION

*Series Editors*

**Manfred B. Steger**
*Royal Melbourne Institute of Technology
and University of Hawai'i–Mānoa*

**Terrell Carver**
*University of Bristol*

"Globalization" has become *the* buzzword of our time. But what does it mean? Rather than forcing a complicated social phenomenon into a single analytical framework, this series seeks to present globalization as a multidimensional process constituted by complex, often contradictory interactions of global, regional, and local aspects of social life. Since conventional disciplinary borders and lines of demarcation are losing their old rationales in a globalizing world, authors in this series apply an interdisciplinary framework to the study of globalization. In short, the main purpose and objective of this series is to support subject-specific inquiries into the dynamics and effects of contemporary globalization and its varying impacts across, between, and within societies.

Supported by the Globalization Research Center at the University of Hawai'i–Mānoa

# GLOBALIZATION AND AMERICAN POPULAR CULTURE

## LANE CROTHERS

### THIRD EDITION

ROWMAN & LITTLEFIELD PUBLISHERS, INC.

*Lanham • Boulder • New York • Toronto • Plymouth, UK*

Published by Rowman & Littlefield Publishers, Inc.
A wholly owned subsidiary of The Rowman & Littlefield Publishing Group, Inc.
4501 Forbes Boulevard, Suite 200, Lanham, Maryland 20706
www.rowman.com

10 Thornbury Road, Plymouth PL6 7PP, United Kingdom

Copyright © 2013 by Rowman & Littlefield Publishers, Inc.

*All rights reserved.* No part of this book may be reproduced in any form or by any electronic or mechanical means, including information storage and retrieval systems, without written permission from the publisher, except by a reviewer who may quote passages in a review.

British Library Cataloguing in Publication Information Available

**Library of Congress Cataloging-in-Publication Data**

Crothers, Lane.
  Globalization and American popular culture / Lane Crothers. — 3rd ed.
    p. cm. — (Globalization)
  Includes bibliographical references and index.
  ISBN 978-1-4422-1495-8 (cloth : alk. paper) — ISBN 978-1-4422-1496-5 (paper : alk. paper) — ISBN 978-1-4422-1497-2 (electronic)
  1. Popular culture—United States. 2. Mass media—Social aspects—United States. 3. Globalization—Social aspects—United States. 4. Civilization, Modern—American influences. 5. United States—Foreign economic relations. 6. United States—Foreign public opinion. I. Title.
  E169.12.C74 2013
  306.0973—dc23
                                                                    2012016678

∞™ The paper used in this publication meets the minimum requirements of American National Standard for Information Sciences—Permanence of Paper for Printed Library Materials, ANSI/NISO Z39.48-1992.

Printed in the United States of America

For Martha and Austin
You are here.

# Contents

# TABLES

# Acknowledgments

In 2007, when this book appeared in its first edition, Facebook had been open to the public for less than a year. Myspace was the dominant social network. Twitter was not even imaginable. Napster, one of the early file-sharing websites, had been shut down, although others had risen to fill the void Napster's closing left behind. Almost no one in the world had an iPhone. Much of the Arab world was governed by a series of strongman dictators who had been in power for decades and who, it could be reasonably assumed, would remain in power for the rest of their inevitably long lives. And I was not a father worried about helping my young son understand and navigate the world.

Today, all of this has changed. Facebook has exploded in size and seems on a path to enroll its one-billionth subscriber in the not-too-distant future. When it hits that threshold, something like one in every seven people on the planet will be a member of the service. Twitter too has grown exponentially, and hundreds of billions if not trillions of songs, television programs, and movies have been electronically downloaded around the world—both legally and illegally. The iPhone and its competitor smartphones have become ubiquitous and have spawned a new generation of digitally connected devices like netbooks and tablet computers. Many of the seemingly immovable Arab dictators have been chased from power by revolutions that, as is discussed in chapter 5, were facilitated by social networks like Facebook and Twitter and by the smart devices that connect users to the Internet seemingly everywhere they go. And I am indeed now the father of a young son—a father who is wondering what it is going to be like to try to raise a child in a world where he can have virtually unlimited opportunities to access a world of information . . . whether I want him to see it or not.

This third edition tries to grapple with the way that things like smartphones, the Internet, and social networking services like Facebook and Twitter have affected the scope and impact of American popular culture in an increasingly connected, globalized world. This edition, of course, updates much of what was already in the book—e.g., the reasons that American audiovisual cultural artifacts like movies, music, and television programs became prominent and even dominant on the world stage; the ways that other aspects of American culture, like food products, clothing styles, and sports, have shaped contemporary globalization; and the fact that the attractiveness of these products and the power of the values they embody have combined to both excite and frighten large numbers of people around the world facing what they see as an onslaught of American popular culture possibly undermining their cultural ideals. But the book also explores the ways that newer phenomena like social networking and wirelessly connected mobile devices have remade global access to American popular culture. Large portions of the world's population today can access information, entertainment, news, e-mail, text messages, and web search sites virtually all the time. This is a new world reality that can be seen to shape—and reshape—both the world's access and reaction to American popular culture.

I hope this book is as interesting and as engaging to read as it was to write. That said, although I wrote this book, no book is ever the product of one person's efforts. It is important to acknowledge the many people who have helped in the creation of this work.

I owe thanks to the different editors who have reviewed, commented on, and otherwise nurtured this book from its earliest imagining: Susan McEachern at Rowman & Littlefield and series editors Manfred B. Steger and Terrell Carver. The book is stronger for their work. Manfred Steger is owed particular thanks for the many conversations, discussions, and words of encouragement he shared with me regarding this project and many others. His early insights into the project profoundly shaped its outcome, and he deserves special credit for this. The conversation continues, which is a good thing.

Tammy Johnson of Illinois State University provided invaluable research support for the first edition of this project. I also owe thanks to Steve Bragg at Illinois State University and Mary Lou O'Neil of Kadir Has University in Istanbul for being both sounding boards and stimulators of thought as the project unfolded. I also appreciate the opportunity the Department of Politics and Government at Illinois State University gave me to work on a project that, on its face, seems to fall outside the mainstream of political science academic research—although, as I found, popular culture is a central issue in debates about contemporary globalization. As I hope the people who read this book agree by the time they are done with it, anyone studying globalization needs to think closely about the role popular culture plays in the modern world.

This book was made better as the result of experiences I had serving as the Eccles Centre Visiting Professor in North American Studies at the British Library in London from September 2007 through February 2008. While this is not the project I was working on at the British Library, the opportunity I had to live in London for six months gave me unique insights into the ways American popular culture engages with cultures around the world. While there, I took advantage of opportunities to travel to Amsterdam, Rome, and Istanbul and thereby broaden my experience in invaluable ways. I need to thank the Eccles Centre for its support. I also want to thank the Illinois State University donor who supported my time in the wonderful but remarkably expensive city of London.

Finally, a special thanks to Dr. Martha Horst, who gives the time and the energy and the love that makes all of life exciting and challenging, leaving me anxious to explore more of the world every day.

As I noted in the acknowledgments to both the first and second editions, the life of an academic is a privileged one. We are given the freedom to think about things we like to think about, to talk about things we like to talk about, and to write about things we like to write about. This is a rare gift in the modern world, and I appreciate the many teachers, family members, and friends who have supported me over the years as I have worked to fully inhabit life as an academic. It is a rare thing to know one is doing what one is meant to do. I have the privilege of living that knowledge every day.

Thanks to you all. This book would not have been possible without you. Any errors and weaknesses are mine alone.

# CHAPTER 1

## AMERICAN POPULAR CULTURE AND GLOBALIZATION

This book examines the ways that American movies, music, and television programs shape and are shaped by contemporary globalization. It also examines other features of American pop culture in this light, including fast food, clothing, sports, and social networking. As will be seen, audiovisual media like movies, music, and television provide a significant means by which images of the "American" way of life, whether political, social, or economic, are transmitted around the world. Likewise, fast-food restaurants like McDonald's, drink companies like Coca-Cola and Pepsi, sports like NBA basketball and major league baseball, and clothing like Levi's jeans are global cultural icons. Facebook and sites like it serve as hubs through which American popular culture reaches ever-widening parts of the world. It is through these artifacts (and many others) that the rest of the world sees American values and lifestyles.

## POPULAR CULTURE AND GLOBAL POLITICS

At first glance, the idea of writing—or for that matter, reading—a book on the relationship between the profound economic, social, political, and cultural changes going on in the modern world that are collectively labeled "globalization" and the movies, music, and television programs (among other features) that compose American popular culture may seem a bit odd. Globalization, after all, seems "heavy": it is the result of numerous powerful forces and is fundamentally remaking the way the world works. Popular culture, by contrast, seems "light": whether in theme or in impact, it is intuitively hard to see how even a movie megahit like *Avatar* could play a meaningful role in such a profound thing as globalization.

Yet popular cultural entertainments have been central to the new era of globalization. For example, by 1998 trade in movies, music, and television programming had become the leading U.S. export.[1] This was true even without factoring in the economic and cultural power of American brands like McDonald's, Levi's, and Starbucks. American pop culture is a global phenomenon.

The end of the Cold War and the emergence of new technologies like the Internet, cellular phones, and small-dish satellite television systems have allowed American popular culture access to an ever-bigger global market. This spread has served both to enhance the profits of U.S. corporations and to highlight and augment cultural tensions that exist between the United States and the nations and communities into which American popular culture has expanded. After all, most people around the world will never visit the United States or meet an American in person. They will never have a Peace Corps volunteer work in their town, village, or city. They may work in factories that produce goods intended for the American market, but their managers will probably be locals, and the rules that govern the factory will be those imposed by the native government, not by the United States. And despite the increased U.S. global military presence after the terrorist attacks of September 11, 2001, most people live in countries and communities that will never be attacked, much less occupied, by U.S. forces. Accordingly, what people are likely to see of America and what they are likely to know about America will be filtered through the lens of American popular culture. As sociologist Todd Gitlin has put it, American popular culture is "the latest in a long succession of bidders for global unification. It succeeds the Latin imposed by the Roman Empire and the Catholic Church, and Marxist Leninism."[2] Put simply, the global spread of American popular culture has been at the heart of the contemporary era of globalization, and it is simply not possible to fully understand the ways in which globalization is reshaping the contemporary world without understanding the role that American popular culture plays in this emerging world order.

The linkage of American popular culture and global politics can be illustrated with brief analyses of two cases in which American popular culture and global politics have intersected. The first is the Cold War, the nearly fifty-year political and military standoff between the United States and the Soviet Union from 1945 to 1991. The second is the controversial U.S. Global War on Terror (GWoT), launched after the terrorist attacks on New York City; Washington, D.C.; and Pennsylvania on September 11, 2001—typically referred to as 9/11.

During the Cold War, for example, the United States and the Soviet Union established vast international coalitions that promoted their interests, and each tried to check the actions of the other. The U.S.-led coalition was centered in the Americas, Western Europe (which came into being only as a result of post–World War II policies), and the Pacific area of Australasia. The Soviet coalition consisted of the Eurasian landmass on which the Soviet Union was located, Eastern Europe, and at times, China. (China was allied with the Soviet Union after its Communist revolution in 1949; however, it subsequently developed an independent agenda as a Communist nation outside the control of the Soviet Union.) The two sides promoted dramatically different social, political, and economic philosophies: capitalism and liberal representative democracy in the Western, U.S.-led coalition; and communism and state control in the Soviet, Eastern bloc. These coalitions occasionally engaged in armed struggle, usually through proxies, as happened in wars in Korea, 1950–1952; Vietnam, 1964–1975; and Afghanistan, 1979–1989. More often, their fights were at the level of propaganda. Each side insisted its way of life was superior.

Global trade and immigration patterns, social and political ideas, security systems, and even popular culture practices were profoundly shaped by the Cold War. The Western bloc advocated relative freedom in personal choice, economic trade, and immigration, while the Eastern bloc practiced state control, the limitation of personal freedom, and government ownership of factories and other productive enterprises. The West insisted that personal liberty promoted maximum happiness and growth, benefiting most people even if others suffered problems like poverty, crime, and lack of opportunity. The East insisted that government control would allow the products of society to be distributed among all people equally, thereby limiting some people's economic and individual freedoms in order to ensure that everyone had the basics of life.

At least part of this struggle was linked to popular culture. Soviet leaders and their ideological allies regularly referred to the West as culturally corrupt. By this they meant that Western—usually American— cultural products like movies, music, television, fast food, clothing, and the like were insubstantial and meaningless or, worst of all, promoted poor moral values. (Why this might be the case is addressed in detail in chapter 2.) While Westerners insisted that popular entertainment and performers like the singer-superstar Elvis Presley or television shows like *Leave It to Beaver* provided individuals with opportunities to create, invent, and provide joy and pleasure to others, Soviet leaders argued that the values expressed in these acts and programs tended to erode public morals and social order. Soviet rulers, accordingly, worked hard to keep Western-style pop culture away from the Soviet people.

Yet in working to exclude Western entertainment from their societies, the leaders of the Soviet-Communist bloc (including the People's Republic of China) actually stimulated interest among their citizens in American popular culture. By making the fruit forbidden, the leadership made it attractive. A vigorous black market developed across the Soviet Union and its allies as people smuggled or otherwise brought Western popular culture products like books, magazines, food, clothes, and other products into their lives. Western popular culture was thus present in the Communist bloc well before the Soviet Union finally collapsed in 1991.

Western leaders exploited the lure of their popular culture during the Cold War. They created radio and television stations such as Radio Free Europe/Radio Liberty to broadcast as much popular culture material into the Soviet bloc as could be programmed. This programming was done to achieve the very purpose the Soviets accused it of: to westernize the values of those who watched or listened to it. Western leaders used the power and appeal of American popular culture to help win the hearts and minds of people inside the Communist bloc.

In using American pop culture as a tool of the Cold War, Western policymakers were exploiting what political scientist Joseph Nye has referred to as "soft power."[3] The notion of soft power refers to cultural, social, intellectual, and ideological ideas, values, attitudes, and behaviors that influence human life. Nye distinguishes these soft forms of power from "hard power," which is typically associated with the use of violent, coercive tools of social action like armies and economic sanctions. Soft power is a significant factor in global politics, Nye argues, because it is subtle and indirect and thus less likely to promote resentful, angry reactions to its use. As such, it provides a way for one people—in the case of the Cold War, people in the political West—to change the attitudes and behaviors of other cultures without resorting to war or other forms of coercion that inevitably lead the loser to hate and resent the winner. Soft power can achieve these results because those who experience soft power may not even be aware they are subject to its effects, so they never think to grow resentful or angry as they see their societies change around them. Indeed, they may change their ideals and values and practices toward those favored by an enemy or alien government willingly.

It would be too much to argue that the Soviet Union fell apart because of the corrupting appeal of American popular culture—although at least one analysis has shown that former Romanian dictator Nicolae Ceaușescu ultimately regretted allowing the 1980s soap opera *Dallas* to be shown in his country, where it inspired viewers to wish for the kind of economic and personal freedom the show demonstrated.[4] (The show's star, Larry Hagman, later became a spokesperson for the Russian company LUKOIL on the grounds that LUKOIL was "The Choice of a True Texan." It is still possible to visit the "Southforkscu" ranch in Romania, modeled after the South Fork ranch that Hagman's character owned.) After all, the forces that led to the dissolution of the Soviet Union were complex and diverse. It is, however, fair to say that in denying their citizens access to the Western movies, music, and television programs and other artifacts they desired, the governments of the Soviet bloc undermined their own legitimacy. Put another way, a government afraid of popular American television programs like *Ozzie and Harriet* or *The A-Team* is probably an inherently weak government that, in time, is likely to fail for a variety of reasons.

American popular culture's role in international affairs has become even more important in the years following the Soviet Union's collapse. New patterns of trade, security, information, investment, ideas, and even the exchange of entertainment have emerged. These changes, collectively labeled "globalization," appeared, at least to many early students of the topic, to be likely to create what President George H. W. Bush called a "new world order," grounded on universal principles of democracy and global free trade. If, for example, a region had a comparative advantage in growing rice but lacked the educational system to have a large high-tech industry, it would export rice and import computers from a region that had lots of software engineers but limited land for rice growing. Similar patterns would emerge in every industry, including the popular culture industry. If one country or culture held a comparative advantage in the production of some consumer good over other countries or cultures, its products would rise to global dominance. No country would produce everything it needed within its borders (or the borders of its coalition), at least not efficiently, and everyone would benefit from lower prices and enhanced choices that would emerge from an integrated global economy.

Advocates insisted that free trade would do more than just create a globally integrated market, however. It would also promote the spread of democracy around the world. Theorists and political leaders insisted that the pressures of competing in a global market would force repressive societies to open up in order to unleash the creative, productive power of their peoples. In turn, engaged, excited, and creative individuals would pressure their governments to open up and become responsive to the needs of their citizens. In time, this would lead to the formation of new democratic governments around the globe. Democracy would inevitably emerge from a global regime of free trade. A new era of economic and political freedom was soon to arrive.

The promise of a fully democratic world freely trading goods, services, ideas, cultures, and freedoms has not come to pass, of course. Indeed, there are good reasons to suppose it never will. The reason for this skepticism is simple. As a practical matter, few people care where their rice is grown or where their computer is built. The exchange of rice for computers is generally understood to take place with little moral impact on either society. There may be long-term economic consequences that derive from the imbalance of trade that exists when one society is rich and developed and capable of designing and programming computers while others are poor and underdeveloped, of course. Moreover, these imbalances may be the result of historical forces like colonialism, racism, repression, and violence that were and remain immoral. Regardless of these problems, however, the specific exchange of some rice for a computer is rarely invested with ethical significance.

By contrast, the exchange of cultural goods is almost always laden with moral meaning. People care where their cultural artifacts come from, what values they express, and how they shape the lives of the people who use them. This is true even of cultural products like movies, music, and television programs since, as is shown in chapter 2, they reflect the maker's culture and values. American cultural artifacts, for example, inevitably bring the ideas, values, norms, and social practices embedded in American popular culture into contact—and often tension—with those of other cultures around the world. As a consequence, the dramatic expansion in the global dissemination of American popular culture that accompanied the end of the Cold War increased rather than decreased the potential points of cultural friction between the United States and its global neighbors.

The fact that cultures resist change also makes the notion of a global market in free trade unlikely. When their norms are challenged, people rarely adopt the "new" point of view easily or quickly (if at all). Instead, as is discussed later in this chapter, they tend to resist, reject, or dismiss the different ideas as wrong, immoral, or false. This reaction is particularly intense when the new point of view seems to attract children, who are generally seen as culturally vulnerable, naïve, and manipulable. This reaction is also likely when the source of such cultural changes is distant, alien, and seemingly beyond one's ability to influence—something that is certainly true of Hollywood-made popular culture, for example. People almost always become concerned when they perceive that their friends, families, neighbors, and children are adopting new, different, and even alien rituals, behaviors, norms, and values. Cultural power may be "soft," in Joseph Nye's phrase, but it is power nonetheless. Simply calling it "soft" does not mean that people will easily or readily adopt the values, ideals, practices, and rituals of a cultural "other." Soft power simply does not guarantee peaceful contacts among people.

The boundaries of cultural conflict in the modern world came into horrific view after the terror attacks of September 11, 2001. By destroying the two towers of the World Trade Center in New York City and severely damaging the Pentagon outside Washington, D.C., the terrorists of 9/11 set in motion a series of events that led the United States to undertake two wars, one in Afghanistan that started in October 2001 and one in Iraq that began in March 2003. Insisting that its actions were necessary as acts of self-defense, the United States deployed hundreds of thousands of soldiers to these two countries, ultimately leading to the overthrow of each nation's government. It additionally established a global effort to track and detain suspected terrorists, often without trial or recourse to courts either in the United States or elsewhere in the world. The ongoing U.S. post-9/11 operations remain both highly controversial and central to contemporary international relations.

As was the case with the Cold War, the U.S. GWoT has several cultural dimensions. For example, the 9/11 hijackers rejected both American foreign policy and Western norms, values, and cultural practices. They were advocates of a particular form of Islam that calls for an overturning of modernity and a return to values and behaviors they insist were dominant in the earliest days of the emerging Islamic world. Their actual and apparent targets highlight this rejection: the World Trade Center towers stood as symbols of global free trade. The Pentagon is the headquarters of the most powerful military in the world. And while the fourth plane did not hit a target, it was apparently aimed at either the White House or the U.S. Capitol, each a powerful symbol of American power, democracy, and culture. That the hijackers used arguably the most potent symbols of the modern world—jet airliners capable of crossing vast distances and cultural contexts in brief periods of time—as the tools of their terror only serves to highlight the cultural disconnect between their goals and the world they were attempting to change. Any assault on the United States was thus at least in part an attack on the relatively secular, tolerant, human-rights-seeking, and capitalist values that Americans sense are central to their political and social lives. (The nature of American political culture is addressed in detail later in this chapter.) Thus while the strikes of 9/11 were not *only* an assault on American culture, they were in part such an attack.

As they did during the Cold War, American policymakers used cultural tools after 9/11. They recognized the need to win hearts and minds across the world as they sought to deflate international concerns that the United States was simply engaging in a Christian crusade against Arab and Islamic enemies. For example, the United States funded the creation of a new television network aimed at the Arab world, al-Hurra, in an effort to counter what it asserted was biased coverage of the United States and its policies in media like al-Jazeera, an international Arabic-language television network. It also established a public diplomacy project in an effort to present the "good news" about U.S. ideals, values, culture, and people.

Just as cultural tensions lay at the heart of the attacks on the United States and of the U.S. responses to them, cultural tensions also shaped global reaction to both the attacks and the U.S. response. Whatever the intent of U.S. public diplomacy, the global public image of the United States declined dramatically in the months and years after 9/11. The world rapidly shifted from sympathy for the United States and Americans shortly after September 11—for example, in its editorial of September 13, 2001, the French newspaper *Le Monde* famously stated, "Today we are all Americans"—to concern, doubt, and fear about how the United States responded to 9/11. A 2002 study of attitudes in twelve countries regarding Americans and American culture found that respondents believed that U.S. popular culture made Americans "selfish, domineering, violent, and immoral." In 2003, *Time* magazine asked 250,000 people across Europe which country posed the greatest threat to world peace: Iraq, North Korea, or the United States. Only 8 percent of respondents chose Iraq, while 9 percent chose North Korea. A BBC poll taken in eleven countries later that same year supported these findings. Pollster John Zogby found that popular support for U.S. leadership and actions dropped dramatically across the Arab world between 2002 and 2004. Much of the planet's population seemed to agree with the title of an editorial that mystery writer John le Carré published in the London *Times* in 2003: "The United States of America Has Gone Mad."[5]

Yet even as the world seemed to resist U.S. policy and leadership, it continued to embrace American popular culture. The invention and distribution of personal music devices like the iPod and smartphones capable of delivering streaming video and music content directly to users wherever they were (assuming access to a wireless or cellular signal) led to explosive growth in international access to American popular culture. Likewise, high-speed Internet drove the spread of American popular culture even after the GWoT began. For example, based on a global survey of sixty-six countries with 1.6 billion combined viewers, in 2008 the American television program *House* was the most popular show in the world, garnering 81,800,000 viewers worldwide. *CSI: Las Vegas* and *CSI: Miami* did nearly as well. The ABC comedy/soap opera *Desperate Housewives* had 56,300,000 viewers in the same survey, followed closely by *Monk* and *Ugly Betty*. The daytime soap opera *The Bold and the Beautiful* led worldwide contenders for most viewers, with a global audience of 24,500,000 that same year.[6]

In other examples, a Russian version of *Married with Children*, a U.S. sitcom popular in the 1980s, became so popular its producers hired the show's original writers to create new episodes for the Russian market.[7] Hollywood now generates more ticket sales in the global market than it does in the domestic one: in 2003, foreign ticket sales generated $1.7 billion more than did sales in the United States; in 2007, that gap had jumped to $7.4 billion. (By 2010, foreign ticket sales accounted for 68 percent of all ticket sales for American films.[8]) Hours of U.S.-produced television programming on European television screens jumped from 214,000 hours in 2000 to 266,000 in 2006. MTV is now shown in Saudi Arabia, and programs like *Inside Edition* and *Oprah* are popular across the Middle East despite the political tensions that exist between the United States and much of the rest of the world. Indeed, despite—or perhaps because of—the U.S. war in and occupation of Iraq, Iraq has a booming hip-hop subculture.[9] So does Japan.[10] Hip-hop music has also been shown to have played a role in the "Arab Spring," the uprisings that led to the overthrow of numerous dictators in the Arab world from winter 2010 to spring 2012.[11] (The Arab Spring is discussed in chapter 5.) American popular culture clearly has a power and an appeal in the world community that transcends the short-term variations in support for the international policies of the United States. This book explores this appeal and the concerns it engenders across the globe.

## UNDERSTANDING CULTURE, POPULAR CULTURE, AND AMERICAN CULTURE

The question of what culture is and why it matters in social and political life is an old one and is complicated by a literature rife with competing definitions, examples, critiques, and reassertions of culture's significance in human life. It is further complicated by the use of the term in at least two dramatically different ways: as an explanation of a "way of life" for some group or community (the anthropological approach) and as a tool for the normative evaluation of particular behaviors or entertainment ("popular" versus "high" culture). Since both types of meanings are used throughout this book in different contexts, a brief discussion of the complexity of culture is appropriate before we link culture to globalization.

## ANTHROPOLOGICAL CULTURE

As a concept, anthropological culture refers to the root values, ideas, assumptions, behaviors, and attitudes that members of particular communities generally share in an unexamined, automatic way. Cultures provide the context in which economic, social, and political life make sense to their members.

Core to the notion of culture is the assertion that most human behavior is learned. For example, while most human babies are born with the innate capacity for language (barring physical disabilities), they do not speak a particular language at birth. Instead, they have to learn one. Sounds themselves are irrelevant; what matters is how combinations of sounds have meaning to the people who share the same linguistic repertoire. This process then continues for other aspects of human life: people, almost always as children, are socialized into the patterns of culture unique to their communities, learning the tools they need for survival and growth from the environments in which they are raised.

Among the many things that cultures teach their members are normative standards of evaluation—of dress, food, behavior, attitudes, ideas, and many other things. One learns that some things/ideas/attitudes/behaviors are appropriate, while others are not. Institutions such as laws, courts, police, parents, schools, and religions then reinforce what is learned. Culture shapes the attitudes, behaviors, and values of both children and adults, particularly newcomers to a given community. Children are seen to be especially important to every culture, since cultures are sustained by teaching each new generation of people the values and ideals of the local community.

Notably, cultural forces usually work unnoticed: just as children in the cradle never realize they are being taught language as their parents play with them, the agents of cultural socialization embed attitudes of right and wrong, normal and abnormal, moral and immoral in each generation through an array of means, such as pejorative comments or facial expressions, that do not appear as obvious acts of education. Cultural socialization is deep. One simply doesn't usually think about what's right and wrong, for example, because right and wrong are obvious and always have been.

Importantly, cultures contain mechanisms for self-defense. These include the shaming of those who transgress the culture's standards, the making and enforcing of rules governing what should or should not be done in the first place, and the punishment of those who violate the culture's rules. If someone transgresses cultural norms, he or she becomes subject to an array of critical responses that can range from indignant, shame-inducing stares to arrest, ostracism, and even death. Cultures fight back against those ideas and behaviors that challenge the culture's stability and permanence.

The formative and defensive dimensions of culture combine to make cultures generationally stable, reproducible, and relatively resistant to change. Group attitudes about right and wrong, moral and immoral, language and gibberish, or any other feature of a particular culture do not easily change. Indeed, if they did, cultures could not exist across generations. Accordingly, any idea, value, attitude, behavior, ritual, or other dimension of human life that might cross from one culture and contact another has the potential to become a flashpoint of cultural conflict. Such contact need not cause tension, but it can. The dramatic expansion in the trade in and use of American popular culture thus serves as a useful case study of the interaction of cultures in this global age.

### POPULAR CULTURE

The concept of culture has several meanings beyond its anthropological sense. One is normative. The concept has been used to separate people who have "taste" and pursue what Matthew Arnold called "the best that was thought and said" from those who pursue what a character in Shakespeare's *Henry V* refers to as the "base, common, and popular."[12] Indeed, Shakespeare's character, an ordinary soldier named Pistol, actually asks, in challenging someone approaching the position he is guarding, "Discuss with me: art thou officer, Or art thou base, common, and popular?" thus implying a difference in the moral status of people, not just in their tastes and pursuits. To be interested in things popular was to be base and common; to pursue "the best of what was thought and said" was to have "culture."

Much of the distinction between "high" and "popular" culture was developed during the Enlightenment. Intellectuals of the time began to pursue universal standards on which to base principles for human life. These principles were to be the product of human thought and exploration rather than derived from mystical superhuman sources. Then, since only the educated and the elite were trained to understand the components of "real" beauty, those things that were objectively and universally beautiful (at least according to those who interpreted them) became associated with "high" culture.[13] Everything else became "base, common, and popular."

The social split between high and popular culture intensified and expanded with the onset of the Industrial Revolution in the late 1700s. At the beginning of the Industrial Revolution, popular culture became mass produced. Large multinational corporations providing goods and services for profit began to produce it in vast quantities. Their motives were profit seeking: a book, a magazine, or—once the technology developed—recorded music, a movie, a television program, or anything else labeled popular culture was produced only because of its likely sales appeal. This stood in stark contrast with historical conceptions of art as a conscious act of creation with no purpose other than its own existence. The primary purpose of popular culture was to be consumed by users who paid for the privilege of reading a mass-produced book or magazine. Such production was essentially secular in nature, meaning that nothing was sacred or holy—everything was available for marketing and consumption.[14]

As a consequence of the secular, market-driven nature of popular culture's creation and consumption, many of the same theorists who argued that high culture was "good" because it was "aesthetic" insisted that popular culture had no innate value beyond the pleasure it brought to those who consumed it. Put simply, there was nothing aesthetic or "high" in the pop culture products of the Industrial Revolution. As one critic put it, mass-produced popular culture was no more meaningful than chewing gum.[15] Consequently, there was no value in studying or examining the patterns and norms embedded in the products of popular culture. The "real" values of society were contained in its high culture, not its common one.

In the middle of the twentieth century, however, scholars like Herbert Gans, Mary Douglas, and Baron Isherwood led others interested in popular culture to define the cultural meaning of popular mass-produced and mass-consumed items in new and valuable ways. Gans noted that an item did not lose its value simply because it was mass produced; instead, the people who used it derived meaning and value from it. Douglas and Isherwood found that communities of individuals—cultures—tend to share common conceptions of what ought to be purchased, used, and consumed.[16] Mass production does not eliminate meaning. It simply provides another way different groups of people make choices that are meaningful in establishing, reinforcing, and representing particular cultural boundaries.[17]

Popular culture thus provides a way for researchers to learn about the values, needs, concerns, and standards by which different communities of people live. It offers insights about the meanings and values that its users attribute to it. The adoption or rejection of particular pop culture products is thus fraught with social and political meaning. Accordingly, such artifacts are a valuable tool for explaining patterns of belief and behavior within and among societies.

## "AMERICAN" POPULAR CULTURE

What does it mean to say that culture or popular culture is American? After all, the 312 million (at least) people who live in the United States come from a vast array of nations, representing every language, religious, and cultural group on the planet. The first people who arrived in the area now called the United States came thirty thousand years ago; hundreds and thousands of people still arrive daily with the hope of making a permanent home in the country. It is hard, in such a context, to suppose that all these people share a common culture that can be described as "American."

In addition, to describe the culture of the residents of the United States as "American culture" can be stunningly arrogant. The Americas, after all, constitute two continents in the Western Hemisphere. These are further divided into four areas: North, Central, and South America and the island nations of Caribbean America. Nearly 930 million people live in forty-seven countries across the region.[18] To refer to any one of these countries or areas as "America" and its inhabitants as "American" is at some level a remarkable act of hemispheric appropriation.

The "Americanness" of American culture lies in what Marc Howard Ross has called "public culture." Public culture refers to the common terms of reference, symbols, rituals, and ideologies within which different groups and individuals press their claims for power, policy, and identity. Such terms are not a matter of private conscience; instead, they can be found, among other places, in public documents, speeches, campaigns, and political symbols referred to by others as they promote their agendas. Such public cultural symbols constitute a shareable language through which different groups and individuals can press for their goals, define meaning, and create rules and standards of conduct. Different groups and individuals express their alternative political programs through shared cultural frames. The public culture contains the terms in which political debate and struggle can occur in particular communities.[19]

The public culture of the United States is generally termed "civic."[20] That is, the values, ideas, and expectations that people who live in the United States refer to when explaining what they believe, why they believe it, and which programs they favor are usually couched in norms like democracy, individual rights, tolerance, and so on, which are seen to cumulatively constitute a civic culture. Americans tend to focus on several specific ideas and values to justify their plans and programs: liberty, particularly "negative liberty," the sense that government should leave people alone so that individuals can think and believe and act as they please[21]; political equality, meaning that everyone is entitled to equal political rights; individualism, the idea that individuals have rights that should be protected by government, even as most individuals are expected to be responsible for their own decisions and their own fate; democracy, especially in the form of citizens electing others to represent them in government, with the expectation that those elected will promote the interests and values of their constituents across an array of local, regional (state), and national (federal) governments; tolerance, the idea that since individuals have rights and responsibilities, and those rights and responsibilities are the most important part of the political and social system, everyone has to let everyone else practice their values in order to preserve the opportunity for themselves; exceptionalism, the idea that the United States is a special nation ordained by God to fulfill an important role in the world; and capitalism, understood as an economic system in which individuals buy, sell, and trade goods and services with the intention of making a profit determined largely by market forces of supply and demand that establish who gets what, when, and for how much.

Over time, as a result of forces like the nation's religious founding, its colonial history, and its success integrating millions of immigrants into the national community, this culture has come to be labeled "American." Rather than sharing a common ethnicity, language, or some other bond, Americans are seen to be defined by their faith in an ideology—civic nationalism. This ideology is so deeply embedded and unquestioned that some scholars have suggested it should be understood as a civic religion: a sacred text expressing eternal truths on which judgments of right and wrong, good and evil, ought to be based.[22]

It is of course true that these cultural values have not been applied fairly or consistently to all Americans throughout the nation's history. Democracy, economic opportunity, and religious tolerance were not afforded to slaves in the American South, for example. Indeed, many of the men who signed the Declaration of Independence owned slaves, despite that document's insistence that "all men are created equal" and that they are "endowed by their Creator with certain inalienable rights." Similarly, the Constitution denied women the very rights it accorded to men. In a large sense, the history of the United States is a chronicle of the violation of what are recognized to be the nation's core cultural values—suggesting that these values are little more than window dressings designed to obscure the true forces shaping American political life—class, perhaps, or structural racism and misogyny. Any account of American political culture must account for the disjunction between the culture's core public values and the discriminatory practices that have been associated with them. How, it is fair to ask, can a culture claim to be civic and yet practice discrimination?

In part, these disjunctions can be explained, but not excused, by reviewing how the people of the time defined the practical implications of American civic values in their lives. For example, slaveholders tended to believe that their liberty and economic livelihoods were dependent on keeping slaves, while abolitionists insisted that liberty for all men meant freedom for slaves, too. Likewise, women were denied the right to vote and own property in much of the early United States on the grounds that they were not fully rational beings capable of properly enjoying freedom and its associated benefits. The public culture provided the terms on which political and social debate centered, even as people came to different conclusions about how cultural values applied in daily life.

Louis Hartz has suggested that much of American political debate has involved groups of Americans who argue that the nation is not living up to its best principles precisely because it is violating the rights it claims to believe in.[23] African Americans, women, and others have called for political change on the grounds that national policies violate the nation's political cultural promises. In each case, the struggle to have their rights respected was long and difficult—and, in the long run, essentially successful. For example, in 2008, a woman was a finalist for a major party's nomination to be its candidate for president of the United States, another woman was a major party candidate for vice president of the United States, and an African American man was elected president. None of these accomplishments excuse historical discrimination, nor do they guarantee that the rights of women, racial and ethnic minorities, and other groups will be respected in America in the future. However, these victories do serve to reinforce the nation's confidence in its civic culture and civic nationalism. Americans reaffirm their public commitments by overcoming their past failures to live up to them. The public, civic culture is thus renewed, not undermined, by recognition of the nation's imperfections. This confirms the "American" in American popular culture.

As will be seen in chapters 3 and 4, the values and ideals of American public culture are expressed through American popular culture and then marketed across the planet. American public culture is inevitably embedded in the products of popular culture. Issues of culture are thus intrinsically linked to globalization in the modern era.

## GRASPING GLOBALIZATION

So what is globalization, and how is the concept used in this book? Manfred B. Steger has offered a concise, highly usable approach to understanding globalization that both accounts for its many dimensions and informs the analysis offered in this work. Steger defines globalization as a *"set of social processes* that are thought to transform our present social condition into one of globality." Globality, in turn, is seen as "a *social condition* characterized by the existence of global economic, political, cultural, and environmental interconnections and flows that make many of the currently existing borders and boundaries irrelevant." A combination of economic, political, and cultural factors promote globalization by (1) making it possible to create new and increased ties among people, social networks, and ideas that span traditional nation-state boundaries; (2) linking people in new ways, making it possible for work or travel or shopping or other activities to take place twenty-four hours a day around the world; (3) advancing the speed of communication and the expectation of instantaneous contact, in effect making global events and issues local ones as well; and (4) shaping and reshaping individuals' ideas and identities as they are exposed to this increasingly complex world. Hence, while globalization is dynamic, uncertain, and insecure, its direction is toward the state of globality—what Steger describes as "interdependence and integration."[24]

Globalization may be a set of processes tending to promote a condition of globality, but it also seems to create movements and reactions in opposition to it. As is addressed throughout this book, the forces shaping globalization seem to both draw people together through trade and increased cultural contacts *and* to anger, frustrate, and frighten many groups and individuals in various (and varied) communities. Political scientist James Rosenau coined the term *fragmegration* to describe the integration-fragmentation dynamic that shapes globalization today. Fragmentation and integration occur at the same time, profoundly shaping the dynamics of globalization. Moreover, fragmegration affects different individuals, groups, sectors of the economy, and communities in varying ways.[25] Thus, whether for economic, political, or cultural reasons, or some combination of these, globalization seems to drive some people apart even as it promotes new international connections among other people around the world. To understand globalization, then, it is necessary to assess how economic, political, and cultural forces that stimulate the growth of shared social institutions and values bring some people together while at the same time pushing others apart.

As will be seen throughout this book, American popular culture is an agent of cultural globalization. It is a conduit by which values, ideas, and experiences in the world at large can become known to Americans, only to be adapted and reflected back out into the world again. Moreover, popular culture is a business run by megacorporations and marketed across the globe. Accordingly, it has an impact on the economic dimension of globalization. This economic activity inevitably has both cultural and political effects, as the sudden intrusion of new forms and modes of communication, entertainment, and lifestyles promotes tensions in local communities. Globalization is not simply *good*. It is multidimensional, dynamic, and transformational in both desired and unintended ways.

## ECONOMIC GLOBALIZATION
## AND AMERICAN POPULAR CULTURE

The economic dimensions of globalization are perhaps the best-understood and most-studied feature of contemporary globalization. In fact, so common are the assertions of those individuals and groups who favor economic globalization that Manfred Steger argues they have combined to form a powerful political ideology, globalism, to legitimate and promote their preferred policies.[26] Since economic globalization interacts with the cultural dimension of globalization, a brief accounting of this arena of globalization is appropriate here before we move on to the cultural.

One of the central features of contemporary globalization is the degree to which the economic livelihoods of people living in many different countries are now linked through world trade, international finance, and the operations of transnational corporations. This is a remarkable change from the way global economics worked even fifty years ago. For most of the last five hundred years or so, most countries (and, if they had one, their associated colonial empires) pursued their economic interests in competition with the other nations and empires of the world. For example, rather than cooperate to build ships or grow food, nations attempted to grow all the food they needed within their own borders (including the boundaries of their colonies), as well as to produce all the ships they needed. Indeed, the desire to go it alone in economic practices was one of the major stimuli that led the European powers to pursue colonies: lacking sufficient resources and markets at home to keep their industrial factories working, they conquered foreign territories from which they could extract natural resources and to which they could sell finished products. (The U.S. expansion across the continent of North America served much the same purpose in the nineteenth century.) The goal of such practices was to protect the profits and jobs of the workers and owners of the home country.

Near the end of World War II, the United States and its allies (with the notable exception of the Soviet Union) decided that such go-it-alone policies were not the best way to ensure their economic futures. They decided that competition for economic resources had in part caused the horrific violence of the First and Second World Wars. They further decided that the economic collapse of the Great Depression in the 1920s and 1930s had been caused and deepened by protectionist trade policies. Finally, they decided that they needed to establish a new kind of economic and political alliance to counter the growing power of the Soviet Union, which espoused communism as its organizing philosophy. With this context as background, they began the process of economic globalization that shapes the world today.

The core of the economic dimension of globalization as developed by the United States and its allies rests on the ideal—if not the perfect practice—of free trade. Free trade is a principle of economic theory that holds that there should be few, if any, restraints on the flow of goods, services, and even people around the world. The theory holds that goods and services should be produced wherever they can be most efficiently made—a concept known as comparative advantage. This is held to be true whether the product in question is a pound of rice, a computer, or a television program. Restraints on trade inevitably make the prices of some goods and services artificially high and prevent those areas that might make a product more cheaply from having the opportunity to develop. Similar problems emerge if capital, people, ideas, or anything else is constrained by legal or social regulations from flowing freely around the planet. While there may be social and political disruptions as industries, jobs, and markets redistribute themselves around the world, free trade is expected to be good overall, at least in the long run.[27]

The major powers of the West began the process of expanding trade and reducing barriers among themselves near the end of World War

II. They agreed to stabilize their currencies in relation to the U.S. dollar; established institutions like the General Agreement on Tariffs and Trade (GATT) and the International Monetary Fund (IMF) to oversee currency exchanges and trade rules for member states; and supported treaties and organizations to enforce the rules governing free trade, to which the major powers agreed. In subsequent years, free trade agreements proliferated, and regional free trade zones like the North American Free Trade Agreement (NAFTA) and the European Union (EU) were set up. With the end of the Cold War in 1991, new areas of trade emerged, global financial markets were deregulated, and it became possible to invest—and compete for capital—around the world. Services, too, became global as communication technologies like the Internet and cellular phones made it possible to outsource work (e.g., customer service phone operations) formerly done in the corporation's home country. Finally, with the deregulation of financial markets and the emergence of global free trade, new institutions rose to exploit the economic opportunities afforded on a worldwide stage. This led to the emergence of transnational corporations. Companies like General Motors, Honda, or Airbus (a joint European enterprise to build commercial aircraft) are now global enterprises spread across the world pursuing profit for investors.[28] Relatively free trade is, as a consequence, the dominant mode of global economic exchange today.

Yet free trade has a dark side, a side that has become increasingly evident over time. As globalization promotes greater economic integration around the world, for example, people whose skills can be replaced at lower cost often lose their jobs. This certainly happened in the case of low-skill factory jobs like those in the textile industry in the United States in the 1980s and 1990s. But people who lose their jobs lose more than just their work. They also lose their identities—the ability to perform their role as providers to their families and friends through work they imagine doing for a lifetime. They then lose connection to their extended neighbors in the national community as people move, jobs are realigned, and state policies shift to accommodate the pressures of globalization. Again, this tends to be true whether the industry or economic enterprise affected by globalization is a farm, a factory, or a music production studio. Each change may serve to integrate the people living in newly developing areas to the larger world, but each of these processes, and many others, also transform the economic, social, and political order of developing as well as developed nations in diverse ways with varying effects. As a consequence, some people have gotten phenomenally wealthy over the last fifty years while others—even some who were once well off—have been reduced to abject poverty. Economic globalization has costs as well as benefits.

In addition, while the United States is the rhetorical leader of the world's free trade movement, its behavior has not always matched its cheerleading. As it happens, the United States works to protect its domestic industries from foreign competition even as it pressures other governments to open their borders to American products. For example, for years the United States has kept in place policies like subsidies to farmers of globally uncompetitive crops like cotton because U.S. farmers of these crops put pressure on their elected officials to maintain subsidy programs. Accordingly, American trade negotiators also seek to insert language into free trade agreements that favors American-produced goods on the global market. Restrictions on trade in certain kinds of computer chips or other high-tech devices serve to protect American manufacturers, as do patent and other laws governing the use of inventions created in the United States. Thus, while the United States has been the world's great free trade advocate, it, like other nations, seeks trade arrangements that are favorable to its citizens' interests.

The United States does this, it should be noted, even though subsidies guarantee that the price of a crop like cotton will be higher for domestic consumers than it would be if cotton were freely traded on the global market. It also supports American cotton farmers even though promoting free trade in cotton would provide many developing nations with a lucrative source of revenue they could use for domestic development. (As will be seen in chapter 5, similar tactics and practices are used by nations seeking to protect their domestic popular culture industries from threats perceived to come from American products.) American practice does not always live up to its promise.

As was suggested earlier in this chapter and is addressed in detail throughout this book, popular culture is a central element in contemporary international trade. As such, it has the potential to provide substantial, enjoyable, affordable entertainment and other products to literally billions of people—the ideal of free trade in general. However, American producers of popular culture have powerful advantages of capital, knowledge, and distribution networks compared to local producers in most of the rest of the world. Accordingly, American producers have the ability to drive local producers of popular culture out of business. For economic reasons alone, then, diverse groups and communities may either favor or oppose the global trade in popular culture as economically beneficial or harmful to their interests. Contemporary globalization is inevitably shaped as a consequence of these choices.

## POLITICAL GLOBALIZATION
## AND AMERICAN POPULAR CULTURE

Politics are central to any discussion of globalization for the simple reason that economic and political life cannot be separated to any meaningful degree, especially since the world is divided into a series of nation-states that govern peoples in discrete territories known as countries. Nations have historically attempted to control the economic activities that occur within their borders. Moreover, the United States and its allies made a political choice to promote free trade in the aftermath of World War II. Economic matters have political consequences, and vice versa.

The right of a nation-state to impose whatever laws it desires on its people is at the heart of any discussion of globalization. This principle, known as sovereignty, has been the central organizing principle of international relations at least since the Peace of Westphalia was adopted in Europe in 1648. The general rule by which nations conducted their relationships from 1648 through the end of World War II was that so long as one state did not threaten or otherwise interfere with another, the two had no just cause to go to war or to attempt to influence each other's internal politics. While this rule was never observed faithfully, it nonetheless provided international relations with an organizing principle around which states could make rules, attempt to govern their citizens, and otherwise conduct their business in ways that made sense to them.

Economic globalization, especially free trade in goods and services, poses multiple challenges to nation-states. For example, both free trade and transnational corporations are new phenomena in global politics, phenomena that test a nation's power to pass laws to control its own economic destiny. After all, if a state passes restrictive laws protecting workers' rights at home, a transnational corporation might simply relocate to friendlier shores. The state's ability to control what businesses do is seriously constrained in such an environment. In addition, the notion that government regulation of trade is harmful for consumers is a political claim that, if accepted, necessitates political changes to a nation's trade laws. It is also common for peoples to ask their governments to take actions that will protect the community's interests and livelihoods when they perceive that their cultures, economies, and ways of life are under assault. Predictably, then, political movements intended to limit any negative consequences of globalization have emerged as a consequence of the dislocations associated with globalization and free trade.

Some authors argue that global free trade heralds the end of the nation-state. For these thinkers there are few problems, if any, that the market cannot solve more efficiently and fairly than governments can. Thus the answer to almost any social problem (poverty, crime, economic inequity, etc.) is to free markets from constraints and allow them to work: goods and services will be produced and consumed across the globe according to which area can do so most productively and efficiently. By extension, states need to get out of the way—even if they mean to help their citizens, globalists claim, governments that pass policies in opposition to free trade will ultimately undermine their peoples' chances for a happy, full, democratic life.[29]

Empirically, however, neither politics nor states have gone away in favor of all-encompassing markets. Instead, states and state policies are adapting to the pressures of economic globalization in three ways. The first can be seen in the emergence of new forms of international political organization that transcend traditional state boundaries but have legal power over the residents of member states. For example, since globalization leads to increased contacts among people, it makes sense that globalization has a regional component: links of geography and culture tend to promote contacts over time.[30] Similarly, as our knowledge of human rights and other abuses around the world have grown, largely as a result of emerging communications systems like Facebook and Twitter, the work of nongovernmental organizations that focus on human rights, environmental regulation, and the like have become more prominent.[31] New political relationships, made by states to regulate both state and nonstate actors, have emerged to govern the economic and cultural consequences of contemporary globalization.

The European Union stands as a key example of such regional governance systems.

A second role for states derives from their role in the creation and management of globalization in the first place. After all, the neoliberal policies of free trade and increased flows of capital that emerged in the West at the end of World War II were the result of choices of specific nation-states made at particular moments in time. Governments set rules for trade, communication, and environmental policies (to name a few).[32] Logically, then, governments might choose to change the regulatory regimes through which they instituted free trade and market liberalization. Indeed, as is discussed in chapter 5, states have proven quite willing to assert a right to protect local culture and local industry despite the logic of free market globalization. One of the central areas of concern has been the power of American popular culture to corrupt native values, often on the grounds that U.S. producers of popular culture will exploit their economic power and threaten local producers and products.

The U.S. response to the terrorist attacks of September 11, 2001, has demonstrated a third means by which states can exert control over economic and social forces in the global era. The creation and deployment of the world's military forces means that states will remain an agent in world affairs for some time to come. For example, after 9/11 the United States restricted immigration and asserted its right to use military force to defend itself anywhere it perceives a threat to its interests across the globe. Other nations, some of which are discussed in a series of case studies in chapter 5, have used their power to control the laws of their societies to limit the ways in which their people interact with American popular culture. Notably, nations that have taken these actions have remained economically and politically viable, even powerful, regardless of globalists' claims that such acts violate the spirit and inevitable benefit of free trade.

Free trade and economic globalization have also promoted the rise of a loosely coordinated global movement of groups that engage in political protest activity to encourage governments to pass policies that protect people from negative effects associated with globalization. The groups and individuals involved in this movement range from hardcore isolationists who eschew any international contacts among nations to advocates for economic and political justice who fear that the unfettered global pursuit of the cheapest goods will result in outcomes that are harmful *both* to the people who produce products for virtually no earnings *and* to the people who consume these items. This movement seeks to pressure governments and corporations to set and follow rules that protect jobs and livelihoods in developed countries while also protecting health, safety, environmental, and other types of standards in the rest of the world. As will be seen in chapter 5, while this movement has had only a modest influence in the globalization debate, it has had its biggest successes in its efforts to limit the free trade of American popular culture. Popular culture is in fact among the most heavily regulated components of international trade, even in the modern era of globalization. Trade in audiovisual entertainment is treated quite differently under international trade agreements than is trade in cars or steel or grain. This, in turn, derives from its perceived importance in cultural affairs. Political systems act to protect local cultures and culture-producing enterprises. As such, popular culture is an element of political as well as economic globalization.

## CULTURAL GLOBALIZATION
## AND AMERICAN POPULAR CULTURE

In broad terms, analysts of cultural globalization focus on the question of how Western goods, services, ideas, values, and media affect local, usually non-Western, cultures once they enter the new markets opened by globalization. Some analysts, relying on a view of culture as a set of fixed, rigid ideas, values, and practices that make peaceful cultural change unlikely, are fairly pessimistic about the likely resulting effects. They see three kinds of negative effects emerging from the global spread of American popular culture in the years since the fall of the Soviet Union in 1991: (1) cultural corruption, (2) cultural imperialism, and (3) cultural homogenization. Other cultural analysts focus on the concept of cultural hybridity to offer a more hopeful sense of cultural interaction over time.

### CULTURAL CORRUPTION

Many critics who are concerned that cultural corruption follows from American popular culture build on the research of a school of thought known as the Frankfurt School. As expressed in works of scholars like Theodor Adorno, Max Horkheimer, and Jürgen Habermas, adherents of the Frankfurt School begin with the idea that the Industrial Revolution broke the traditional ties that oriented people to life in their societies. Where once people lived in small communities governed by rules established by church, political, and familial authorities who lived in the same small towns, the Industrial Revolution drove people into large cities where traditional authority structures could not function. When millions of people moved from rural areas to cities to take jobs in the new factories, they were separated from the institutions and values that had previously served as the teachers and enforcers of moral behavior. This separation was significant because life in the cities, at least in contrast with the bucolic image of life on the farm offered by critics of town living, was nasty, dirty, and immoral. Brothels, crime, and disease flourished, for example, even as new forms of entertainment like dime novels and the penny press found markets peddling stories of lust, violence, and exploitation. In turn, life became dominated by new values like consumerism, the pursuit of entertainment, and the pursuit of individual interests regardless of their social effects. In such circumstances, people became profoundly isolated despite living together in large numbers: lacking traditions of trust and authority like those embedded in their rural communities, new urban migrants were often left to their own devices to survive. As a result, people's life orientations shifted from dedication to the social good of their communities to the autonomous desire to satisfy the self.

Frankfurt School analysts emphasized the way that new forms of communication, particularly mass communications and entertainment like newspapers, radio, and the movies, could promote false or harmful ideas to their mass audiences. Without historical moral anchors like local church and community leaders to offer alternative points of view on crucial issues of the day, all that people living in the mass isolation of large cities could know or care about was what they were told by newspaper publishers, radio broadcasters, movie producers, and other agents of mass communication. This shift from social to private consciousness made people susceptible to manipulation by outside forces. Thus, two great transformations occurring at the same time—the social and manufacturing changes associated with rapid urbanization and the Industrial Revolution, and the rise of mass communication and entertainment to fill the urban market—created a world in which mass media and entertainment could lead to the undermining of moral society in favor of some corrupted new order.

Another set of contemporary critics of American popular culture typically espouse a version of Frankfurt School thought known as mass society theory. For adherents of mass society theory, the moral decay of urban society (compared to agrarian, rural societies) is a result of the messages and meanings embedded in the communications of mass entertainment.[33] As people are separated from the rural, traditional social and political institutions that define their lives and provide them with meaning, they are exposed to exploitative, manipulative media. The media replaces traditional forces in socializing behavior and attitudes: immoral behavior in novels and magazines is inevitably mirrored in lustful violence in the real world. Individuals are, essentially, helpless victims of those who control the media. This is seen to be particularly true for some individuals or groups—particularly children—who are believed to be particularly gullible and prone to manipulation.[34] Thus critics employing mass society theory argue that people need to be protected from "bad" cultural products and messages for their own good, echoing—or perhaps foretelling—the arguments of Soviet leaders about the corrupting influence of American popular culture during the Cold War.

### CULTURAL IMPERIALISM

A second group of critics of the globalization of American popular culture focuses on its capacity for cultural imperialism. As a concept, cultural imperialism suggests that the interaction of different cultures will inevitably be conflictual. Members of each culture will seek to destroy or eliminate the other. This might occur through outright violence or by undermining the alien culture and installing a new, dominant culture in its place. Samuel Huntington, for example, argues that civilizational/cultural boundaries constitute the ultimate cleavages on which political conflict will inevitably arise.[35] In Huntington's model, cultural interactions tend to stimulate civilizational conflicts, as members of each group seek to expand or defend their cultural turf. Benjamin Barber makes a similar, more developed argument when he notes that the values, products, and processes of globalization can and must provoke what he calls "jihad," defined as "bloody holy war on behalf of partisan identity that is metaphysically defined and fanatically defended."[36] Jihad is counterpoised against "McWorld"—the integrated, sophisticated, and even cosmopolitan world reflected in the notion of global free trade and cultural interaction. Jihad can occur *between* societies—the highly integrated globalized societies of the West, for example, and those of the less developed, less linked world. But it can also emerge *within* nations (e.g., coastal communities heavily dependent on trade as opposed to upland areas in the same polity). Under such circumstances, increased cultural contacts associated with globalization are likely to generate violence and fragmentation, not the new world order promised by globalism's proponents.

## CULTURAL HOMOGENIZATION

Those critics concerned with the concept of cultural homogenization agree that American popular culture may well dominate the world; however, rather than worrying about imposing supposedly "American" values on local populations, these critics fear that corporate-produced mass entertainment will ultimately move everyone's values toward those associated with mass consumer capitalism. One scholar has termed this "McDonaldization."[37] Corporations like McDonald's are expected to have such advantages in economies of scale, organization, predictability, and efficiency that, combined with superior marketing, they will drive traditional providers out of business. The same logic applies if the corporation in question is Walmart, Home Depot, or Starbucks. The fear is that in time everyone everywhere will end up eating the same thing, reading the same thing, and wearing the same thing. Under such circumstances, cultural diversity would be lost forever. What would be left is a world of soulless consumers just looking for the next thing to buy that is exactly like what everyone else in the world already has and wants until the corporations generate the next must-have item. One culture, consumer capitalism, would dominate the world.

Accordingly, whether they fear corruption, imperialism, or homogenization, many people, groups, communities, nations, and cultures around the world can be expected to resist the spread of American popular culture even as American movies, music, and television programming have become a central component in global trade. Indeed, as is addressed throughout this book, many have. In this context, it simply makes no sense to try to understand globalization's recent history or to estimate its likely future without analyzing the critical role American popular culture plays in globalization today.

## CULTURAL HYBRIDITY

There are, however, less skeptical analysts of cultural globalization. One group focuses on the concept of cultural hybridization.[38] Roughly defined as "mixing," hybridization has been defined as "the ways in which forms become separated from existing practices and recombine with new forms and new practices."[39] Such mixing is common in global affairs. Christianity emerged from Judaism and retained many of Judaism's core values before being adopted and integrated into the Roman Empire, for example; it then served as one source for the creation of Islam. Contemporary English is the result of the mixing of an array of cultural and linguistic traditions that began at least a thousand years ago. There were no horses in the Western Hemisphere until Spanish colonists brought them in the sixteenth century; accordingly, the iconic image of Native Americans chasing bison across the plains in the American West was made possible only when two widely different and profoundly hostile cultures came into contact—and indeed when one quite literally made an effort to annihilate the other. What seem to be core dimensions of discrete cultures often turn out, on closer inspection, to be hybrid forms.

Brought into the context of contemporary globalization, the interaction of Western values, institutions, products, and services does not necessarily have to lead to the elimination of local norms and desires in favor of rational, efficient Western alternatives. Instead, businesses can adapt their practices to fit the needs of their workers and the culture of their clients.[40] Or Western corporations may develop a profit interest in celebrating and protecting the diversity of the cultures in which they operate.[41] Cultural communication and hybridization can be a two-way process; Western societies can be as influenced by non-Western ones as non-Western communities are influenced by the West. Jan Nederveen Pieterse has referred to the result as a global mélange.[42] Marwan M. Kraidy suggests that hybridization is the inherent end of globalization.[43]

Hybridization does not always lead to equal cultural exchange, however. Roland Robertson has coined the term *glocalization* to describe the ways globalization can change cultures in favor of the needs, interests, and values of the dominant trading partners. Paying particular attention to questions of identity—how individuals and groups define their values, ideals, and communities—Robertson sees glocalization as a "massive, twofold process involving *the interpenetration of the universalization of particularism and the particularization of universalism.*"[44] Put another way, glocalization describes a process in which established cultures both shape and are undermined by the emergence of a new cosmopolitan culture whose values and ideals are to a large degree determined by the demands of globalization. Robertson thus argues, "The contemporary capitalist creation of consumers frequently involves the tailoring of products to increasingly specialized regional, societal, ethnic, class, and gender markets—so-called micro-marketing." In turn, while the broader global community experiences new products and ideas, the local community is integrated into the global economy as another group of consumers.[45]

Popular culture, as cultural artifacts and products that are marketed around the world, stands in the center of the glocalist/hybridized/globalist dynamic. Different groups and individuals can respond to pieces of popular culture from American sources in diverse ways. As is shown in chapter 5, many groups and nations resist American popular culture as an element of globalization. However, as is addressed in chapter 6, these concerns may be misaimed; globalization is a complex phenomenon, and American popular culture is both less fixed and less permanent than is often supposed. In any case, American popular culture is at the heart of contemporary globalization.

## CONCLUSION

The economic, political, and social dimensions of globalization described above offer an array of perspectives and expectations about globalization's present nature and future course. These range from the promise of a democratic, free market future to the prospect of global cultural war. This book examines the ways that the messages and mechanisms of American popular culture are a force for fragmegration in contemporary globalization. It focuses on the way American public culture is expressed on a global scale in movies, music, television programs, fast-food franchises, sports, and styles of clothing. As will be seen, what is appealing about the American dream for some is repellent to others. What is admirable about a civic culture to one group is proof that people have lost their moral values to another group. What is hopeful in globalism's promise for many is a symptom of the end of uniqueness in another's vision. What is free choice for some is petty consumerism for others. What promises a vision of inexpensive, enjoyable entertainment for some threatens others' livelihoods. Teasing out these dynamics is the task that follows through the rest of this book.

## NOTES

1. Paul Farhi and Megan Rosenfeld, "American Pop Penetrates Worldwide," *Washington Post*, 25 October 1998.

2. Farhi and Rosenfeld, "American Pop Penetrates Worldwide."

3. Joseph S. Nye, *Soft Power: The Means for Success in World Politics* (Cambridge, Mass.: Public Affairs, 2004).

4. Nick Gillespie and Matt Welch, "How *Dallas* Won the Cold War," *Washington Post*, 27 April 2008.

5. Adapted from Toby Miller, "Anti-Americanism and Popular Culture," paper prepared for the Center for Policy Studies, Central European University, 2005.

6. *Foreign Policy*, "World's Most Popular TV Shows," http://www.foreign policy.com/articles/2009/10/19/the_worlds_most_popular_tv_shows (accessed 23 November 2011).

7. Except where noted, these points come from Tim Arango, "World Falls for American Media, Even As It Sours on America," *New York Times*, 20 November 2008, http://www.nytimes.com/2008/12/01/business/media/01soft .html (accessed 29 February 2012).

8. Lauren A. Schuker, "Plot Change: Foreign Forces Transform Hollywood Films," http://online.wsj.com/article/SB10001424052748704913304575 371394036766312.html?KEYWORDS=movie+foreign (accessed 16 September 2011).

9. Tim Arango and Yasir Ghazi, "An Embrace of the U.S., Spun and Mixed by Iraqis," *New York Times*, 12 October 2011.

10. Ian Condry, "Japanese Hip-Hop and the Globalization of Political Culture," in *Urban Life: Readings in the Anthropology of the City*, ed. George Gmelch and Walter Zenner (Prospect Heights, Ill.: Waveland Press, 2001), 357–87.

11. Ulysses, "Hip Hop and the Arab Uprisings," openDemocracy, http://www.opendemocracy.net/ulysses/hip-hop-and-arab-uprisings (accessed 24 February 2012).

12. David Steigerwald, *Culture's Vanities: The Paradox of Cultural Diversity in a Globalized World* (Lanham, Md.: Rowman & Littlefield, 2004), 29.

13. Steigerwald, *Culture's Vanities*, 29–33.

14. Todd Gitlin, "Television Screens: Hegemony in Transition," in *Cultural and Economic Reproduction in Education*, ed. M. Apple (London: Routledge & Kegan Paul, 1981), 202, quoted in Robert Burnett, *The Global Jukebox: The International Music Industry* (New York: Routledge, 1996), 33.

15. Quoted in Steigerwald, *Culture's Vanities*, 38.

16. Cf. Herbert Gans, *Popular Culture and High Culture: An Analysis and Evaluation of Taste* (New York: Basic Books, 1974); Mary Douglas and Baron Isherwood, *The World of Goods* (New York: Basic Books, 1979).

17. Steigerwald, *Culture's Vanities*, 40.

18. "Countries by Continents: Countries of the Americas and the Caribbean," Nations Online, http://www.nationsonline.org/oneworld/america.htm (accessed 16 September 2011).

19. Marc Howard Ross, "Culture and Identity in Comparative Political Analysis," in *Comparative Politics: Rationality, Culture, and Structure*, ed. Mark I. Lichbach and Alan S. Zuckerman (New York: Cambridge University Press, 1997), 42–80.

20. The following discussion rests on a number of works. See, for fuller discussion, John Kenneth White, *The Values Divide: American Politics and Culture in Transition* (New York: Chatham House, 2003); John W. Kingdon, *America the Unusual* (New York: Worth, 1999); Daniel Judah Elazar, *American Federalism: A View from the States*, 3rd ed. (New York: Harper & Row, 1984); Daniel Judah Elazar, *The American Mosaic: The Impact of Space, Time, and Culture on American Politics* (Boulder, Colo.: Westview, 1994); Richard Ellis, *American Political Cultures* (New York: Oxford University Press, 1993); Louis Hartz, *The Liberal Tradition in America* (New York: Harcourt, Brace, 1955); Richard Hofstadter, *The American Political Tradition and the Men Who Made It* (New York: Vintage, 1974); Samuel P. Huntington, *American Politics: The Promise of Disharmony* (Cambridge, Mass.: Belknap, 1981); Seymour Martin Lipset, "American Exceptionalism Reaffirmed," in *Is America Different? A New Look at American Exceptionalism*, ed. B. Shafer (Oxford: Oxford University Press, 1991), 1–45; Frederick Jackson Turner, *The Frontier in American History* (New York: Holt, Rinehart and Winston, 1962); and Aaron Wildavsky, *The Rise of Radical Egalitarianism* (Washington, D.C.: American University Press, 1991). See also Daniel J. Boorstin, *The Genius of American Politics* (Chicago: University of Chicago Press, 1953); James Davison Hunter, *Culture Wars: The*

*Struggle to Define America* (New York: Basic Books, 1991); Seymour Martin Lipset, *American Exceptionalism: A Double-Edged Sword* (New York: Norton, 1996); Charles Lockhart, *The Roots of American Exceptionalism: Institutions, Culture, and Politics* (New York: Palgrave Macmillan, 2003); Deborah L. Madsen, *American Exceptionalism* (Jackson: University of Mississippi Press, 1998); and Trevor B. McCrisken, *American Exceptionalism and the Legacy of Vietnam: U.S. Foreign Policy since 1974* (New York: Palgrave Macmillan, 2003).

21. Isaiah Berlin, *Two Concepts of Liberty* (Oxford: Clarendon Press, 1958).

22. Cf. Sidney E. Mead, *The Nation with the Soul of a Church* (New York: Harper & Row, 1975); Sacvan Bercovitch, *The American Jeremiad* (Madison: University of Wisconsin Press, 1978); Sacvan Bercovitch, *The Puritan Origins of the American Self* (New Haven, Conn.: Yale University Press, 1975); Robert N. Bellah et al., *The Good Society* (New York: Knopf, 1991); Robert N. Bellah et al., *Habits of the Heart: Individualism and Commitment in American Life* (Berkeley and Los Angeles: University of California Press, 1985).

23. Hartz, *Liberal Tradition*.

24. Manfred B. Steger, *Globalization: A Very Short Introduction* (New York: Oxford University Press, 2003), 7–12.

25. James N. Rosenau, *Distant Proximities: Dynamics beyond Globalization* (Princeton, N.J.: Princeton University Press, 2003).

26. See Manfred B. Steger, *Globalism: Market Ideology Meets Terrorism*, 2nd ed. (Lanham, Md.: Rowman & Littlefield, 2005) for a full discussion of this argument.

27. For more expanded explorations of this summary, see Robert Kuttner, *Everything for Sale: The Virtues and Limits of Markets* (New York: Knopf, 1997); Harvey Cox, "The Market as God: Living in the New Dispensation," *The Atlantic*, March 1999, 18–23; Edward Luttwak, *Turbo-Capitalism: Winners and Losers in the Global Economy* (New York: Harper & Row, 1999); Robert Reich, *The Work of Nations* (New York: Vintage, 1992); and Robert O. Keohane, *After Hegemony* (Princeton, N.J.: Princeton University Press, 1984).

28. Steger, *Globalization*, 37–55; Steger, *Globalism*, 24–28. See also Robert J. Holton, *Globalization and the Nation-State* (New York: St. Martin's, 1988); James H. Mittelman, *Globalization: Critical Reflections* (Boulder, Colo.: Lynne Rienner, 1996); and Roland Robertson, *Globalization: Social Theory and Global Culture* (London: Sage, 1992).

29. Cf. Lowell Bryan and Diana Farrell, *Market Unbound: Unleashing Global Capitalism* (New York: Wiley, 1996); Kenichi Ohmae, *The End of the Nation-State: The Rise of Regional Economies* (New York: Free Press, 1995); Kenichi Ohmae, *The Borderless World: Power and Strategy in the Interlinked World Economy* (New York: HarperBusiness, 1990); Lester Thurow, *The Future*

*of Capitalism: How Today's Economic Forces Shape Tomorrow's World* (New York: Morrow, 1996).

30. Jan Nederveen Pieterse, *Globalization and Culture: Global Mélange* (Lanham, Md.: Rowman & Littlefield, 2004), 12–13.

31. Steger, *Globalization*, 67.

32. Nigel Harris, *National Liberation* (London: I. B. Tauris, 1990); Francis Adams, Satya Dev Gupta, and Kidane Mengisteab, eds., *Globalization and the Dilemmas of the State in the South* (London: St. Martin's, 1999); Philip G. Cerny, *The Changing Architecture of Politics: Structure, Agency, and the Future of the State* (London: Sage, 1990); Michael Connors, *The Race to the Intelligent State: Charting the Global Information Economy in the Twenty-first Century* (Oxford: Capstone, 1997); Liah Greenfield, *Nationalism: Five Roads to Modernity* (Cambridge, Mass.: Harvard University Press, 1992).

33. For fuller discussion of each of these points, see Warren Agee, Phillip Ault, and Edwin Emery, *Introduction to Mass Communication*, 10th ed. (New York: HarperCollins, 1991); John R. Bittner, *Mass Communication: An Introduction*, 4th ed. (Englewood Cliffs, N.J.: Prentice Hall, 1986); Stanley J. Baran and Dennis K. Davis, *Mass Communication Theory: Foundations, Ferment, and Future* (Belmont, Calif.: Wadsworth, 1995); Ronald T. Farrar, *Mass Communication: An Introduction to the Field* (St. Paul, Minn.: West, 1988).

34. Donald K. Emmerson, "Singapore and the 'Asian Values' Debate," *Journal of Democracy* 6, no. 4 (1995): 95–105.

35. Samuel Huntington, *The Clash of Civilizations and the Remaking of World Order* (New York: Simon & Schuster, 1996).

36. Benjamin Barber, *Jihad vs. McWorld: How Globalism and Tribalism Are Reshaping the World* (New York: Ballantine Books, 1996), 9.

37. George Ritzer, *The McDonaldization of Society: An Investigation into the Changing Character of Contemporary Social Life* (London: Sage, 1993).

38. Cf. Arjun Appadurai, *Modernity at Large: Cultural Dimensions of Globalization* (Minneapolis: University of Minnesota Press, 1996); Ulf Hannerz, *Cultural Complexity: Studies in the Social Organization of Meaning* (New York: Columbia University Press, 1992); Ulf Hannerz, *Transnational Connections: Cultures, People, Places* (London: Routledge, 1996); Pieterse, *Globalization and Culture*, 52–55.

39. William Rowe and Vivian Schelling, *Memory and Modernity: Popular Culture in Latin America* (London: Verso, 1991), 231.

40. James L. Watson, ed., *Golden Arches East: McDonald's in East Asia* (Stanford, Calif.: Stanford University Press, 1997).

41. Marwan M. Kraidy, *Hybridity, or the Cultural Logic of Globalization* (Philadelphia: Temple University Press, 2005).

42. See Pieterse, *Globalization and Culture*, for a full discussion of this point.

43. Kraidy, *Hybridity*.

44. Robertson, *Globalization*, 100 (emphasis in original).

45. Robertson, *Globalization*, 100–102.

# CHAPTER 2

## "AMERICAN" POPULAR CULTURE IN MOVIES, MUSIC, AND TELEVISION

To write (or read) a book on the effect(s) of American popular culture on contemporary globalization is to assume, perhaps without being aware of it, that there is something uniquely American about the popular culture made or developed in the United States and consumed around the world. Chapter 1 introduced the notion that American public culture contains an array of values, norms, and practices that distinguish it from other cultures. In particular, American public culture was shown to be "civic": members of the political community publicly declare that Americans believe in ideals and values that promote the dignity and rights of all individuals—whether they actually practice what they preach or not. These values include particular forms of liberty, political equality, individualism, democracy, tolerance, exceptionalism, and capitalism.

Yet the global popular culture corporations that control much of the world's trade in popular culture (see chapters 3 and 4 for discussions of them) have an interest in not appearing to be agents of one culture or another. Cultures often conflict, after all, and as was discussed in chapter 1, people often resent and resist cultural products that come from foreign, distant places and that seem to undermine the ideals and values of local people, especially children. Global corporations have an incentive to be secular, not cultural. Put another way, a cultural content producer that is seen to be overtly "American" may have a hard time selling its goods on the global market. Corporations might well try to avoid being labeled "American" as a consequence.

Whatever pressures exist to the contrary, popular culture can be seen to reflect the values of the nation from which it emerges. According to Ernest Gellner, this is the result of the Industrial Revolution, which made the creation of mass-produced popular culture possible in the first place. Gellner notes that achieving a goal in an industrial community requires more than walking from one end of a field to the other with a plow. Instead, running a complex machine or managing money or overseeing people as they work requires a sophisticated understanding of others' ideas, expectations, and goals. People in an industrial society need to understand how their work connects with the work of an entire system of processes, actions, and actors if they are to create a car, balance a corporation's accounts, or coordinate the efforts of an entire factory floor. The Industrial Revolution thus required that millions of formerly illiterate, uneducated peasants learn to read, work mathematical equations, and engage in a variety of abstract thinking activities that had previously been undertaken only by political and social elites. As a consequence, education and social systems had to change to accommodate the new economic reality. Universal education, at least to the level of literacy and abstract thought, became standard, for example, and social and legal codes that kept people in rural communities were changed to promote migration from rural areas to cities. The majority of the community's citizens became part of its "high" culture rather than its "low" one.[1]

Importantly, Gellner notes that to say a culture is "high" is not to say it is "neutral." Access to high culture is not just a matter of being educated, literate, and capable of understanding instructions on how to operate a machine because one understands the principles on which the machine operates (abstract reasoning). Instead, high culture "has to be articulated in some definite language, such as Russian or English or Arabic, and it must also contain rules for comportment in life; in other words, it must contain a 'culture.'" As a consequence, "modern industrial High Culture is not colourless; it has an 'ethnic' colouring, which is its essence. The cultural norm incorporates expectations, requirements and prescriptions, which impose obligations on its members."[2] In the end, then, the products of the Industrial Revolution necessarily express the values and ideals of the culture that produced them. This is true whether the product is language, a car, or popular culture artifacts like movies, music, and television programs or clothes, eating establishments, sports, and cars.

This chapter explores the "Americanness" of American popular culture. It examines how national culture can be reflected in popular culture and summarizes academic studies that link popular culture and American culture. It also explores the many formulas, genres, and conventions that shape American popular culture products in specific and predictably American ways, even in a global era.

## AMERICAN CIVIC CULTURE AND AMERICAN POPULAR CULTURE

There is empirical support for Gellner's theoretical linkage of national and popular cultures. For example, Allen McBride and Robert K. Toburen offer a useful and interesting explanation of how the values of American civic culture are expressed in American popular culture in their work "Deep Structures: Polpop Culture on Primetime Television."[3] McBride and Toburen analyze the content of fifteen of the twenty most popular television programs from the 1992 broadcast year. (They did not examine programs that lacked a continuing story line, like news magazines or clip shows such as *America's Funniest Home Videos*.) Thirteen of the programs were situation comedies; the others were hour-long dramas of various sorts.

The specific focus of their analysis was conflict: how it arose, who resolved it, and how and when it was resolved. For McBride and Toburen, conflict serves as a useful indicator of the cultural values of a given community. Different cultures can be expected to both initiate and resolve conflicts differently. In a traditional community, for example, conflict would likely emerge when an individual challenged his or her assigned place in the system, and the conflict would likely be resolved through appeal to community standards and norms. In an individualist society, by contrast, simply challenging hierarchical norms would likely be insufficient to start a conflict, and an appeal to comply with group values is unlikely to resolve a conflict with a person motivated by the desire to improve his or her personal lot in life.

McBride and Toburen's central finding is consistent with the idea that the United States has a civic culture organized around the rights of individuals. They show that individualist values dominate both conflict and conflict resolution on popular American television programming. In the programs they studied, most conflicts were between individuals, at least one of whom was usually seeking some personal benefit for himself or herself or a friend or loved one. The conflict was usually resolved through interpersonal negotiation, bargaining, and cooperation—although the fact that many of the shows involved family relationships guaranteed that many conflicts were resolved through an appeal to an authority figure like a parent. In any case, McBride and Toburen show that the core civic value of individualism is omnipresent in popular American television shows.

Conrad Kottak's analysis of Brazilian television provides additional confirmation of the individualism apparent in American television programming, while adding additional insights to this finding. Kottak notes that compared to American programming, Brazilian television shows are more focused on the importance of extended traditional families. Rather than showing adults who live far away from home and have interesting or important jobs, for example, Brazilian programs show adults living at or near home and interacting with their family members instead of bosses, social leaders, or members of the broader community. Similarly, Kottak finds that Brazilians have less expectation of privacy than do Americans. Family members, servants, and others can easily walk into or out of homes or overhear personal conversations through the usually open doors and windows of Brazilian homes. Brazilian programming emerges from a web of social interdependence and accountability, while American programming derives from the deep individualism of American life.[4]

Kottak also sees the value of political equality reflected very differently in Brazilian and American television. Issues of social and eco-

nomic class, for example, are largely absent from American programming (even though they certainly exist in American life), but class and
status are central to Brazilian television. Few American programs make
the economic class of their stars a central focus of their story lines. The
characters in American programs rarely, if ever, link their social and
economic status to political or financial factors beyond their control,
even if the shows focus on working-class families or characters. Likewise, better-off characters like doctors and lawyers are usually seen to
have achieved their status by their own hard work, not as the result of
some racial, ethnic, gender, or class bias. By contrast, Kottak notes that
Brazilian programming reflects the social, political, and economic in-
equalities in Brazilian life. The class and racial foundations of Brazilian
programming stand in stark contrast to the egalitarian ethic that is one
of the defining characteristics of American public culture and is usually
reflected in American popular culture.

Kottak is also insightful on issues of race in both Brazilian and American societies. In the United States, race is a fairly rigid category that is
ascribed to a person at birth. It is fixed through some combination of
color, appearance, parentage, and culture. In contrast, race in Brazil is
fluid. There are few if any markers like color, hair type, or background
that Brazilians use to ascribe racial categories to individuals. As a consequence, characters are rarely defined by race in Brazilian programming.

Yet Kottak notes that black characters have been both more common and more popular in the United States than they are on Brazilian
television. This is true even though the major audience for U.S. programming is white. *The Cosby Show*, for example, was both the number
one show in the United States for a number of years in the late 1980s
and early 1990s and one of the most distributed programs worldwide.
It focused on the lives of an African American family, the Huxtables.
However, its story lines usually revolved around typical family situations rather than the complexities of living as a black family in a racist
nation. The Huxtable parents had jobs—one as a doctor and the other
as a lawyer—that they had earned as a result of their hard work. They
were able to provide their children with a healthy and comfortable
home. They lived in a large New York City house and interacted easily
and comfortably with a diverse range of Americans. In other words, the
Huxtable family was self-sufficient, individualist, egalitarian, and tolerant—quintessential Americans.

Notably, white Americans celebrated this vision of an employed, educated, and successful African American family. The Huxtables reflected the broad patterns of American public culture in ways that reinforced the ideals Americans claim to value—such as hard work, tolerance, capitalist success, and so on. The correlation between the Huxtables' lives and the values of American public culture made it easy for white Americans to embrace the Huxtables as an African American version of the American dream. Put another way, it is hard to imagine a television show being as popular as *The Cosby Show* was if the family were dysfunctional and headed by a single woman working several jobs or receiving welfare who decried her fate as a black female in a racist America. Her story would not fit American cultural values as closely as the Huxtables' story did.

Timothy Havens has offered an extended analysis of *The Cosby Show*'s popularity as "the biggest show in the world." For Havens, *The Cosby Show* was noteworthy for its ability to address issues of race, racism, and economic inequality in a way that was recognizable and appealing to audiences worldwide. Thus, rather than making economic hardship and social exclusion a central theme of the show (a theme that would be hard to pull off given the economic and social status of the parents in the show), the program addressed questions of race and discrimination in indirect ways. For example, the Huxtables' son, Theo, had an "Abolish Apartheid" sticker on his bedroom door. Show plots included discussions of the significance of the civil rights movement both in the past and in contemporary life. African American art hung on the Huxtables' walls, while jazz and blues, musical forms often associated with black performers, played in the house. In other words, *The Cosby Show* could appeal to diverse audiences because it provided an appealing vision of a happy, integrated African American family enjoying the full promise of American life.[5]

The Huxtables do more than just express an American way of life, however. They manifest the notion of transparency. Scott Robert Olson explains that American popular culture, as a result of a unique mix of cultural factors addressed further in chapter 3, "has a competitive advantage in the creation and global distribution of cultural taste." This advantage is transparency, which he defines as "any textual apparatus that allows audiences to project indigenous values, beliefs, rites and rituals into imported media or the use of those devices." Thus, Olson continues, "This transparency effect means that American cultural exports, such as cinema, television, and related merchandise, manifest narrative structures that easily blend into other cultures."[6]

Havens finds transparency in the reaction of international audiences to *The Cosby Show*. Drawing on other research, Havens quotes a resident of Barbados as noting, about *The Cosby Show*, "Black people in this show are not isolated, no fun is made of Blackness, and the characters are shown as leading wholesome moral lives." Similarly, a black South African viewer simply explains, "The show makes me proud of being black." Another black South African even sees hope in *The Cosby Show* for educating and persuading white South Africans to treat blacks with dignity and respect: "*The Cosby Show* . . . is saying, 'Come on, you white guys [in South Africa], the blacks are not so bad as you make them out to be. Look at us, we are having a good life and normal problems here in America. Give those guys down there a chance. Let's change for the better and live together, not apart.'" Havens even finds nonblack audiences identifying with the Huxtable family: a Lebanese Shiite man notes, "American blacks are a little like us. They have big families."[7] American stories and contexts as depicted in *The Cosby Show* are thus both American and transparent across a wide variety of cultures. This combination makes it relatively easy for American popular culture to spread across the globe—particularly when it is distributed as described in chapters 3 and 4.

At least one other study has highlighted the cultural content of American programming. Daradirek Ekachai, Mary Hinchliff-Pelias, and Rosechongporn Komolsevin examined the influence U.S. media have on the perception of the United States by regular consumers of U.S. movies, music, and television in Thailand. Thailand has a long history of showing U.S. programming. Television shows like *Dallas*, *L.A. Law*, and *Magnum, P.I.* were popular in Thailand, as were movies like *Jaws*, *Raiders of the Lost Ark*, and the *Rambo* and *Die Hard* series. Thais have also regularly been exposed to sports programming from the NBA, the NFL, and boxing. Researchers polled Thai viewers of American programming and found results that Conrad Kottak's Brazilian audience might well recognize. Thais believe Americans are individualistic and committed to their rights to self-expression and personal development. In particular, Thais see Americans as individualistic, pleasure loving, scientifically minded, passionate, impulsive, athletic, musical, persistent, practical, and efficient. In contrast, Thais thought Americans were *not* traditional, naïve, loyal to family, lazy, or quiet. The researchers also found that frequent TV viewers were 47 percent more likely to believe that the depictions of American life they saw accurately reflected American reality than were occasional or infrequent viewers. Fifty-six percent of those who saw four or more American movies per week believed that those films accurately captured life in the United States, compared with 43 percent of moderate viewers and 33 percent of occasional viewers.[8] At least for Thais, then, American popular culture was seen to have an explicitly American content.

## "AMERICAN" STORIES

Empirical studies provide a useful look into the ways America's civic culture can be seen to inform the popular culture products produced in the United States, but they are not the only way such influence can be seen. It is also possible to disentangle the threads of culture and see how they ground pop culture products. Even as American political and social values are manifested in American popular culture, they are enmeshed in products that link those political and social values with images, themes, and content that often anger and frighten people both in the United States and around the world. Understanding the stereotypical formulations in which American popular culture is presented to the world is an important part of understanding how American popular culture feeds contemporary globalization.

*The ubiquity of American English.* One aspect of American popular culture that needs discussion is something that, to a native speaker of American English, is perhaps so obvious as to be ignored: the fact that almost all of it is produced in American English. Throughout most of its period of dominance in world entertainment, American popular culture has been made, sold, and even consumed in American English. (There is a growing market of American-made content in Spanish, as will be discussed in chapter 5.) People worldwide have had access to programming and other cultural artifacts that are expressed in "American." And while some of that programming might be available dubbed in the local language or presented with subtitles, not all of it is: I, for example, watched *Crocodile Dundee* in English (American and Australian, in this case) one rainy night in Amsterdam. (I later saw it dubbed into Italian in Rome.) This simple fact—that American audiovisual entertainment is conceived and distributed in American English—helps explain the global reach of American popular culture.

Moreover, the marketing tie-ins to which the products of American popular culture are linked (discussed in chapter 3), whether Mickey Mouse's ears or a *Star Wars* T-shirt, are often recognizably and obviously both American and in English. Accordingly, whether directly (watching a movie in which the dialogue is in American English) or in consuming products derived from American popular culture, the use and consumption of American popular culture has a distinctively American character—a character that, as discussed in chapters 3, 4, and 5, can provoke concerns from people who believe that the language in which movies, music, and television programs are being presented is systematically destroying indigenous cultures.

*Happy endings.* Another remarkably consistent feature of most American audiovisual entertainments is the happy ending. On America's televisions and movie screens, problems almost always resolve themselves in the allotted time: the situation comedy ends with a homily about family love; the cop show's bad guy goes to jail; the hero of the action-adventure movie is reunited with his or her child/family/ buddies. Even *Titanic*, one of the most popular movies of all time, manages a happy ending amid the horrors of that ship's sinking: the heroine loses her lover to the frigid waters of the North Atlantic, but she is improbably rescued as a sole survivor in a sea of corpses, escapes her hated fiancé, marries for love, and has a wonderful family—all while keeping her ship-borne love in her heart forever.

Notably, the centrality and significance of the happy ending in American popular culture contrasts sharply with the endings offered in many European-produced works. For example, directors like Ingmar Bergman (Sweden) or Federico Fellini (Italy) created works that depicted disturbing, even painful, stories that, like real life, often, if not always, end badly or even bizarrely. In European movies and programs, bad guys are not always caught, lovers do not always find each other by the closing credits, and people do not always learn lessons about life from which they can grow into better people.

The happy ending is a central feature of American popular culture for several reasons, not the least of which is the role played by social forces like the Production Code, the McCarthy hearings, and FCC regulations. To anticipate the analysis of these forces to be offered in chapter 3, the early producers of American movies sought to put an American stamp on their work and mandated that the good guys, however defined (white-hatted cowboys, police detectives, and the like) *had* to beat the bad guys in all their films. This mandate expressed itself in endless serialized films shown to millions of audience members year after year after year. It set an audience expectation that could be challenged only at the risk of running afoul of public and political pressure. Moreover, once established, this formula served as the foundation for producing the endless number of television shows and movies needed to fill the growing market for popular culture. The happy ending thus made both business and political sense as a central feature of American popular culture.

*Triumphant individuals.* The happy ending is more than a "feel good" close to an American movie or TV show, however. It also serves to emphasize the importance of the individual in determining his or her own fate and happiness. The happy ending is, in large measure, an audiovisual manifestation of the myth of the self-made man expressed in nineteenth-century tales like the Horatio Alger stories. Horatio Alger wrote hundreds of dime novels in which anyone, no matter his life circumstances, could succeed through hard work, perseverance, and dedication. One's class background was irrelevant: a poor boy could become rich through effort. In fact, one's station in life was ultimately one's own responsibility: since everyone could succeed, failure to succeed was the obvious result of one's laziness.

Happy endings teach Alger's lesson to contemporary audiences. Bruce Willis might have to run (improbably) across broken glass in his bare feet while fighting the heavily armed, well-trained, numerous bad guys in *Die Hard*, for example, but because he is willing to do it and committed to his task he is able to defeat the obviously European terrorists who are holding his wife and her co-workers hostage. Similarly, Scarlett O'Hara may have had her house burned down and lost her lover by the end of *Gone with the Wind*, but "tomorrow," she says, "is another day," as she swears she will never be hungry again. No problem is too big for the individual to overcome; no limitation is determinative of one's fate. The happy ending is triumphant American individualism made real on screen.

*Spectacle.* Likewise, the visual spectacle of dramatic special effects offers a lure to audiovisual culture that few non-Hollywood products can offer. As a practical matter, the concentration of talent and financing available to American movie, music, and television makers allows their products to be made to a standard that far exceeds that which can be met by most global competitors. The most obvious example of this phenomenon lies in big-budget, "blockbuster" films: whether *Die Hard*, *Star Wars*, or *Avatar*, American films are far more likely to be extremely expensive to make, with elaborate special effects to carry the story forward. Indeed, elaborate special effects have the additional advantage of being transparent: an exploding spaceship tracing a fiery arc as it burns up in an alien planet's atmosphere requires no culturally sensitive nuance to understand. It is its own meaning.

There is another form of spectacle evident in American audiovisual popular culture: opulent consumerism. Whether it is rap music videos filled with Cadillac Escalades, ever-larger gold crosses proclaiming the wearer's Christian faith, other sources of "bling," or the luxurious setting of Southfork ranch in *Dallas*, most American movies, music, and television programs create fantasy worlds of extraordinary wealth. Even television shows set among the allegedly poor—*Roseanne* and *Grace under Fire* stand as useful examples—have their families living in relatively large houses surrounded by refrigerators, microwave ovens, dishwashers, televisions, VCRs, cars, and other assorted consumer goods that are unimaginable extravagances in much of the world. The trend toward wealth in families, particularly on television, has led to a relative doubling in the salaries paid to TV fathers of contemporary programs versus those of the 1950s.[9] As a consequence, American popular culture presents a vision of Americans as wealthy, consumerist, and self-interested.

As was the case with happy endings and triumphant individualism, spectacle and consumerism can be seen as a logical extension of American cultural values. Material wealth can stand in as a marker of individual success, for example, and thus it can seem that the more you have the more successful you are. This isn't always true, of course, but it's a common perception. Wealth, opulence, and excess are symbols of a particular form of individualism, and they reinforce the "me-ness" of American life.

*The morality of violence.* In addition to being filled with happy individuals enjoying vast wealth, American audiovisual popular culture is also a remarkably violent place. The popularity of police procedural television programs like *Law and Order* and *CSI*, for example, ensures that popular American television programming, especially the programming popular around the world, is awash in violence. Shows like *CSI* take as much advantage of computer graphics in presenting violence as films do. Through computer animation, audiences see bullets penetrate skin, shatter bones, and slice through arteries, leading to arcs of blood spurting across the screen and splattering across walls. Some rap musicians have linked violence and the acquisition of wealth in their songs and videos; in the Doors' hit "The End," lead singer Jim Morrison imagines murdering his father and raping his mother. Garth Brooks, in his country hit "Papa Loved Mama," describes a jealous man driving his eighteen-wheel truck into the motel room where his wife is cheating on him, killing both his wife and her lover. The country band The Dixie Chicks joyfully sings about murdering Earl, the wife-beating bad guy in their number one song, "Goodbye Earl." Unlike the husband in "Papa Loves Mama," the wife and friend who kill Earl get away with their crime and prosper after his death. Indeed, according to one report, the average American child sees eight thousand murders depicted on television before finishing grade school.[10] Given how many hours of television American children watch, they may see an average of ten thousand rapes, assaults, and murders each year.[11]

Importantly, violence is not necessarily a bad thing, at least as presented in American movies, music, and television programs. Instead, it can have a moral purpose that legitimizes its use. Take, for example, the inevitable plot of an action-adventure movie. Pick one—they are all quite literally the same. These plots are transparent, to use Olson's phrase: the plot is so formulaic that audiences around the world can recognize it instantly. Such films usually show individual, heroic action in defense of what are often offered as or assumed to be American values or the American way of life. (Superman's actual purpose as a superhero was to defend truth, justice, and the American way, for example.) A hero—almost always male—stands as a lone individual facing some great evil. (In some cases the hero is reluctant; in others, anxious.) Usually heroes are people with some special training or power—for example, Special Forces veterans or, depending on subgenre, superheroes of some kind or another. In a few cases they are recognizably ordinary, however. The odds are usually overwhelming and the stakes are typically high: a child is being held hostage, or the safety of the world or some other grand fate hinges on the victory of the hero. Then the bloodbath begins. The hero slaughters untold numbers of the enemy and either escapes unharmed or is wounded only enough to enhance the dramatic tension. In this modern era of computer graphics, much of this destruction is accompanied by extraordinarily vivid explosions, graphic depictions of mangled flesh, and a soundtrack that drives the action at a frenzied pace. All this violence, of course, is depicted as necessary for achieving whatever goal the hero must accomplish; anything less and the child dies or the world explodes or evil conquers the innocent. We may see dozens (and more!) slaughtered, but since either they deserved it or it was necessary to secure the community, the violence is appropriate and laudable. (As an aside, the Dixie Chicks' "Goodbye Earl" tells essentially the same story, only in this case with a female as the defender of the communal good.)

What is important here is the use to which violence is put. When violence defends and expands community values and norms, it is laudable and worthy. Violence in defense of Americanness is thus a moral act, not an immoral one.

*Gendered popular culture.* American audiovisual culture is also deeply embedded in American cultural stereotypes on gender. In part this can be seen in the fact that most action hero individualists in American films are male. (Ellen Ripley, played by Sigourney Weaver in the *Alien* series, is a notable exception.) More broadly, the question of what roles men and women ought to play in society is a regular source of controversy in social and political life around the world. American popular culture has certainly employed issues of gender in its products; these images and themes have been and continue to be controversial both in the United States and across the rest of the globe. And, notably, they have tended to reproduce American social patterns for global audiences to emulate or fear. For better and for worse, American audiovisual culture depicts a particular vision of American life for the world's movie, music, and television audiences.

At least four stereotypes of women's roles in society can be identified in American audiovisual products, for example. One is the woman as sex object. In this role, women serve as little more than eye candy for the sexual enjoyment of the audience. A linked stereotype is that of woman as victim. In this role, females are dominated, often through sexual violence, into accepting the will of an authority figure—usually, although not always, a man. Another common gender stereotype in American popular culture is that of the traditional wife and mother. Explored and ultimately enshrined in such 1950s television classics as *Leave It to Beaver* and *Father Knows Best*, this image usually depicts a woman whose life is devoted to her family. She is the master of the private realm of family life, working endlessly to cook, clean, care for the children, and support her husband as he interacts with the outer, public world. Admittedly, over time this role has evolved along with the American family—Carol Brady, in the 1970s TV hit *The Brady Bunch*, had to deal with a blended family, for example—but the basic pattern of the role has remained relatively unchanged. A final female stereotype is that of the "strong woman," which usually comes in one of two forms: the superwoman who balances family and career to be a success in the world at large, or the victimized woman who throws off her oppressors and becomes a new, independent person.

For males, the range of gender roles tends to be more limited. As a rule, men are either (1) strong and assertive or (2) wimpy and effeminate—even implicitly or explicitly homosexual. Those males who are seen to have appropriately "male" values tend to be in positions of authority or athletes; in both cases, they are defined by their endless pursuit of sexual conquests. By contrast, "failed" males hold weak positions at work, are dominated and mocked by colleagues and families, or are incompetent at sexual gamesmanship. While there has been a noticeable shift toward an acceptance of gay male characters, particularly on television programs like *Modern Family* and *Queer Eye for the Straight Guy*, these characters almost always conform to the effeminate notion of homosexuality—and so, by extension, make the life of a nonassertive heterosexual male all the more complicated by allusion to gayness. Rap music is particularly noted for its expressive homophobia. Other conceptions of maleness rarely make it to the screen, the CD, or the multiplex.

*The lure and challenges of sex.* Sex and sexuality are also central to American popular culture. Sexuality, like violence, is enticing, engaging, and likely to hold an audience, particularly when it tests social limits on sexual expression. And, as was the case with depictions of gender, the treatment of sexuality in American movies, music, and television provides a frame on which global audiences can either be enticed or shocked by the lure of sexual freedom, or by the horror of it.

Much sexual activity in American movies, music, and television programming is focused on the immediate gratification of individual desire, for example. In scene after scene, people are seen to meet and bed one another quickly and readily. Such couplings are rarely consequential: few people get pregnant or are infected with venereal diseases; people connect because they want to "hook up" and then move on. In almost all cases, these events are presented in individualist, hedonist, self-interested terms. Movies like *The Brown Bunny* have shown established, award-winning actors engaged in explicit sex acts, and one famous episode of the popular television comedy series *Seinfeld* was organized around a contest to see who among the program's cast could resist masturbating for the longest period of time. Indeed, entire series—notably the HBO hit *Sex and the City*—have been organized around the sexual adventures of the program's stars.

Music, too, has emphasized the fun and freedom of sexual activity. The apparent sexual energy and movements of rock and roll have been a matter of public concern at least since Ed Sullivan ordered the cameras on his 1950s-era show not to film Elvis Presley's gyrating hips during the star's first televised performance. In retrospect, such concerns seem quaint. Lyrics like those in the peppy Beach Boys' hit "I Get Around," which asserts "and we've never missed yet with the girls we meet," have evolved through the Beatles' classic "Why Don't We Do It in the Road?" and beyond. Kelis, in her 2003 rap song "Milkshake," is a virtual prostitute advertising her sexual skill and superiority when she asserts: "My milkshake brings all the boys to the yard / And they're like, it's better than yours / Damn right, it's better than yours / I could teach you, but I'd have to charge." The Bloodhound Gang managed to create an entire new vocabulary of implied sex acts by describing their desire to "power drill the yippee bog / With the dude piston" and to "put the you know what in the you know where" in their rock song "Foxtrot Uniform Charlie Kilo"—the military call signs for the letters F, U, C, and K. Britney Spears offered a similarly circumspect double entendre in a 2009 hit song in which she explained, "All the boys and all the girls are begging to 'If You Seek Amy.'" The disco classic "Lady Marmalade" explicitly asks: "Voulez-vous coucher avec moi?" ("Do you want to sleep with me?") The country classic "Help Me Make It through the Night" insists: "I don't care what's right or wrong / I won't try to understand / Let the devil take tomorrow / 'Cause tonight I need a friend."

The link between music and sexuality is nowhere more explicit than in contemporary music videos, which are among the most globally popular products of American popular culture. Song lyrics that are already aggressively sexual are regularly framed in highly erotic or sexually suggestive images and situations. From Madonna's "Like a Virgin" video, in which she rolls on the floor wearing a wedding dress and making moaning sounds while describing herself as being "like a virgin, touched for the very first time" at her lover's caress, through the Pussycat Dolls' "Don't Cha," in which scantily clad women tease a potential boyfriend with provocative dancing and questions like "Don't cha wish your girlfriend was hot like me? / Don't cha wish your girlfriend was a freak like me?" music videos have traded on sexually stimulating imagery to sell their products. Indeed, there has been something of a "race to the bottom" as once-scandalous images (Madonna kissing an African American statue depicting Jesus Christ, which brings the figure to life, for example, in "Like a Prayer") become bland. Lady Gaga has made a career of transgressing established norms—including the norms she herself sets. The next video, then, needs to capture the attention of an audience that has, quite literally, seen it all.

Issues of sex and sexuality do not stop at the depiction of heterosexual sexuality, of course. Accordingly, American popular culture also depicts other aspects of sexuality, some of which, such as homosexuality and transgendering, are controversial. The first mainstream American television program to feature a leading male character who was gay was the 1970s comedy *Soap*. Another 1970s show, *Three's Company*, revolved around the efforts of a straight male character to pass as a gay man in order to live with two female friends whose landlord was opposed to gender cohabitation. The popular comedy *Modern Family* features central characters that are gay. The 1970s film *Dog Day Afternoon* featured Al Pacino as a bank robber motivated by the desire to raise funds for his homosexual lover's sex-change operation; twenty years later, Robin Williams and Nathan Lane played a gay couple of long standing who run a business together in a highly sympathetic portrayal of homosexuality in *The Birdcage*. Notably, the business is a nightclub in which men perform in elaborate cross-dressing extravaganzas dressed as famous women.

Lesbianism, too, has been a common feature of American popular culture's products. The 1982 film *Personal Best*, in which Mariel Hemingway's character engages in a torrid affair with another woman, was the first significant depiction of lesbianism in a popular American movie. A similar first was broken in the 1980s sitcom *Roseanne* when Roseanne's sister kissed another woman on primetime TV. Today such depictions have become commonplace. For example, a cottage industry of *Girls Gone Wild* videos, recording the alleged antics of college-aged women across America as they kiss and fondle and expose one another, has sprung up, and the comedian Ellen DeGeneres, perhaps Hollywood's most famous lesbian, has her own daily talk show. Music videos, particularly rap and rock videos, regularly show their male stars surrounded by groups of women touching and kissing each other. If anything, contemporary American popular culture seems to celebrate lesbians—at least in the case of attractive women who appeal to men (or other women) by making sexual contact with other attractive women.

Even issues of transgendering are regular, if not common, elements of American popular culture. The shock rock star Marilyn Manson often appears on stage wearing a plastic body suit that makes him appear both nude and without genitalia. An earlier generation of rock stars, the members of the band Kiss, made themselves famous by wearing outrageous costumes and elaborate makeup. Actress Hilary Swank won an Academy Award for her portrayal of a woman who is ultimately beaten to death for hiding her gender behind male clothes and restrictive undergarments in *Boys Don't Cry*. Another Academy Award–winning film, *The Silence of the Lambs*, records the efforts of law enforcement officials to find a serial killer who, it turns out, wanted to undergo a sex-change operation but was rejected as psychologically unstable. In American popular culture, boys will not always just be boys.

*The intersection of sex and violence.* At least one other aspect of sex and sexuality needs to be addressed if the link between American popular culture and global reactions to it is to be understood: its link to violence. Sex and sexuality are, of course, among the most emotionally charged aspects of human life; given the extraordinary tension that accompanies human sexuality, it is perhaps not surprising that violence is one aspect of the experience of sex. Linked to the evident marketing appeal of violence, the sex and violence dimension of American popular culture should be expected. Thus, as many of the examples of movies, music, and television programs listed above suggest, violence is a regular part of the depiction of sexuality in the products of American political culture. As was noted earlier, Hilary Swank's character is beaten to death for hiding her biological sex, and Al Pacino's character is willing to rob a bank and risk killing innocent people in order to fund his lover's operation. In other cases, the sex-violence linkage is more purely prurient: its sole purpose is to shock and horrify its audience with the image of a paralyzed woman being raped and murdered. Whether as an accurate expression of the pains and tensions of human emotions, or as a virtually pornographic tool of exploitation and audience appeal, violence is often linked to sexuality in American popular culture.

*The nuclear(ish) family.* When families are depicted in American popular culture, they tend to appear in three forms, two of which are profoundly dysfunctional and the third of which is, at best, improbable. The first form is at the root of many, if not most, situation comedies. It centers on hapless and incompetent fathers, faithful and persistent wives (if they exist in the show—many such programs feature only divorced or widowed fathers) who really hold the family together, and an array of loud-mouthed, basically disrespectful children who provide the family tensions around which the show revolves. The children, in turn, may or may not be biologically related to either or both parents. If the program admits that parents have parents themselves and includes the grandparents in the program, the grandparents are as often a burden as a help—an adult version of the show's children. Every half-hour, some problem is introduced, chaos ensues, and order is restored through the love everyone actually feels for one another.

A second dysfunctional family form appears on one of the most globally popular forms of American programming, the soap opera/melodrama, especially on television. Such melodramas regularly use the family as their dramatic focus; however, families in the serial universe are not mutually supportive bastions of strength to help each other through a troubled world. Instead, soap opera families are internally competitive and vicious. Brothers and fathers scheme to sleep with each others' wives and girlfriends; sisters and mothers engage in a constant barrage of gossip and criticism that intends only to undermine another's self-confidence and self-worth and so enhance the gossiper's chance of sleeping with the other person's husband or boyfriend. While the members of the family are often alleged to have important jobs that generate great wealth, no one actually ever goes to work; instead, everyone spends all their time attacking and manipulating each other emotionally as well as sexually. While everyone is well dressed and has expensive possessions, family is an obstacle, not a key, to happiness.

The third typical family form in American popular culture derives from the power woman stereotype. In this convention, the mother is often important and powerful and well off; her problems, such as they are, come from struggling to find time to balance the competing pressures of job, family, and romance. More often than not, however, the family is relatively harmonious with happy children and a satisfied spouse, even if the families are blended among two or more divorced/ widowed couples. Unlike the 1950s, when father knew best, housework is now a shared responsibility, as is care of the children. The end result is well-adjusted children enjoying a middle-class lifestyle—or better.

*Race and ethnicity.* Race and ethnicity is yet another area of human life in which American popular culture broadcasts stereotypical, often offensive, images and themes. Indeed, many of these stereotypes predate the emergence of electronic media and stand as legacies of the racist and ethnically discriminatory policies that the United States has adopted and defended throughout much of its history. Thus, in general, whites, especially the white Anglo-Saxon Protestants known as WASPs, have been shown to be the best educated, most effective, most law-abiding members of society. They are seen to fill most positions of authority in the political, economic, and social system. Notable exceptions to these patterns have been Catholics, Jews, and gay people: they, along with poor, usually Southern, whites constitute the only Caucasian groups that American films, music, and television programs consistently mock or assign cultural stereotypes to. None of this should imply that whites are only presented in heroic or positive terms; indeed, many films, television programs, and pieces of pop music make it clear that whites, typically men, are the bad guys of the piece. However, when whites are presented as evil, their evil is rarely ascribed to their cultural background—unless they are Catholic, Jewish, gay, or Southern. Instead, they are responsible for their crimes—or their heroism—as individuals. It matters less what color they are than it does who they are as people.

The situation is not as positive or hopeful regarding the popular culture images of members of other races and ethnicities in America, however. African Americans, in particular, have been subject to centuries of savage, horrific portrayals in U.S. social and political life. These images perpetuate. One image, for example, is that of the black male as criminal. Established during the era of slavery as a means to justify the violent control of black males, as well as a tool to frighten white women into compliance through their husbands' and fathers' threats that leaving the house made them vulnerable to attack by black men, the image of the black male as an out-of-control, sexually aggressive predator has recurred throughout American history. Indeed, the first major multi-reel movie, D. W. Griffith's *Birth of a Nation*, was based on *The Klansman*, a novel that depicts the horrors of black violence against innocent white women in the aftermath of the U.S. Civil War. Its heroes are members of the Ku Klux Klan, who save the women from an attack by evil blacks. (*Birth of a Nation* is still considered a classic groundbreaking film.) Contemporary popular culture is awash in images of violent black males, whether as sports stars, gang members, prisoners, or drug dealers. As was noted earlier, the entire genre of gangsta rap exploits and reinforces this imagery. Sympathetic portrayals of professional African American men are few and far between. (The comedian Robert Townsend mocked the limited range of roles available to African American actors in his film *Hollywood Shuffle*.)

The situation for African American women is hardly any better, with one major exception: the daytime talk show host Oprah Winfrey. Black women are regularly shown as un- or underemployed, usually single mothers who are inevitably lifetime welfare recipients. (Former U.S. president Ronald Reagan once famously referred to such women as "welfare queens," implying that they were living lives of comparative luxury on government handouts.) These women are also generally depicted as drug or alcohol addicted. Alternatively, particularly in rap videos and music, they are depicted as objects of sexual desire who exist, mostly, to satisfy the sexual demands of various male partners. Only rarely are sympathetic images, such as Claire Huxtable on *The Cosby Show* or those associated with Oprah Winfrey, who has become one of the wealthiest people in entertainment, manifested in American popular culture. This pattern has continued in recent years despite the fact that in the real world, an African American woman, Condoleezza

Rice, was U.S. Secretary of State during the presidency of George W. Bush—and, of course, the fact that the United States now has its first African American president and first lady.

The lives of Latinos and Latinas are similarly dire, at least as depicted in American popular culture. Early images of them were the grossest form of stereotypes of an alien "other" with which few Americans would have ever come into contact. The male image of the Mexican bandito, which was a staple of Western movies and television programs in the 1930s, 1940s, and 1950s, morphed into a 1970s cartoon character selling the snack food Fritos by singing, "Ay, ay, ay, ay, I am the Frito Bandito," while stealing various victims' snack chips. This, in turn, fed into images of Latinos as gang members, drug dealers, and drug lords in innumerable movies, television shows, and songs set in the context of the international drug trade in the 1980s and 1990s. The only other types of Latinos commonly shown were prisoners—usually arrested for gang and drug activity—and, in a few cases, police officers intent on rescuing the neighborhoods in which they had grown up from the ravages of the drug trade.

Latinas are given even less diversity in their presentation in American popular culture. The earliest images of Latinas in U.S. films centered on the character of Carmen Miranda, an attractive woman who became a famous entertainer while wearing seductive clothing and a bowl of fruit on her head. Since then, most Latinas have been shown to be sexual attachments of the men in their lives, and thus—given the distribution of Latino characters—members or associates of gangs engaged in or managing the drug trade. They are seen to raise the men's children. On occasion one woman is shown to resist or challenge the corrupt values of the local community, but more often than not, Latinas are active participants in the criminal lives of their men. Indeed, there is not a single major sympathetic portrayal of a Latina in contemporary American popular culture.

There is really only one stereotype of Asian Americans in contemporary popular culture—that of a hard-working but potentially dangerous person, whether he or she is a nerdy hard-working student, an entrepreneur, or a crime boss. This image derives from earlier cultural stereotypes about Asians in America. During World War II, for example, Asians were usually seen as devious, dangerous people who attacked the United States without warning on December 7, 1941.

(Little distinction was made between Japanese and other Asians; Asians as such were usually believed to be a threat to the United States.) This perception itself emerged from Anglo fears of Asian migration in the nineteenth and early twentieth centuries: as Asians immigrated to the Western areas of the United States in the aftermath of the Civil War, usually for economic opportunities associated with the gold rush or the building of the transcontinental railroad, local Anglo-Americans passed restrictive rules against Asian employment and access to education. These were later codified by the U.S. Congress to include limitations on the numbers of Asians who could immigrate to the United States, as well as laws that barred Asians from owning property or becoming naturalized citizens of the United States. The three contemporary images of Asian Americans manifest this historical concern that Asian Americans are undermining the American way of life. In each case there is the sense that, whether student, enemy, or immigrant, Asians are so different that they will work to replace American ideals and values with their own—that they will not become fully American.

Native Americans are perhaps the only ethnic group that has seen a full-scale reversal in its characterization in American popular culture. Early in the history of electronic media, Native Americans were "savages" who brutalized settlers trying to make new lives for themselves in the American West. At best, if they cooperated with Anglos, Native Americans could serve as scouts and supporters (never leaders) of Anglo troops and wagon trains. At worst, Native American tribes were bloody raiders of innocent villages or alcoholics on reservations. All this has changed since the 1970s. It is now rare to see a negative portrayal of a Native American in American popular culture. If anything, the images of Native Americans have become stereotypically positive, as tribes are presented as environmentally sensitive, peace-loving people who acted only in self-defense against rapacious Anglos.

It is important to remember here that while each of the issues addressed above—gender, sexuality, violence, and the like—was discussed individually, they are experienced cumulatively. No film or video or song or program features only one of these controversial aspects; each inevitably contains several, if not all, of these concerns. Thus, sexual violence can be used to dominate women and pressure them into accepting traditional gender roles that bring them access to great wealth and security, particularly as protection against an alien, dangerous other—be he or she African American, Latino/a, poor, or any of a number of other fear-inducing persons or groups. Any or all of this can be and often is objectionable, offensive, and norm challenging both in the United States and around the world. Much of this material is further embedded in cross-marketing tie-ins, meaning that violence, sexuality, diversity, gender, and other complex social phenomena can become associated with fast-food restaurants, cell phone ring tones, clothing choices and styles, or any other commodity that can be sold through a movie, a piece of music, a performer's endorsement, or a television program. As will be seen in chapter 5, such linkage to the cultural values embedded in American popular culture provides endless ammunition and evidence for those who oppose both American values and the process of globalization.

## AMERICAN CULTURE IN MOVIES, MUSIC, AND TELEVISION

This section offers a series of extended analyses of representative examples of American movies, music, and television programs that have been popular worldwide. Rather than just relying on the broad descriptions available in academic research or in scans of popular cultural products, it offers a detailed examination of the ideals, values, and themes contained within American popular culture and links them to the features of American public culture analyzed in chapter 1. Its goal is to establish the "Americanness" of American movies, music, and television programming.

### AMERICAN MOVIES

Three movies are given an extended commentary here—*Titanic* (1997), James Cameron's megahit that was the most successful movie (in terms of ticket sales) of all time until it was knocked off its pedestal; *Avatar* (2009), the James Cameron movie that replaced *Titanic* as the highest-grossing film of all time; and *Blade Runner* (1982), a dark, dystopian vision of a future in which the values of American public culture combine to create a nightmare version of a globalized world. Any number of films might have been analyzed here, of course, so this list should not be seen as comprehensive. Instead, what follows is intended as an exegesis of how American culture is expressed in movies using these three films as particularly useful examples.

## *TITANIC*: CLASS AND THE AMERICAN DREAM

*Titanic*'s success was stunning. Many people rushed back into the theater to watch the film a second and third consecutive time despite the movie's extraordinary length. It set numerous box office records on its way to smashing the all-time high-water mark at $1.8 billion in ticket sales alone—$600 million in the United States, and $1.2 billion globally.[12]

This success is seemingly out of proportion to the story. Essentially a love story framed in the foreshadowing context of the *Titanic*'s doomed ocean voyage, the movie follows the trials of Jack (played by Leonardo DiCaprio) and Rose (played by Kate Winslet) as they meet, fall in love, and struggle to survive while the *Titanic* sinks. Jack is a down-and-out working-class youth trying to return to America; he only gets on board the ill-fated ship because he wins a third-class ticket in a last-second poker game. Rose, by contrast, is the daughter of a formerly elite Philadelphia family that has fallen on hard times; she is to be married to an American millionaire to restore the family fortune. Where Jack is lucky to be on the *Titanic* at all, Rose is berthed in the lap of luxury in first-class accommodations.

Despondent over her pending forced marriage, Rose decides to commit suicide by jumping off the *Titanic*. Jack, who has snuck onto the first-class deck, saves her by threatening to join her in her plunge. The two quickly establish a relationship as the poor but talented Jack sketches Rose, reads her poetry, and otherwise acts like a perfect romantic hero. By contrast, Rose's fiancé is a petty, disinterested, possessive man of little integrity or merit to recommend him other than the size of his bank account—which he himself did not earn. When Jack's relationship with Rose is discovered, conflict ensues: as the *Titanic* sinks, Jack is imprisoned and nearly drowns before being saved by Rose, returning his earlier favor, and Rose and Jack spend the last hour of the movie slowly moving toward the back of the sinking ship—the place where they had met just a few days before. They barely survive the *Titanic*'s final plunge beneath the waves and share a last good-bye moment before Jack freezes to death in the frigid waters of the North

Atlantic. Rose is rescued, but when she has the opportunity to resume her former life by joining her fiancé, who has survived by claiming a small child was his and using this excuse to join one of the few lifeboats *Titanic* manages to launch before it sinks, she hides. She tells a questioner that her name is Rose Dawson—Jack's last name, not her own. Love has survived tragedy.

Whatever the merits of this story—and it is told effectively, with good acting and stunning special effects—it is hardly unique or innovative. Accordingly, something else must account for its popularity. As will be seen, much of the film's success derives from the ways the values of American public culture emerge in the movie. They provide a transparent foundation on which others can build their interpretations of the film's significance in their lives.

At least part of the movie's appeal can be seen to lie in the everyman-versus-privilege story, for example. Despite being a poor, working-class kid, Jack is romantic, loving, engaging, poetic, artistically talented, self-sacrificing, heroic, and, above all, happy. Jack is self-made, self-confident, and successful in the most important ways: he risks his own life to save Rose, risks his personal safety to maintain a relationship with Rose despite threats and humiliations, tries to save several passengers (including children) as the *Titanic* sinks, and insists to his last breath that Rose must live, no matter what. By contrast, despite his supposedly superior parentage, Rose's fiancé Cal is shown to be deceitful, manipulative, and uncaring for Rose or for the young child he claims is his in order to escape in a lifeboat. (He hands the child off the second he takes his seat.) He orders his butler to kill Jack. Whereas Jack is a skilled artist, Cal has no interest in art or other social finery. Having money, clearly, is not the same thing as having class.

Not only is having money not the same thing as having class, but having money is also seen to undermine the true development of human character. Cal is not the only character whose life of privilege has served to promote personal selfishness. Rose's mother is horrified by the thought of a life without wealth and essentially prostitutes Rose to Cal to ensure the family fortune. She slaps Rose when she finds out about Rose's relationship with Jack. Similarly, most of the first-class passengers treat Jack badly when he is invited to a dinner party. By contrast, the one first-class passenger the audience sees who treats Jack with dignity and mocks the values of the alleged upper class was born middle or working class. Molly Brown, a portrayal of a real woman who would later be called the Unsinkable Molly Brown for her actions as the *Titanic* sank, treats Jack well and also shows real courage in pushing her boat mates to return to the sinking ship to try to rescue dying passengers. Meanwhile, her supposedly superior upper-class lifeboat mates are paralyzed by fear.

Rose finds a different reception when she joins Jack on the lower decks. She is immediately embraced and immersed in a web of dancing, friends, and shared food and drink. The working class seems authentic, sincere, honest, and decent. By extension, then, there is no need for Jack or the members of *Titanic*'s audience to be jealous of others' wealth. Such jealousy might, of course, encourage the audience to favor strong welfare policies or high taxes—after all, if the rich are idle and vain while the workers are decent and caring, why should the rich get to keep their money? In *Titanic*'s telling, however, the rich deserve pity more than envy. Wealth is better avoided.

As was discussed in chapter 1, the sense that class is not the key to happiness or even a guarantee of good behavior is central to American public culture. Jack has to live by his wits, uncorrupted by the luxuries of wealth. He may be working class, but he has a heart of gold. He will clearly be successful and happy wherever he might go. Cal, of course, will never be happy, and indeed the film notes as it closes that Cal kills himself during the Great Depression. A central theme in the film is thus that class—the control of wealth—is unimportant. Indeed, class provides no constraints on either behavior or opportunity: since Jack can win Rose's heart, the barriers of class mean nothing.

Jack's story also emphasizes the moral importance of the individual in human life. Jack is a plucky, optimistic individualist. He gains admission to the ship through his own wits and talents, figures out how to stop Rose's suicide attempt, charms his way onto the first-class deck, and is even invited to a formal dinner (which he attends wearing a borrowed tuxedo, which, since this is a love story, fits perfectly and looks beautiful). All he has are his talents and his intelligence. With them, however, he is able to establish a rapport with most of the first-class passengers and to be invited back again and again despite the disapproval of Rose's family and fiancé. Ultimately, Jack and Rose only survive the *Titanic*'s fateful final plunge beneath the sea because Jack reminds Rose to never quit and always struggle against the ship as it pulls her into the deep. This same pluck lets her survive and call for help as everyone else around her freezes to death. Likewise, it is Molly Brown's spunky character, formed outside the halls of privilege and sloth, which makes her heroic. Individuals, not social backgrounds, matter.

Titanic's popularity rests at least in part on the values and variables of American public culture. The irrelevance of class, the importance of individualism, the lure of capitalism, and the distribution of talent across society are all foundations of American civic culture. In reflecting them, Titanic told a story that reached out to the world. The world responded.

## AVATAR: THE TRIUMPH OF THE INDIVIDUAL

Avatar's success was, like Titanic's, stunning. Conceived and shot as a 3-D movie, the film is a straightforward good-guys-versus-bad-guys tale set on an alien moon. Its story resonated to a global audience, generating almost $2.8 billion in total ticket sales: $700 million from U.S. audiences, and more than $2.0 billion from moviegoers around the world.[13]

While the film is wrapped in extraordinary—and extraordinarily expensive—special effects, the story Avatar tells is quite simple: humans are mining a mineral paradoxically called "unobtanium" on a moon called Pandora in an extraterrestrial solar system. Pandora is, as it happens, home to an indigenous people—nine-foot-tall blue beings called the "Na'vi." Mining operations threaten the homes of the Na'vi, which sets in motion the dramatic tension that carries the film's narrative forward.

The primary story line Avatar offers involves the efforts of a human, Jake Sully, to learn the Na'vi way of life. At first he does this to spy on the Na'vi on behalf of the corporation that is mining unobtanium, as well as to assist the mercenary forces the company has hired to protect its operations. In time, however, Sully comes to love the Na'vi and their connection to the natural world; he also falls in love with a Na'vi woman named Neytiri.

Notably, the Na'vi sense of community and connectedness is in fact literal: their bodies are adapted to physically connect with the life-forms of their world. This turns out to be an important part of Sully's transformation from company spy to Na'vi freedom fighter: he and his fellow humans who work closely with the Na'vi actually live among the Na'vi in Na'vi-human hybrid bodies—avatars. The humans working with the Na'vi transfer their consciousness to genetically engineered bodies that are almost identical to Na'vi bodies. As a consequence, when Sully and other humans interact with the Na'vi, they experience the world the way the Na'vi do—through Na'vi bodies, and with the Na'vi sense of real connection to the life around them.

The Na'vi sense of peace and community contrasts sharply with the mechanized destruction being wrought on Pandora by the human miners and their mercenary army. Where the Na'vi preserve, the humans exploit. Where the Na'vi honor, the humans ravage. Where the Na'vi love, the humans covet.

Eventually, Sully "goes native" and helps the Na'vi fight to protect their home—literally called "home tree." While that effort fails, Sully leads the Na'vi as they defeat the human mercenaries and drive the miners from Pandora. The moral order is thus restored to Pandora: those who care and nurture are liberated from the oppression of abusers and exploiters.

On its face, *Avatar* might not seem a good candidate for analysis of "American" values. After all, the bad guys in the film all have American accents, and the mining company that is exploiting Pandora for unobtanium has a distinctively American management. Moreover, by the end of the movie some humans are at civil war with others: several humans join Sully in his quest to beat the humans trying to destroy the Na'vi. How is any of this "American"?

First, it should be noted that this story is a fairly straightforward American action movie. One person—usually, as in this case, a man— with some kind of special skill (Sully is a former Marine) leads the community to a greater good. As is typically the case with such films, the odds are overwhelming; the stakes are high. And, of course, there is the requisite happy ending: the Na'vi may have only bows and arrows and flying creatures they can ride as they attack, but properly led, they are able to beat a mechanized army with the most modern of arsenals.

Sully certainly plays the role of the typical American action movie hero. It is his inspirational leadership that helps the Na'vi recover when home tree is destroyed. The Na'vi share such a close connection with nature that when their home is destroyed they are overwhelmed with despair. It is only when Sully, in his avatar body, enacts a Na'vi legend and links with a particularly powerful flying creature that the Na'vi are inspired to again challenge the humans. It is Sully's inspirational leadership that jump-starts the Na'vi will to fight.

Additionally, the film makes it clear that while the mining company and the mercenaries are human—indeed, even American—they have lost their moral compass. For the company manager, the only thing that matters is money. For the commander of the mercenaries, genocide seems like a perfectly acceptable strategy for dealing with the Na'vi "problem." These are immoral—or perhaps worse, amoral—people. They have lost the sense that the purpose of wealth and power is not more wealth and more power—it is providing an opportunity for citizens to lead just, moral lives.

The gap between the company's actions (and those of its mercenary protectors) and ordinary standards of right and wrong provide a final way to see the "Americanness" of *Avatar*: the film's evocation of the notion of redemptive violence as a tool of social restoration. The human rebels like Jake Sully are not seen to be committing crimes when they kill their fellow humans; rather, they are living up to a moral code that the other humans have lost sight of. Violence and death may be regrettable, but they are necessary components in restoring social and political order. Thus, when the audience witnesses the Na'vi standing on either side of the gangway guarding the humans being forced from the planet, it senses that the right thing has been done. Individual heroism has overcome great odds and restored social justice for the community.

### BLADE RUNNER: THE EMPTINESS OF CONSUMER CAPITALISM

Ridley Scott's 1982 film *Blade Runner* offers a strikingly different vision of American life and civic values than does either *Titanic* or *Avatar*. Never as popular as the other two films described in this section—*Blade Runner* only did $33 million in the U.S. market when it was released—the film has gone on to become a cult classic in its dystopian vision of a globalized future.[14] Yet its imagined dystopia is every bit as derived from the content of American public culture as the other two films discussed above are. It simply offers a negative vision of the way American attitudes and preferences might play out over time. As such, it provides useful insight into why some people might react negatively to the values presented in American popular culture.

In the world of *Blade Runner*, society has been transformed into a disconnected mass of polyglot consumers with no evident purposes or goals other than consumption. The film is set in a future Los Angeles where it always rains, a setting that serves as a powerful symbol of the general alienation that characterizes the mood of the film, as humans have managed to change even the environment from its natural order.

*Blade Runner* hinges around the actions of a police officer, Deckard (Harrison Ford), who works in a special unit designed to track down and kill androids (called replicants) who return to Earth. In this future, humans have begun to colonize other worlds. Much of the dirty work of colonization, whether working in hostile environments, serving the needs (including sexual needs) of human workers, or serving as soldiers in various wars, is performed by androids. Most of the time this is a good deal for humans: machines take on much of the hard, dangerous work of colonization and combat.

The replicants are sentient, however. They are aware of the moral implications of the things they do. They are also aware of their own mortality: they have an internal clock that limits their lives to only a few years. *Blade Runner* tells the story of a group of replicants who return to Earth to confront their maker—the Tyrell Corporation and its genius owner, Dr. Tyrell—to force him to adjust their life clocks so they can extend their lives. Deckard works to find and kill them—a task he ultimately completes only because one of the replicants, Roy, chooses not to kill Deckard when he has the chance. Instead, in an affirmation of the value of life, Roy saves Deckard and then dies.

*Blade Runner* is striking in its lack of any direct examination of the politics and social life that ground its vision. There are not even any oblique references to any governing authorities. Instead, the dystopia it offers and the lessons it draws about a particular human future have to be teased out of the background—which is its ultimate political point.

Of particular importance in this vision is the dominance of the global/galactic megacorporations. Tyrell Corporation is clearly one of the megacorporations that run society. Its power is symbolized in its towering obelisk of a building that rises, along with those of other megacorporations, above the crowds and rain that now dominate a culturally and environmentally corrupted Los Angeles. Yet this dominance seems so well entrenched that no one finds it remarkable.

Deckard and his fellow agents seem to work largely at the will of the Tyrell Corporation. Their agency exists only to solve problems caused by Tyrell, and they kill replicants on crowded streets with little consideration for the safety of innocent civilians. Indeed, even Deckard never challenges the logic of his work: a problem exists that has to be solved, and even when Deckard falls in love with a replicant and works to save her life, he never considers that laws might be changed to make Tyrell accountable for the problems it causes. No discussion ever occurs about the need to limit Tyrell's power, either.

The social isolation of being a member of a mass population is another important dimension of the vision of the future *Blade Runner* offers. The streets literally teem with people. Individuality is lost in the rain and decay of lower-level Los Angeles. One can buy artificial replacement body parts for only a few credits. No one appears to be going anywhere in particular or doing anything important. The endlessly circling electronic billboards that advertise cola and other products offer what action there is on the street. There is no other end to life than that of shopping.

An additional example of the anonymity of the mass is the language of the street. Most people speak a language amalgamated from German, English, Japanese, and Spanish. The face and garb of the model on the floating billboard is clearly Asian, probably Japanese, and the mix of people on the streets constitutes a true melting pot. Styles, trends, languages, and ethnicities are all commodities to be exchanged and merged in a giant marketplace. Notably, most people pass each other without consideration or concern. Everyone is self-involved to the exclusion of any sense of community or the common good.

The anonymity and isolation of *Blade Runner*'s streets highlight the irony that, while it is possible to buy other forms of artificial life (eyes, pets, and the like), artificial humans, the replicants, are banned from Earth. Only humanoid replicants are bad. Everything else is acceptable, regardless of its artificiality.

*Blade Runner* thus offers a vision of the dark side of American public culture. Individualism inspires isolation, not participation. People are anonymous, not engaged. There is no exceptionalist crusade to make things better and spread truth and justice across the world, because there is no group, organization, or government with any kind of social conscience with which one might work if one desired to make the world a better place. At the root of all this empty existence is the dominance of consumer capitalism. When freedom becomes the freedom to shop for whatever one might like (including life itself), life holds no meaning or value. When liberty becomes nothing more than the freedom to choose one from a series of options on the shelves of street vendors, it is an empty concept.

## AMERICAN TELEVISION

Three programs are examined here: *Star Trek*, *The West Wing*, and a post-9/11 hit series about American counter-terrorism agents run amok, *24*. *Star Trek* offered perhaps the single clearest example of an idealized vision of American culture leading to quite literally universal happiness. *The West Wing* was an immensely popular television drama that spread its vision of American democracy in practice around the world. *24* was, in many ways, doppelgänger to *The West Wing*: it explored the consequences of American rejection of its core values.

## THE UNIVERSE OF *STAR TREK* AND THE UNIVERSE ACCORDING TO *STAR TREK*

*Star Trek*, originally broadcast on NBC from 1966 to 1969, was a ratings failure in its original run. It has since grown into a global phenomenon. Its episodes have been rebroadcast for decades, its fans have developed a global subculture, and its creators have spun off eleven movies and four television series from the original series. Combined, the films have generated over $1 billion in sales in the U.S. market alone; the eleventh film, a reboot of the old series with an altered timeline and changed series of events, sold nearly $128 million in tickets overseas the year it was released.[15]

Much of the continuing popularity of *Star Trek* lies in its vision of a globalized, ethically driven, rights-respecting, democratic future—American culture made manifest on a galactic scale. While most fans and casual observers of the *Star Trek* phenomenon focus on the characters, stories, and technology that lie at the heart of the series' storytelling, it is important to note that this action takes place in a well-developed political-social context: the Federation. The Federation, organized along lines similar to the U.S. political structure, is the political agency served by those in Star Fleet—Kirk, Spock, McCoy, and their colleagues. Star Fleet is the military arm of a political order made up of a federation of planets that elect representatives to a central governing council. The Federation—formally titled the Federation of Planets—is organized along classic federal principles: each member planet has broad discretion to enact its politics as it pleases; however, the central authority does hold certain powers through which it can establish and enforce peaceful relations and protect the safety of its members from both internal and external threats. The existence of Star Fleet is one such power.

The parallels with American federalism extend beyond the name and the existence of a central governing body. In addition to electing representatives to the Federation's governing body, planetary members elect a president and a Federation council. These leaders make policy that is then ratified (or not) by the Federation's elected officers. These officials operate in the context of the rule of law and are bound by their oaths to respect the rights of all people to self-determination. Indeed, during the course of the series and films, several senior political and military officers are arrested or otherwise removed from office for violations of their legal responsibilities. In many ways, then, the Federation manifests the ideals of American democracy in actual practice. The world of *Star Trek* expresses the ideals that are at the core of American public culture.

The key to the Federation's success is warp technology. Warp technology allows humans to travel faster than light. With warp technology, humans set out—like the Puritans coming to America—to bring their way of life to the galaxy at large. After a slow process of exploration, interaction with other species, and wars, humans sponsor the creation of the Federation. This coalition of species and cultures shares relatively common values and political practices, and its members work together to promote and defend their ideals against internal threats like officials and others who would use their power for their own good, as well as against external threats like political and military competitors such as the Romulans and the Klingons. In its political, military, social, and economic dimensions, the Federation is a shining symbol of the capacity of technology, integration, and procedure to bring nearly universal benefits to all who embrace the Federation's vision.

At the core of this ethical expansionism is a concept the show's fans developed only after the original series went off the air: IDIC. IDIC stands for "infinite diversity in infinite combinations" and is used to represent the way the many cultures of the *Star Trek* universe can respect each other's particular practices and values while working together in a collective, healthy way. Many of the show's plots deal with struggles to both accept others and explain when it can be appropriate to intervene in diverse cultures.

The *Star Trek* vision of a global—indeed galactic—democratic future is profoundly optimistic, mirroring the claims of contemporary globalists. People are not displaced by technology; they are empowered by it. Disruptions in a former way of life do not cause pain; they are liberating. There are no fundamental tensions among cultures and communities; instead, virtually all problems that arise at the intersection of cultures can be bridged successfully. Life in the Federation is not simply rich, it is rewarding. Technology and politics work to free people from pain, want, and repression.

This vision of the relationship between globalization and democracy is as pure an example of American public culture made real as has ever been presented in popular culture. Tolerance promotes order, growth, opportunity, and education; democracy and a respect for rights ensure freedom; and individuals pursuing dreams leads to social harmony. The world of *Star Trek* is that of an idealized America projected onto a galactic stage.

## THE WEST WING AND THE DEMOCRATIC EXPERIMENT

*The West Wing* offered an idealized, compressed vision of the workings of American democracy. It dealt in detail with the processes of politics in the United States. It featured episodes on the filibuster, the appointment of Supreme Court justices, the use of force in international affairs, the problems of racial violence in America, support for human rights overseas, the invocation of the Twenty-fifth Amendment of the U.S. Constitution, a terrorist attack on the United States, and the attempted assassination of the president. Each of these story lines, and many more, offered extended commentaries on the formal rules and informal practices of American democracy. They also invoked the ritualistic aspects of the presidency, as President Bartlet called the parents of American troops wounded in combat, lit the national Christmas tree, gave the State of the Union address, and offered his annual pardon of a Thanksgiving turkey. To watch *The West Wing*, even casually, is to be offered an object lesson in the workings of American government.

The world of *The West Wing* is an exceptionally tolerant and diverse one. President Bartlet is Catholic; two of his senior aides are Jewish. Most of the rest are Protestant. Bartlet's personal aide is a young African American male, an obviously subservient role for a black character; however, for the bulk of the show's run, the powerful chairman of the Joint Chiefs of Staff was an African American man. Women also play important roles in the Bartlet administration. They serve in jobs ranging from the first lady to press secretary to national security adviser. They fight as effectively and as passionately for their causes as do their male counterparts. The administration even nurtures recovered alcoholics. Notably, this diversity melds together almost seamlessly to create a cooperative and successful harmony of committed, caring individuals dedicated to achieving their goals on behalf—they say—of the American people.

It is only when its members fail to respect the inherent decency and dignity of everyone everywhere that the Bartlet administration finds itself in trouble. In an episode dealing with a terrorist attack on the United States, for example, Leo McGarry, the president's chief of staff and one of the show's main characters, ruthlessly interrogates a Muslim White House employee who happens to have the same name as a suspected terrorist. As he conducts this questioning, McGarry questions the employee's patriotism and assumes his guilt on the basis of his skin color and religion. Tellingly, however, when the employee is found innocent, McGarry is ashamed. (In a sign of religious and personal tolerance, the employee returns to work after his interrogation.) Likewise, it is only when the staffers demonize their political opponents or when the president himself loses faith in the American people (as he did by covering up an illness during his first election) that the administration gets into trouble.

The story of *The West Wing*, then, is the story of the best parts of American civic culture, played out with sufficiently realistic touches to make the politics seem real. It bears little or no relevancy to how the U.S. presidency actually works, of course. The people are too attractive, everyone is too smart and too selfless, the staffers have far too much ease of access to the president, people sublimate their agendas to the good of the group far too easily, and above all everyone spends too much time talking to and about everyone else to accurately simulate the frenetic, disjointed experience of working for the president of the United States. Likewise, the show offers little insight into how laws are actually developed and passed: the tedious hours of drafting, revising, reconsidering, and negotiating that go into the legislative process for just one of the hundreds of significant laws passed every year would make stunningly boring television. Instead, in *The West Wing*, the audience sees noble people trying hard to follow the Constitution and do what is right. It expresses what Americans want to believe about their government in a manifestation of their deepest cultural hopes and beliefs.

### *24* AND AMERICAN ILLIBERALISM

*24* was a groundbreaking show on the Fox network that sought to portray events in real time. The events shown in each episode were intended to take the length of time they were shown to take on screen, and the entire arc of a season's story was to be developed over the course of one 24-hour day. Hence viewers were to be drawn into a real-time drama in which a crisis was introduced and resolved in one day—even though that day was spread across 24 one-hour episodes of *24*. The show ran from 2001 to 2010.

*24* is centered on the life of Jack Bauer, played by Kiefer Sutherland, an agent for a U.S. government agency called the Counter Terrorist Unit (CTU). Bauer and his colleagues were charged with preventing terrorist attacks in the United States. Examples included preventing the assassination of an African American candidate for president of the United States and preventing the detonation of nuclear weapons on American soil.

Premiering in November 2001, *24* was profoundly informed by the terror attacks of September 11, 2001. The show was infused by a "get it done at all costs" mentality that saw Bauer regularly torture suspects and then, in other story arcs, being tortured himself. Some CTU agents were corrupt; others aided and abetted the corrupt agents for reasons ranging from ignorance to misplaced loyalty. And, in an effort to keep the dramatic tension high, Bauer and his fellow agents were seen to have home lives as well—e.g., families and problems that shaped their work. (Bauer's daughter Kim seemed to have a remarkable propensity to get kidnapped, for example.) Part of the show's melodrama was grounded in the struggles CTU agents had in balancing the professional and personal aspects of their lives.

Like *Blade Runner*, 24 is at its most "American" in the values and ideals it violates rather than those it upholds. As Louis Hartz and others have explained, American civic culture embodies a dark, illiberal dimension in which the very ideals that ground the nation's best qualities can become tools of repression and dominance. For Hartz, for example, the cause of this illiberalism lies in the consensus that undergirds American civic culture: precisely because no one has to think about whether American ideals are good or not, Americans as a people are not very skilled at recognizing that others may not share these goals or may believe that Americans are hypocritical when their practices don't match their rhetoric. Thus, when Americans find their ideals challenged, they don't reason or argue or recognize that the challenge is one of ordinary politics, to be addressed by winning elections, persuading others of the rightness of the American cause, or similar acts. Rather, the challenge gets cast in existential terms: to reject American values is seen as an attack on America itself, and since America's values are global and universal, an assault on American ideals can be seen as an attack on things like freedom and liberty and the rights of the individual as such.[16] In such circumstances, the credibility of the threat—could the "enemy" really achieve such a goal?—gets tossed aside in the frenzied fear that any diminution of American strength or unity constitutes a threat to the future of human liberty itself.

One area where such ideological fear manifested itself in 24 lay in the use of torture to extract confessions or information from suspects. While the empirical evidence about torture shows that it doesn't work—people will tell you anything to get the torture to stop, and it is not clear that they would not have divulged true material while undergoing conventional interrogation techniques—such evidence becomes irrelevant in a world in which an audience believes its way of life is in an existential struggle for survival. In such a context, all that matters is survival, and if people need to be tortured, well, so be it. Thus, while 24 was roundly criticized for its depiction of torture as a useful tool of interrogation, especially by civil rights and human rights groups, the show remained popular throughout the 2000s. Torture "made sense" to its audience, even when it violated the straightforward application of core values in American civic culture. (As the show continued, the U.S. government eventually asked its producers to tone down the use of torture, as the depictions of U.S. agents torturing suspects was actually causing a backlash against American efforts to promote a positive public image worldwide.)

In the end, part of what made 24 appealing to its fans was its explicit rejection of the nice, moral side of American civic values, by suggesting that these values were imperiled without the courage to contravene them when necessary. Whatever one thinks of this ethos—and given popular American support for actual torture of actual terror suspects in the U.S. war on terror, it is less clear that Americans as a whole are troubled by the notion that torture can be necessary than they perhaps should be—the moral dilemma reveals the cultural context that underlies it.[17] 24 was a profoundly American show, even if it drew life from the illiberal, paranoid dimension of American civic culture rather than from its rights-affirming, democratic aspects.

## AMERICAN MUSIC

It is not as simple to offer an extended analysis of the way American public culture manifests itself in popular music as it is in the case of American films or American television. Individual pieces of music are usually quite short to fit the time available on commercial radio, so the medium rewards brevity and simplicity rather than complexity. In addition, most songs, even when collected into albums, are rarely linked thematically in the way that television programs and films are. Consequently, individual pieces of music usually lack the substance to provide a solid foundation for analysis.

Rather than focus on a particular song or group of songs, the analysis offered here describes the evolution of the three forms of American music that have become the most important in global trade: country, rock, and hip-hop. While each history is brief, it highlights the roots of each of these forms of music and describes their genesis in the United States. Many performers not born in the United States have become famous and rich by performing in these genres, and it is of course true that there are many forms of music other than country, rock, and hip-hop. However, these three emerged in the United States and spread across the globe. They are American forms wherever they may be performed.

## The Culture of Country

Country music emerged first among the three types of musical forms addressed in this section. Country established its modern form in the 1920s and was the first music extensively broadcast on radio: WSM-Nashville began broadcasting the *Grand Ole Opry*, a weekly variety show featuring a combination of established and up-and-coming acts, in 1925. Its weekly broadcasts drew vast audiences across rural America, particularly in the South. The show's popularity led Victor Records in Bristol, Tennessee, to sign Little Jimmie Roberts and The Carter Family to recording contracts in 1927.[18] Country music was born.

Country is an amalgam of bluegrass, folk, Appalachian mountain, and Western cowboy music. While bluegrass and Appalachian mountain music are themselves derived from Celtic folk music, by the 1920s, Celtic forms had been transformed into a distinctively American sound. In terms of instruments, for example, country emphasized the twang of steel guitars and the distinctive tone of the Appalachian violin, often referred to as a fiddle. Acoustic sounds dominated in a world in which most people learned to play without electricity in their homes or communities. Multiple traditions of music combined with acoustic instruments to create a distinctive country sound.

Country music is also distinguished by its subject matter. Country has long prided itself on reflecting the lives of real people, particularly working-class, rural Americans. Country's topics have chronicled the struggles of the individual as he or she tries to make it in a dead-end job, in a difficult marriage, or even through addiction to drugs or alcohol. Additionally, country regularly sings the virtues of hard work, traditional love, the glory of a loving family, and unabashed patriotism. The real America, country seems to say, is the America in which people struggle but take responsibility for their personal fates. Americans fight for their honor and dignity as ends all their own.

These stories of individual struggle and sacrifice are mirrored by populist resentment of elites and others whom country artists define as undeserving of the benefits they enjoy. Like the depiction of the upper class in *Titanic*, country music usually insists that elites are wimps, sycophants, and otherwise unmanly, to adopt a gendered phrase that nonetheless captures what country music asserts. Big-city folks don't really love America, country songs opine, and poor people in urban areas just wait in welfare lines for handouts rather than hitching up their pants and getting to work the way that rural people do. The real, authentic America, then, is a country America.

By the 1950s, the country music industry became centered in Nashville, Tennessee. Aspiring artists wanted to get to Nashville to show their talents, and Nashville housed the recording studios for the major labels producing country music. More importantly, the Nashville recording studios developed "the system," a way of doing business that still operates today. In the system, labels hire songwriters full time. It is the songwriter's job to take the core themes and sounds of country music and shape them into three-and-a-half-minute hits. Country stars then review these songs and choose the ones they want to record. Big stars can place holds on particular songs they like, reserving the right to record the song in the future so that competitors cannot record it in the meantime. This system has made it possible for country stars to remain popular for decades. Country music flourished as songwriters fashioned new material that established stars could sell through the Nashville marketing machine.

The Nashville music machine has helped country music achieve global prominence despite the tight linkage of American culture and American country music. Country star Garth Brooks is one of the best-selling artists of all time, for example, and he is in fact the most successful solo performer in the history of recorded music.[19] The industry draws performers from many foreign nations, including Australia and Canada, and country-themed clubs exist in places like London and Paris. Cover bands perform classic hits to delighted audiences across the world. Country has grown from humble roots to global prominence, all the while asserting its message of authentic America.

## IT'S ROCK AND ROLL

If country is the music of rural Americans, rock and roll is the music of America's suburban youth—especially middle-class whites. As a musical form, rock and roll is closely associated with the generation that rapidly expanded in the 1950s and 1960s and brought rock music along on the journey: the Baby Boom, the generation of Americans born between 1946 and 1964, after the end of World War II. Rock and roll exploded onto the global music scene in the same period. The world has never been the same.

Like country, rock is an amalgam of other forms—including country itself. However, where country emerged from a combination of predominantly white forms of music, rock is an extension of music types popular among both whites and African Americans. In addition to white styles of music like country and folk, rock grew out of the blues music popular among African Americans and concentrated in big cities up and down the length of the Mississippi River, like New Orleans, Memphis, St. Louis, and, off on a branch, Chicago. African American musicians took the chord progressions popular in blues music and sped them up. They also took blues subjects—love, sex, yearning, and other emotions—and matched them to a driving beat. The music was built on electric guitars and drums rather than on steel guitars and fiddles.

African American artists may have created rock and roll, but they did not popularize it. Radio stations and recording companies often refused to record or play African American groups, usually on the grounds that the white audience did not want to listen to black performers. Instead, in 1953, Bill Haley and the Comets, who were white, recorded the first rock and roll song to break through on the charts. Later, Elvis Presley and Jerry Lee Lewis played important roles in introducing black music to white audiences. By the mid-1950s, rock and roll was a booming enterprise, making millions of dollars as a fast-growing teen audience enjoyed it.

Rock and roll was as much about lyrics as instruments and chord progressions. At its heart were energy, excitement, and rebellion. Rock musicians tapped into their fans' adolescent dreams and fears to offer brief but compelling stories of teen love gone wrong, the hope for a better tomorrow, and the simple need to get up and dance. It was music of individual freedom and expression. Both the music and the culture that surrounded it seemed to reflect the needs and desires of the large generation of teenagers it both appealed to and seemed to define as a generation.

Rock and roll had its critics, of course. It still does. The core of these critiques has been grounded in the same concerns long ago expressed by the Frankfurt School and mass society theory advocates. Put simply, the fact that millions of young people were attracted to rock music was taken as proof that rock and roll had (and has) some kind of special, dangerous hold on young people. This fear was grounded in the coincidence that rock became popular at the same time the new generation of the Baby Boom exploded in America's schools and universities, just as it remains popular with teenagers today. Rock, after all, expresses rebellion, energy, and individualism—as do teenagers. The causality seemed self-evident: children who were once compliant and sweet suddenly became angry, resentful, and often quite sexual. Rock must have been the culprit. The notion that the reverse was true, and that rock was popular because it was expressing the angst that teenagers feel whether they listen to rock and roll or not, was generally not considered. Instead, parents tried to limit sales of rock music—a phenomenon discussed in chapter 3. Likewise, parents claimed that rock was corrupting their children, a claim that remains common today. Its popularity became proof of its danger.

Whatever parents at the time thought, rock expanded across the world. The 1960s saw the so-called British Invasion, as British groups like the Beatles (still the best-selling group of all time despite having broken up in 1970) and the Rolling Stones mixed African American musical traditions like the blues with established rock styles to create what is today termed "classic rock." They helped spawn new generations of rock artists who explored rock with jazz overtones (Pink Floyd and the Grateful Dead, for example), operatic inflections (The Who and Pink Floyd again), and metal (Led Zeppelin and AC/DC). Rock became a global music phenomenon, with artists emerging from all corners of the globe innovating new derivations like punk, grunge, and indie rock.

The core of rock's global success was its transparency. The yearnings, questions, and dreams of adolescence are universal. So, too, is the rebellion against authority that accompanies the establishment of one's individual identity. Rock and roll emerged as a compelling template on which young people around the world could express their hopes and their fears. As a consequence, a musical form that grew in the unique cultural environment of the United States became global. It is at the center of contemporary globalization.

## DON'T STOP HIP-HOP

Hip-hop and its associated musical form, rap, is a relatively recent addition to music history. It was born in New York City of a fusion of African American, Jamaican, West African, and other forms. Crucially, it emerged in polyglot neighborhoods filled with immigrants and native-born Americans whose musical styles found new expression in the rhythms and lyrics of hip-hop. The first generally recognized hip-hop hit was The Sugarhill Gang's "Rapper's Delight" in 1979.

Fundamentally, hip-hop is an electronic musical form. Its genesis lay in the clubs of New York in which the DJs (pronounced "deejays"), the people who played the records that club patrons danced to, became stars in their own right for the creative ways they mixed songs. They also drew note for developing the technique of scratching, which entails rapidly spinning a record backward and forward under the player's needle to create a distinctive sound. Hip-hop performances did not actually require the musician to play instruments. Instead, the music was often already recorded: the talent was in spinning the music and keeping the crowd excited.

DJs were usually accompanied by MCs (pronounced "emcees"), who introduced the songs, urged people to dance, and otherwise kept the party moving. In time, the role of the MC changed from just introducing songs to making up accompanying rhymes, stories, and lyrics. DJs, too, began to exploit electronic technologies to sample parts of songs and remix them with new beats. MCs could then make up new lyrics for these remixed songs.

As a style, hip-hop emphasizes heavy beats and interesting, creative rhymes. While hip-hop acts may have accompanying bands to provide the music for their songs, this is not essential. Instead, all a budding hip-hop star needs is a stereo on which to blast the rhythms they sing along with—or a good sense of rhythm that they can express using their hands or their voice. The simplicity of the instruments needed to make hip-hop music made it readily accessible to poor urban kids. It also made it easy to make free-form compositions that could integrate the different styles of music wafting around big-city streets. Hip-hop quickly became the music of urban, usually African American, youth.

Hip-hop and rap expanded rapidly across the United States in the 1990s. Stars like Tupac Shakur and Public Enemy put out albums that became nationwide hits. Youth across America responded to the innovative rhythms and rhymes of hip-hop. This included white youth, who would in time became the largest consumers of hip-hop simply because they tended to be middle class and as such generally had more discretionary income to spend on music.

Young people also reacted to the lyrics. Emerging as it did from the streets of major U.S. cities, hip-hop offered a trenchant critique of life in modern America. If country celebrated traditional values and patriotism, and rock and roll energized the ambitions of a generation to change the world, hip-hop expressed the anger and frustration of a long-repressed community that had many grievances in what it described as a racist America. Public Enemy's "Fear of a Black Planet," for example, continued the band's narrative journey accounting for and describing the ways racism in America worked to repress African Americans. Hip-hop also reflected a raw form of street sexuality in which suggestive language was common. Other performers offered explicit accounts of their sexual desires and fantasies.

As happened when rock music exploded on the American landscape, a backlash followed hip-hop's emergence. Ironically, this reaction often manifested the racism that many hip-hop artists asserted was central to American life. Hip-hop, after all, was a disproportionately African American musical form, and its lyrics often complained about police violence against the African American community, along with poverty, drug dealing, and other features of life in the urban inner city that are usually seen as unattractive, dangerous, and scary. Not only were such issues inherently troubling, but the fact that it was African Americans, a group long viewed as outsiders by white Americans, addressing these problems also frightened many people. The obvious conclusion, at least to so many unknowing adherents of mass society theory and the Frankfurt School, was that hip-hop was dangerous. It could corrupt the young. It could hurt children. Meanwhile, of course, no meaningful effort was made to address the problems hip-hop complained about. Instead, the black Other had to be controlled.

It is going too far to insist that all resistance to hip-hop was racist, however. It is one thing to complain about police corruption and quite another to fantasize about being a cop killer and running a criminal organization—themes that were common in a style of hip-hop called gangsta rap. Many critics of hip-hop have also complained that hip-hop acts regularly demean women by reducing them to nothing but sex objects, particularly in music videos. In addition, an actual war broke out between purveyors of East Coast rap and their West Coast competitors. This war led to the shooting of Christopher Smalls, also known as Notorious B.I.G. or Biggie Smalls, and is alleged to have led to the death of early rap star Tupac Shakur in a drive-by shooting. Gangsta rappers took an obvious pleasure in presenting angry, defiant, and criminal personas to the public. Mainstream society may well have been racist, but the forms in which hip-hop presented itself, at least in some cases, played off that racism while reinforcing it at the same time.

Regardless of attempts to limit it, hip-hop spread rapidly both in the United States and outside of it. Hip-hop acts crossed genders, races, and finally international borders. There are thriving hip-hop industries in countries ranging from Japan to India to Turkey. Meanwhile, U.S. acts have achieved global prominence. Hip-hop formed in the unique cultural mix of major U.S. cities in the 1970s, but it did not stay there. Like country and rock before it, its themes, styles, and appeal transcended nationalities to become a worldwide phenomenon. Like country and rock before it, the American form became a global one, with American artists and corporations at its center.

## CONCLUSION

American popular culture, particularly as manifested in movies, music, and television programs, has a relatively specific content. American television shows, movies, and music inevitably emerge from the core variables of American civic culture. While the individual values evident in American public culture may be mixed in different proportions in different works and may even be used to paint a negative portrait of those values in some cases, these values substantially shape the message and meaning of particular television programs, music, and films. The products of American popular culture are further embedded in formulas and narrative conventions. These factors combine to define the Americanness of American popular culture as its products go out to the world.

## NOTES

1. Ernest Gellner, "From Kinship to Ethnicity," in *Encounters with Nationalism* (Cambridge, Mass.: Blackwell, 1994), 39.

2. Gellner, "Kinship to Ethnicity," 40–42.

3. Allen McBride and Robert K. Toburen, "Deep Structures: Polpop Culture on Primetime Television," *Journal of Popular Culture* 29, no. 4 (1996): 181–200. All subsequent references to this research are from this source.

4. Conrad Phillip Kottak, *Prime-Time Society: An Anthropological Analysis of Television and Culture* (Belmont, Calif.: Wadsworth, 1990). All subsequent references are from this source.

5. Timothy Havens, "The Biggest Show in the World: Race and the Global Popularity of *The Cosby Show*," in *The Television Studies Reader,* ed. Robert C. Allen and Annette Hill (New York: Routledge, 2004), 442–56.

6. Scott R. Olson, "Hollywood Planet: Global Media and the Competitive Advantage of Narrative Transparency," in *The Television Studies Reader,* ed. Robert C. Allen and Annette Hill (New York: Routledge, 2004), 114.

7. Havens, "Biggest Show," 451–52.

8. Daradirek Ekachai, Mary Hinchliff-Pelias, and Rosechongporn Komolsevin, "Where Are Those Tall Buildings: The Impact of U.S. Media on Thais' Perceptions of Americans," in *Images of the U.S. around the World: A Multicultural Perspective*, ed. Yahya R. Kamalipour (Albany: SUNY Press, 1999): 265–78.

9. Dan Malachowski, "TV Dads: Real-Life Salaries Nearly $200,000," http://www.salary.com/tv-dads-real-life-salaries-nearly-200-000/ (accessed 1 March 2012).

10. Internet Resources to Accompany the Sourcebook for Teaching Science, "Television and Health," http://www.csun.edu/science/health/docs/tv&health.html#influence (accessed 1 March 2012).

11. Sen. Orrin J. Hatch, Chair, Senate Judiciary Committee, Executive Summary, *Children, Violence, and the Media: A Report for Parents and Policymakers* (Washington, D.C.: U.S. Government Printing Office, 1999), http://www.indiana.edu/~cspc/ressenate.htm (accessed 1 March 2012).

12. "All Time Box Office," http://boxofficemojo.com/alltime/world/ (accessed 29 September 2011).

13. "All Time Box Office."

14. "Blade Runner," http://boxofficemojo.com/movies/?id=bladerunner.htm (accessed 29 September 2011).

15. "Star Trek," http://boxofficemojo.com/franchises/chart/?id=startrek.htm (accessed 29 September 2011), and "Star Trek," http://boxofficemojo.com/movies/?page=intl&id=startrek11.htm (accessed 29 September 2011).

16. Louis Hartz, *The Liberal Tradition in America* (New York: Harcourt, Brace, 1955).

17. "Poll Finds Broad Approval of Terrorist Torture," http://www.msnbc .msn.com/id/10345320/ns/world_news-americas/t/poll-finds-broad-approval -terrorist-torture/#.ToTrB09sQVc (accessed 29 September 2011).

18. Roughstock, "History of Country Music: The Beginnings," http:// www.roughstock.com/history/begin.html (accessed 14 January 2009).

19. "RIAA Presents Garth Brooks with Special Career Award Representing Highest-Selling Solo Artist," http://www.riaa.com/newsitem .php?id=FD3FAA5C-B993-0852-CBA4-71A29CABC50D (accessed 22 September 2011).

# CHAPTER 3

## THE GLOBAL SCOPE OF AMERICAN MOVIES, MUSIC, AND TELEVISION

This chapter focuses on the global spread of American movies, music, and television programs. It analyzes how the audiovisual (AV) popular culture industry developed as it has and assesses the global dominance of American AV culture. It also offers an assessment of the types of American AV culture that play a particularly important role in contemporary globalization. As is discussed in detail in chapter 5, these pervasive, message-rich AV media play a very significant role in globalization today.

Before exploring this issue in detail, however, it is important to note here that a countercase can be made that (as a result of the hybrid way by which a great deal of AV entertainment is produced today) "American" movies, music, and television aren't that American at all. As a practical matter, much filmed programming (whether movies or television programs) seen worldwide today is made in a truly global marketplace. Independent producers seek studio financing from wherever they can find it. They seek to lower production costs by searching for international actors, venues, and markets for their films, and the behind-the-scenes talent that supports a film or television production can be from anywhere in our digital age. In such circumstances, it is not necessarily the case that a movie or television show will be purely American. (The ease with which music can be downloaded and manipulated around the world means that music, too, is not necessarily American, even if its performers are.)

To offer an empirical example of this conundrum, consider the *Pirates of the Caribbean* franchise. *Pirates of the Caribbean* has become one of the most globally successful movie series of all time, occupying four of the top fifty slots for highest grossing films in history. It is based on a ride at the Disney theme parks—and Disney, as is discussed below, is one of the most important globalizers of American popular culture. Accordingly, *Pirates* can be seen as an American product, infused by the Disney ethos from which it was born.

Yet as filmed, the *Pirates* movies have no particularly American content. They star Americans like Johnny Depp but also British citizens like Keira Knightley. They are set in colonial times (at least in the U.S. sense of the word "colonial"), but none of their themes or story lines seems to obviously express an American sensibility. Hence it is possible to consider the *Pirates* movies not as American, but as international— carefully calibrated to meet the demands and desires of a global audience while void of meaningful, culture-specific content.

Accordingly, assessing what is or is not an "American" popular culture product is a judgment call. Here, several criteria are used: the nature of the financing, the locale in which the film was set, the nationalities of the central actors (and, where evident, the nationalities of the characters the actors portray), and the type of movie it is (e.g., film noir, big budget blockbuster, and so on). It is therefore possible for the director and actors of a given movie to be international but the movie to be American in type and financing; such hybridity is, today, the norm rather than the exception. (Note: by this rubric, the *Pirates of the Caribbean* films are not considered "American" movies in this book.)

## THE MOVIE, MUSIC, AND TELEVISION MACHINE IN THE GLOBAL ERA

Most popular AV culture produced today is made or otherwise controlled by a select group of popular culture–producing corporate giants. Moreover, while not all AV popular culture is controlled by American-based corporations, as will be seen later in this chapter, the early U.S. dominance in the creation of movies, music, and television programming has served to create conditions in which much of the global trade in popular culture is done in genres created in the United States under labels traditionally associated with American companies and performers.

Two concepts have been crucial to this concentration of power and control: synergy and convergence. Synergy describes the vertical and horizontal integration of entertainment companies and the products they market. For example, when the same company that produces a performer's album also owns a venue like a radio station on which to play and thus market the album, synergy is said to exist. Synergy is enhanced when the company also can place the song in a popular television program it produces or make it the theme song for a movie it has financed. Multiple marketing outlets reach different audiences to hopefully increase sales. This serves to concentrate profit in the controlling company and also lets the company spread the risk of creating a movie, an album, or a television program across an array of businesses: a movie might not make money in the theaters, for example, but it may sell and rent well enough in the post-theater market that if the same company that produces the movie also controls the companies that produce and rent the videos it can earn a profit.

Another example of synergy can be seen in product placements as described in chapter 1. The soft-drink maker Pepsi, for example, has entered into sponsorship agreements with numerous record labels and pop stars; both Michael Jackson and Madonna had major international tours sponsored by Pepsi in the 1990s. (While filming a commercial for Pepsi, Michael Jackson suffered severe injuries when a pyrotechnic explosion set his hair on fire.) In addition, Pepsi, like most soft-drink makers, seeks placement for its products in other pop culture venues like films and television programs. The association of a big star with Pepsi's products is seen to enhance the marketability of both the star and the product. Synergy thus involves linkages among an array of popular culture products.

*Convergence* refers to the long process by which synergy in the entertainment industry has been created. Alternately known as consolidation, *convergence* is the term used to describe how the many companies and individuals who used to make popular culture have been reduced in number to the few corporations that control the trade today. Essentially, companies merged so that each could control enough products and have enough marketing and distribution opportunities that they could spread the risk of financing any individual project across many enterprises. If one expensive movie bombed at the box office, a large company might survive because other films, music, and television it produces could generate enough income to keep the company alive. By contrast, if a film produced by a small company flopped, the company could easily fail. In the long run, then, only large corporations had the economic power to survive market competition, leaving the popular culture industry in the control of only a few major producers.

Sony, for example, the giant Japanese corporation, is one of the largest movie studios in the world. Its holdings as of August 2011 included Columbia Tristar Motion Picture Group, which was itself composed of Columbia Pictures, Sony Pictures Classics, Screen Gems, and TriStar Pictures among other holdings. Its music holdings included the Columbia/Epic Label Group (American Recordings, Columbia Records, Epic Records, Roc Nation, Star Time International), the RCA/JIVE Label Group (Arista Records, Battery Records Black Seal, J Records, Jive Records, LaFace Records, Polo Grounds, RCA Records, Verity Gospel Music Group, and Volcano Entertainment), and Sony Music Nashville (Arista Nashville, BNA Records, Columbia Nashville and RCA Nashville). Sony also owned Sony Pictures Television. It co-owned the Game Show Network with Liberty Media and shared ownership of Movielink with Paramount Pictures, Universal Studios, and Warner Bros. Studios. Sony, of course, is also the producer of the Playstation video game system as part of its vast holdings in Sony Electronics and Sony Computer Entertainment America. It is a major force in the contemporary popular culture industry.[1]

In 2001, the Internet provider America Online (AOL) merged with Time Warner to become AOL Time Warner. It was at the time the biggest media merger ever at $165 billion. It has also become something of a business object lesson in the failure of convergence: the merger was supposed to create a new model for the delivery of entertainment products online by linking entertainment production (Time Warner) with a new form of distribution (the Internet and AOL). The attempt failed, however, largely as a result of the extraordinary debt the merged company acquired. It simply could not market enough products to pay its debts. As a consequence, in time, a decision was made to revert to the name Time Warner. Time Warner, however, continues to own a host of entertainment companies. As of December 2011, it owned HBO and the Turner Broadcasting System, which itself controlled television networks like CNN, TNT, and the Cartoon Network. Its film industry holdings included the film production studios Warner Bros., New Line Cinema, and DC Entertainment. It could advertise programming for these networks in an array of publications ranging from *Time*, *Sports Illustrated*, and *This Old House* to niche magazines like *Audi Magazine* and many others. It might also promote or distribute its products through online services like NASCAR.com, PGA.com, or any of its other diverse array of Internet holdings.[2]

One of the most famous entertainment conglomerates is The Walt Disney Company. Built from a few cartoon characters first drawn in the early twentieth century, in August 2011 Disney held Walt Disney Pictures, Touchstone Pictures, Hollywood Pictures, Miramax Films, and Pixar. In the area of music production it owned Hollywood Records and Walt Disney Records. Disney was a major player in the television industry, owning or partially owning the ABC network, the Disney Channel, SOAPnet, ESPN, History, and Lifetime, as well as ten television stations and thirty-seven radio stations. Finally, it had a substantial Internet presence through its ownership of websites like the Baby Einstein store, ESPN Zone, and the Disney Store. Disney even owned its own cruise line. Most of all, of course, it owned destination theme parks in California, Florida, France, Japan, and two in China—Hong Kong and Shanghai.[3] It is even planning a television channel in Russia.[4]

Viacom is another media giant, particularly in the fields of film and television. As of August 2011, it owned the film production and distribution studios Paramount Pictures and Paramount Home Entertainment, as well as DreamWorks Studios, Paramount Vantage, MTV Films, and Nickelodeon Movies. In television, it owned or had a significant interest in thirty networks or cable/satellite channels including

MTV, Nickelodeon, CMT, VH1, and Comedy Central. It also owns the digital production house SouthParkStudios.com. The company also had control of the *Star Trek* franchise.[5] This franchise spans eleven feature films, five television series, and innumerable books, magazines, and collectable paraphernalia. One source estimates that the combined revenues of the *Star Trek* franchise have exceeded $100 billion since its inception in the 1960s.[6]

CBS is in one sense a relative newcomer to the pop culture corporate elite: it was spun off from its parent company, Viacom, in 2007 at the behest of the company's majority owner, Sumner Redfield. The newly formed CBS took over Viacom's television operations as well as its print publishing operations. As of August 2011, the CBS network encompassed twenty-eight television stations and more than a hundred radio stations. CBS owns the CBS Television Network and CBS Records, as well as the cable Showtime channel. Finally, it has a major presence in the print industry, owning Simon & Schuster's adult and children's publishing houses.[7]

Rupert Murdoch's News Corporation, associated with the Fox label, controls a wide range of entertainment production in the world today. As of July 2011, News Corp. owned sixteen film production studios, including Twentieth Century Fox, Blue Sky Studios, and Fox Searchlight Pictures. In television, it owned the Fox Broadcasting Company and twenty-seven broadcast television stations. It also owned an array of cable networks including the Fox News Channel, Fox Kids Network, Fox Sports, FX, and the National Geographic Channel. It counted six satellite services, including BSkyB and Sky Italia, among its holdings. News Corp. also owned seven print publishers, with a total of forty-four imprints; four magazines; and dozens of newspapers around the world. It owned forty international television stations and online properties like Americanidol.com, hulu.com, and realestate.com.[8]

Vivendi S.A. is now a comparatively small force in the production of contemporary popular culture, but it remains a significant source of global music production under the Universal Music Group, the labels of which include Island Def Jam Music Group, Interscope Geffen A&M Records, MCA Nashville, Mercury Records, Polydor, Universal Motown, and Decca. Finally, it is a significant producer of television programming across Europe.[9]

The newest entry as a powerful player in the global AV market is the cable television company Comcast. In 2011, Comcast completed the purchase of a 51 percent stake in NBC Universal, which it bought from the global megacorporation General Electric (GE). (GE retains a 49 percent stake in the company.) As of July 2011, Comcast's acquisition of NBC Universal, combined with its own holdings, led to its owning or having a significant stake in a substantial array of movie, music, and web studios and services. Comcast owned thirteen NBC-affiliated local news stations and sixteen Telemundo (Spanish language)-affiliated stations. Comcast owned forty cable television channels as well, including Bravo, CNBC, MSNBC, Syfy, and the Weather Channel. It owned the NBC television network, NBC Universal Domestic Television Distribution, and NBC Universal International Television Distribution. It owned Universal Pictures and Focus Features, and it had majority control of Universal Parks and Resorts and Universal Pictures. It even owned sports franchises like the Philadelphia Flyers and the Philadelphia 76ers.[10]

Not all AV popular culture is produced by these firms, of course. However, as is suggested by the partial listing of the various companies that each of these corporations owns, a remarkable array of global AV popular culture is produced within a remarkably small circle of companies. It is these companies that carry movie, music, and television styles largely created and promoted by Americans to the world.

## THE DEVELOPMENT OF THE MODERN AMERICAN MOVIE, MUSIC, AND TELEVISION INDUSTRIES

This section of chapter 3 traces the historical, economic, social, and political forces that led to the global rise of the American AV pop culture industry. It explores both why U.S. corporations had a particular advantage in the global competition for audiences and how the music, television, and film industries developed in their contemporary forms.

As will be seen at the end of this section, however, recent technological changes in the ways that AV products are made and distributed globally have worked to both expand and challenge American dominance in these pop culture forms. The digitization of AV products, both in their creation and their transmission to an increasingly Internet-connected, wirelessly linked world has provided American movies and music and television products with access to global markets that no producer could have imagined at the height of the Cold War. However, the ease with which such products can be reproduced and retransmitted has profoundly undermined producers' abilities to generate profits from these media. The digital revolution, which hit music first and hardest, has the potential to restructure the ways AV popular culture is made and experienced. American producers may be better positioned to adapt to this changed environment than most other movie, music, and television program makers might be—but the pace and scope of the digital revolution may overwhelm any efforts to maintain historical modes of production, distribution, and profit.

## THE AMERICAN EXCEPTION

Perhaps the first question that needs to be answered in any assessment of one group or community's dominance in a particular field is, why? Why was it possible for this group and not some other group to rise to such a position? After all, while American corporations and American forms of entertainment dominate the global AV pop culture industry today, it did not have to be this way. The first movie ever made that was recognizably a movie in the modern sense of the word was filmed in France, for example; had things worked out differently, Paris, not Hollywood, might well be the center of the world's film business today. Similarly, the first television broadcast was in London and the first recordings of speech and music were made in Europe. At least in terms of origin, then, there was no logical or inevitable reason that the AV popular culture industry would be concentrated in the United States, especially in Hollywood, California.

As was discussed in chapter 1, our ability to communicate, whether through printed matter like books, magazines, or newspapers or through electronic media like movies, music, and television, has generated a great deal of cultural fear across the ages. Frankfurt School and mass society theorists worried that those who controlled the means of mass communication could distort or corrupt the values and ideals of populations that had left their rural homes and traditional lives and moved to big cities. Freed of the social constraints that exist when everyone knows everyone else and lives near the churches they are expected to attend on Sunday, consumers of mass communication were seen to be prone to having their morals undermined by erotic and enticing entertainments.

This fear is as old as movable type itself. Johannes Gutenberg's invention of the movable-type printing press in 1436 initiated a revolution in the creation and dissemination of books, pamphlets, and eventually magazines and newspapers. Notably, printed materials were subjected to religious, political, and economic controls almost as soon as printing was invented. Texts were heavily censored. Put simply, religious and political authorities were afraid that the new media of print would be used to undermine the power of the state or the authority of church officials who claimed to interpret God's will. They would not allow their religious and political authority to be challenged in print. State authorities therefore passed and enforced laws defining what could or could not be printed, and they penalized violators with imprisonment and even death.

Printing freedom was further limited when Europe's printers formed guilds that controlled the industry and limited access to printing by establishing a system of extended apprenticeships. This had the effect of protecting the economic power of the few printers who were in the guild: if people wanted something printed they had to go to one of the few businesses that could operate legally and had to pay the price asked for the work done. As a consequence, printing expanded slowly in most of Europe. Literacy and markets for the printed word grew slowly as well.[11]

Most governments adopted controls on AV electronic technologies similar to those they imposed on the print industry as their native movie-, music-, and television-making industries developed in the twentieth century. The British Broadcasting Corporation (BBC), for example, is a quasi-governmental corporation that has a state-mandated mission to provide specific types of programming to the British people. In particular, the British government has historically set content standards that the BBC had to meet in order to keep operating. More generally, governments used their power to regulate the broadcast airwaves to create state-sponsored media broadcasters that offered programming that met the government's criteria for what ought to be broadcast. Additionally, many governments provided subsidies to private filmmakers in return for state influence over the content of any movie. As a consequence, in most of the world the AV media developed in cooperation with, and sometimes under the direct control of, the political leaders of the nation in which the media were based.

This state-centered evolution of the AV media rested on an important belief about the role of the media in social and political life, a belief that profoundly shaped the future evolution of today's globalized popular culture. Those nations and communities that regulated their communications industries from the beginning, were, like the Frankfurt School and mass society theorists described in chapter 1, worried about the ways in which mass communications could be used to undermine social and political order. As a consequence, they limited the freedom of mass communication industries to create and market whatever these industries thought they could produce and sell to the citizens of their countries. The state's goal in limiting such freedoms was to assure, or to try to assure, that their peoples would not be exposed to ideas, attitudes, values, and behaviors that society's leaders decided were dangerous—especially if elites considered those ideas dangerous to the elites themselves. The AV industries were thus viewed as a tool of state policy. Movies, music, and television programs were another way political and economic elites could try to manage society as they saw best—by controlling the information their citizens got and the entertainments they enjoyed. The AV industries, in other words, were political: they served to promote specific political values.

In the United States, the printing and other mass communication industries developed very differently than they did in Europe. While there were occasional, early efforts to regulate what was printed in the United States, as well as to limit access to printing technology through apprenticeship systems and taxes on paper, these proved relatively ineffective. Instead, printing spread rapidly throughout the American colonies. Literate Americans sought Bibles, entertainment, and the opportunity to advertise their goods and services to the growing population that was quickly spreading across a large territory. Printing provided an ideal means to spread both the word of God and the world of consumer goods to the American people. Mass communication thus emerged as a means of both personal salvation and personal enterprise.

The twin forces of profit and proselytizing would push the American mass communication industry to expand rapidly and to innovate to meet the needs of a diverse market. For example, from 1790 to 1835 the number of American newspapers grew from 106 to 1,258 (more than

1,100 percent), even though the U.S. population grew only 400 percent in the same period (while the number of newspaper subscriptions per 100 households grew from 18 or 19 in the 1780s to over 50 in the 1820s.) By contrast, Great Britain, which was more heavily populated, had only 369 newspapers in the entire country in 1835—only 17 of which were produced daily.[12] In the United States, mass communication became an agent of both God and mammon, as individuals and entrepreneurs explored ways to use it for both their commercial and their ecclesiastical ends. It was not a tool of state power, at least not directly.

What was true for the printing industry was true for the AV industries that followed: telegraph, telephone, radio, recording, film, and television. In general, not only was there less regulation of American industries as compared to European ones, but the American economic environment promoted the creative evolution of AV technologies as they developed. Rather than being limited by strong government regulations—or, perhaps more accurately, working in a vast geographic area and a constitutionally protected legal environment that combined to make effective state regulation of newspaper and other mass media difficult—American mass communication industries were relatively free to develop and market whatever goods and services they thought would satisfy their audience's appetites. Whereas European producers were subject to an array of state controls on their actions, American producers could more easily create whatever they thought would sell. While American popular culture did not develop completely free from state sanctions, as is discussed later in this chapter, it was much freer to develop than was the case in most of the rest of the world. As a consequence, the mass communication industries in the United States became individualistic, capitalist, and entrepreneurial. American popular culture production companies were therefore well positioned to enter the international market as it developed in the nineteenth and twentieth centuries.[13]

Notably, the economic and political freedom that American producers of popular culture products had to create and market their goods coincided with the emergence of a domestic U.S. market that was both globally diverse and sufficiently well off to be able to afford mass market entertainments. As millions of immigrants moved to America, film and music makers had to learn to concoct stories that were appealing across a broad—indeed a global—audience. The existence of a large, financially supportive domestic market that in many ways reflected the cultural diversity of a large part of the world's population led American makers of movies, music, and eventually television programming to develop a style that was, as Scott Robert Olson explained, transparent: it appealed across cultural boundaries.[14] The American AV industries exploited U.S. political and economic freedoms to develop industries that were globally accessible and engaging in front of diverse cultural audiences. The interaction of the size of the American market, its cultural diversity, and the political and economic ability American producers enjoyed to make appealing products worked to promote American pop culture makers as the dominant force in the global market.

## A BRIEF HISTORY OF THE MOVIE INDUSTRY

The first of the three great AV industries to be invented and eventually come under American dominance was the movie industry. While France was the first locus of the nascent movie industry, in time Hollywood emerged as the center of the film universe. Hollywood in turn helped spread American popular culture—indeed, American culture—around the world.

In the early days of filmmaking, individual entrepreneurs, not giant global corporations, dominated the industry. Tinkerers and inventors made short reel films of horses running or people running and jumping or other live action events that would then be shown in nickelodeons at theaters and carnivals around the world. The first recognizable film, in the sense of being a story told over several minutes' duration, was Georges Méliès' A Trip to the Moon. It was made in France in 1902.

France's head start as the home of the film industry did not last long, however. The Edison Company quickly overwhelmed it. Inventor Thomas Edison's company, already an international giant due to its founder's inventive prowess, was able to combine the efficiency of mass production with the marketing advantage of a national and international corporation to turn movies into profit-making endeavors. The Edison Company out-produced small operations by exploiting the ideal movie-making conditions in Southern California to make better movies at lower cost than other, non-Hollywood producers could.[15]

What Edison's company started, other entrepreneurs mimicked. By the 1920s the international movie industry was concentrated in

Hollywood, California. A few companies, such as Universal, Metro Goldwyn Mayer (MGM), First National, and Fox controlled most of the industry. Most of the world's successful writers, directors, producers, and distributors made their living in Hollywood. Stars were signed to exclusive contracts to guarantee the studios profits on the films they showed at theaters they often owned. This combination allowed the studios to generate enormous profits, produce elaborate extravaganzas that no other nation's film companies could duplicate, and take control of the international movie industry. Indeed, by the end of World War I, American films were shown as much as 80 percent of the time on screens in other countries—particularly those that had not established quotas to protect their domestic film industries. By the 1930s, Hollywood earned 35 percent of its income from the overseas distribution of its films, two-thirds of which came from Europe.[16] During this same period, a commentator for the British newspaper the *Daily Express* bemoaned that British movie audiences "talk America, think America, and dream America. We have several million people, mostly women, who to all intent and purpose are temporary American citizens."[17] As early as the 1930s, then, American films were internationally pervasive.

Notably, Hollywood was able to maintain its global dominance of the film industry despite a major shock to its funding model that hit the industry in 1948. That year, the U.S. Supreme Court declared that the production companies' ownership of theaters constituted an unconstitutional restraint on trade—a monopoly. *United States v. Paramount Pictures*, known as the Paramount case, led to a significant change in the way movies were produced and distributed—divorcement. Under the terms of the case, Hollywood production studios had to sell—divorce—their theater chains. This change stripped the production studios of a major source of revenue: ticket sales. In response, the major studios reduced the number and quality of the films they produced, preferring to focus on a smaller number of likely blockbusters. This, in turn, allowed smaller, independent producers to emerge to fill the parts of the market the major producers had abandoned. In time, the major and minor producers developed a series of financial relationships, including one that remains common today: distribution deals. The major companies might contribute some money, but not all, to independent companies that take responsibility for making specific movies. The major company then markets and distributes movies it did not actually make. Profits, if any, are shared according to the terms negotiated in the contract.[18] Subsequently, most of these quasi-independent producers were still based in Hollywood, where the pool of writers, directors, special-effects persons, lighting and stage designers, and all the other specialists it takes to make movies is still largely centered. They simply worked as independent contractors, rather than as employees of the major production studios.

One consequence of the rise of the independent film producers and production companies was the introduction of a degree of economic vulnerability in making and distributing movies. Independent companies were, as a rule, much smaller than the major studios they replaced. As a consequence, independent producers were much more vulnerable to the success or failure of individual movies. A big hit could make an independent a major player in the movie industry, while a flop could destroy a company. Moreover, a hit could provide a company with the resources to buy another, weaker competitor, while a flop could make a company vulnerable to a takeover. Many small producers collapsed and were swallowed up as a consequence of this vulnerability. A few major producers therefore came to dominate the industry.

In recent years, three technological developments in the distribution of movies have changed the economic model on which American movie industry dominance was built, and thereby threatened the U.S. role as the globally dominant film producer. These are videotapes, digital video discs (DVDs), and the Internet. The industry learned how to adapt to the first two and remain profitable. However, the Internet has posed new and ongoing challenges to the film industry, which it is just beginning to address. (All discussion of the effects of the new digital era on the movie industry will be put off into an analysis later in this chapter of how the television and music industries have been affected as well.) As a consequence, while the industry is dominated by a small number of producers today, this may change as the web alters the ways movies are financed and distributed.

Videotapes emerged in the 1980s. They offered home consumers a smaller, cheaper, less sophisticated version of the taping equipment available to broadcasters and film producers. With videotape and a videocassette recorder (VCR), people could copy material from their television sets. This included broadcasts of previously released movies. Alternatively, consumers could watch tapes of films that they rented or purchased from distributors. In either case, videotape posed a significant challenge to the film industry, which had made most of its money on ticket sales in theaters since the industry emerged in the early 1900s. Now, with VCRs, people did not have to go to the theater. The movies eventually came to them. Ticket sales dropped, and numerous production houses struggled as a consequence.

In time, the film industry adapted to the VCR and its electronic successor, the DVD. Some production companies signed contracts with video rental firms to share profits and offer filmed content exclusively in one store or the other for some period of time, while others bought video distribution companies to add that stream of revenue to their portfolios. Movie companies began to market and sell videotapes, and later, DVDs, of their products to the mass audience. In addition, a whole new industry of direct-to-video movies emerged, as filmmakers exchanged high quality and expensive production values for the fast profits available from a cheap movie produced quickly and marketed to consumers' homes without expensive promotion campaigns. Companies that successfully negotiated the challenges and opportunities of the video era emerged stronger and bigger; other companies failed.

The economic twists and turns of the film industry have in large measure worked to create the modern film industry as it stands today. Major corporations have bought numerous other companies and entered into distribution deals with many others. While who owns what is subject to constant change, the basic long-term effect of the economic history of the film industry has been to leave it with only a few dominant producers that share the market with an array of minor, independent houses. Each new economic challenge changed which company was dominant in a given era but ultimately reinforced the relative dominance of American producers and American forms of global popular culture.

In addition to these economic forces, an array of social pressures has shaped the modern film industry. Many people have resented and resisted what they perceived was the power movies had to shape society's culture. From the earliest days of film, many people have strongly opposed popular movies on the grounds that they were culturally corruptive—dangerous to the moral order. For example, *American* magazine echoed Frankfurt School and mass society theorists in 1909 when it worried that "four million people attend moving pictures theaters [*sic*], it is said, every day. . . . Almost 190 miles of film are unrolled on the screens of America's canned drama theaters every day in the year. Here is an industry to be controlled, an influence to be reckoned with." Likewise, in April 1916, *Outlook* insisted: "The version of life presented to him [the audience] in the majority of moving pictures is false in fact, sickly in sentiment, and utterly foreign to the Anglo-Saxon ideals of our nation." In April 1929, *Commonweal* complained:

> And if the speech recorded in the dialogue [of talking pictures] is vulgar or ugly, its potentialities for lowering the speech standard of the country are almost incalculable. The fact that it is likely to be heard by the less discriminating portion of the public operates to increase its evil effects; for among the regular attendants at moving picture theaters there are to be found large groups from among our foreign-born population, to whom it is really vitally important that they hear only the best speech.[19]

As popular forms of entertainment and communication, movies have faced criticism since they were first invented, for failing to uphold high standards of conduct and values.

In an effort to forestall externally imposed censorship, in 1930 the major film producers created a production code under the leadership of former U.S. Postmaster General Will Hays. It remained in force until 1968, when it was replaced with the ratings system still in effect in the United States today. The Production Code eventually governed the behavioral and moral content of movies. For example, the code controlled depictions of sexuality and violence in film, setting up a self-enforced censorship board for the industry. Likewise, the code mandated that characters with "good" values had to be victorious over those who were "bad." As a consequence, the code pushed the studios to adopt acceptable formulas that they repeated again and again, all to the delight of the audience.[20]

Another round of social pressure hit the movies in the late 1940s and early 1950s. This was the result of McCarthyism and the Red Scare. During the Cold War, Hollywood found itself on public trial to prove its "Americanness." Actors, directors, writers, and others were called to testify before Congress—particularly before the evocatively named "House Un-American Activities Committee"—about whether they were, ever had been, or knew members of the Communist Party. Those who refused to testify, or who were identified as party members, found themselves blacklisted and denied the opportunity to earn a living. Others, like Screen Actors Guild president Ronald Reagan, became politically active: Reagan joined the conservative wing of the Republican Party after testifying to Congress against many of his fellow actors and Hollywood professionals. (Reagan parlayed this experience into an active role in Senator Barry Goldwater's campaign for president in 1964, his own election as governor of California in 1966, and his election and reelection as president of the United States in 1980 and 1984.) Hollywood got the message: its films espoused anti-Communism throughout the 1950s.

In 1968, in the midst of changing social standards about issues like sexuality, the proper roles for women and minorities in society, and other contentious matters, the motion picture industry perceived it was likely to face another bout of pressure to regulate its products. In response, the Motion Picture Association of America created a ratings system for movies. This was intended to allow filmmakers to experiment with complicated adult themes while providing parents and community members with sufficient information to make informed choices about which films they and their children went to see. In effect, G and PG movies would tell safe, traditional "American" stories, while R-rated films might provide a zone of freedom for some topics and stories that would not otherwise be produced under the terms of the Production Code.[21] In time, a PG-13 rating was added for movies too violent or sexual for a simple PG label; likewise, an NC-17 rating was established for those films whose content was considered to be too mature for any children to attend at all. (PG-13 films are not supposed to admit children younger than thirteen without parental or guardian permission; NC-17 films are not supposed to admit anyone under eighteen.) Notably, this effort at self-regulation has been only moderately successful: as the need to develop the PG-13 and NC-17 ratings suggests, filmmakers have continued to stretch the limits of what is socially acceptable in the movies.

The Production Code, the reaction to the Red Scare in the 1950s, and the imposition of voluntary ratings in the 1960s were particularly important to the creation and sustaining of the "American" movie. In large measure, the conventions and genres established in response to the code have survived to today. The pressures of these events worked to sustain the "American" movie well beyond the time it was an exclusively American phenomenon. Thus even as foreign companies bought "American" production companies, they purchased the expertise and experience of filmmakers shaped by making American movies for a global audience. In turn, the early U.S. dominance of the industry let it establish many of the conventions and genres in which movies are presented worldwide. It also meant that the labels on many, if not most, of the films distributed around the world are associated with the United States, not other countries. As a consequence, while movies may star non-U.S. actors, be financed from outside the United States, or otherwise be global in production, they are often recognizably American.

So just how dominant are American movies on the global market? There are a number of ways to illustrate the dominance of American movies worldwide. As of the end of 2011, for example, most of the top-grossing films of all time, worldwide, were either made by American or American-based studios, starred Americans, had themes and values recognizably in line with American public culture, or were set in a locale definably American. The list includes the all-time top-grossing film *Avatar*, with worldwide ticket sales exceeding $2 billion, as well as *Jurassic Park*, *Independence Day*, *Star Wars* (three of its six parts), *The Lion King*, and *Spider-Man 2* and *3*. (See table 3.1.) Sixty-six percent, or thirty-three of the top fifty all-time biggest-grossing movies were American. (Of the remaining seventeen films, fourteen were segments of three film franchises: *Harry Potter*, the *Lord of the Rings*, and *Pirates of the Caribbean*.) Moreover, as is made clear in table 3.1, not only were the films American, in almost all cases they generated more sales overseas than they did in the United States itself.

As might be expected, given the percentage of ticket sales for American films purchased worldwide, American films dominate a surprising array of nations' moviegoing. In 2009, for example, the Jim Carrey film *Yes Man* was the most popular movie in Australia, Venezuela, Croatia, and Lithuania, among other countries. *Bolt* took top honors in Argentina, Denmark, Hungary, and Sweden. *Twilight* was the most popular film in Peru, Germany, and France. Meanwhile, Austria and Belgium fell for *The Curious Case of Benjamin Button*.[22]

The global popularity of American films is also evident in direct economic terms. American films took 85 percent of European film revenues in the early 1990s, grossing $1.7 billion of total film receipts of

$2 billion. This dominance occurred despite the fact that France alone produced an average of 150 movies per year during the same period—suggesting that American movies were vastly more popular than their local counterparts. Indeed, by the early 1990s, almost 60 percent of French spending on movies was for attendance at American films. For example, when the American megahit *Jurassic Park* opened, it occupied fully one-quarter of all movie screens in France. Likewise, in Germany, American movies grew from a one-third market share to two-thirds between 1972 and 1991. By the end of this time frame, American movies controlled more than 80 percent of the European market collectively. In return, European movies accounted for less than 2 percent of American ticket sales.[23] Thus, even in competition with European films in the European market, American movies expanded in popularity throughout the post–World War II era.

More recently, in 2007 American films made almost twice as much money in Russia as Russian-produced films did: 8.3 billion rubles ($325 million) as opposed to 4.5 billion rubles for Russian films. By 2010, the difference was even starker, with American films taking five times as much of the Russian market as Russian films did. Similar growth has occurred in China, despite the government allowing only twenty foreign films into the country each year: in 2010, American films grossed $1.5 billion in sales.[24] Notably, China is expected to open thirty-five thousand screens over the next five years, up from the five thousand it currently has.[25]

As might be expected, given the dominance of American movies in the international market, U.S. films are also dominant in the post-theater market in the form of DVDs. Using Amazon.com as a proxy for a global market for DVD sales, for example, shows that of the twenty-five best-selling DVDs in Amazon's history, most replicate the highest-grossing movies list: *Star Wars*, *The Matrix*, *Finding Nemo*, the *Shrek* movies, and *Spider-Man* all make appearances, as do *Saving Private Ryan* and the *Godfather* films. Most of the rest of the list is the same mega-franchises that have dominated global movie screens for the last decade: *The Lord of the Rings*, *Harry Potter*, and the *Pirates of the Caribbean*.[26]

However one examines it, then, American movies have a dominant global presence on the world's movie screens. As will be seen later in this chapter, this dominance is reflected on global television screens as

**Table 3.1. Top-Grossing Films of All Time, U.S. and Foreign Sales**

| Rank | Film | Studio | Total (M $) | U.S.% | Foreign/% |
|------|------|--------|-------------|-------|-----------|
| 1 | Avatar | Fox | $2,782.30 | $760.5 27.3% | $2,021.8 72.7% |
| 2 | Titanic | Paramount | $1,843.20 | $600.8 32.6% | $1,242.4 67.4% |
| 4 | Transformers: Dark of the Moon | Paramount | $1,122.00 | $352.4 31.4% | $769.6 68.6% |
| 7 | Toy Story 3 | Buena Vista | $1,063.20 | $415.0 39.0% | $648.2 61.0% |
| 10 | The Dark Knight | Warner Bros. | $1,001.90 | $533.3 53.2% | $468.6 46.8% |
| 16 | The Lion King | Buena Vista | $928.20 | $421.7 45.4% | $506.5 54.6% |
| 18 | Star Wars I: The Phantom Menace | Fox | $924.30 | $431.1 46.6% | $493.2 53.4% |
| 19 | Shrek 2 | DreamWorks | $919.80 | $441.2 48.0% | $478.6 52.0% |
| 20 | Jurassic Park | Universal | $914.70 | $357.1 39.0% | $557.6 61.0% |
| 22 | Spider-Man 3 | Sony | $890.90 | $336.5 37.8% | $554.3 62.2% |
| 23 | Ice Age: Dawn of the Dinosaurs | Fox | $886.70 | $196.6 22.2% | $690.1 77.8% |
| 26 | Finding Nemo | Buena Vista | $867.90 | $339.7 39.1% | $528.2 60.9% |
| 27 | Star Wars III: Revenge of the Sith | Fox | $848.80 | $380.3 44.8% | $468.5 55.2% |
| 28 | Transformers: Revenge of the Fallen | Paramount | $836.30 | $402.1 48.1% | $434.2 51.9% |
| 29 | Inception | Warner Bros. | $825.50 | $292.6 35.4% | $533.0 64.6% |
| 30 | Spider-Man | Sony | $821.70 | $403.7 49.1% | $418.0 50.9% |

| Rank | Title | Studio | Worldwide | Domestic | % | Overseas | % |
|---|---|---|---|---|---|---|---|
| 31 | Independence Day | Fox | $817.40 | $306.2 | 37.5% | $511.2 | 62.5% |
| 32 | Shrek the Third | Paramount | $799.00 | $322.7 | 40.4% | $476.2 | 59.6% |
| 34 | E.T.: The Extra-Terrestrial | Universal | $792.90 | $435.1 | 54.9% | $357.8 | 45.1% |
| 35 | Indiana Jones and the Kingdom of the Crystal Skull | Paramount | $786.60 | $317.1 | 40.3% | $469.5 | 59.7% |
| 36 | Spider-Man 2 | Sony | $783.80 | $373.6 | 47.7% | $410.2 | 52.3% |
| 37 | Star Wars | Fox | $775.40 | $461.0 | 59.5% | $314.4 | 40.5% |
| 38 | 2012 | Sony | $769.70 | $166.1 | 21.6% | $603.6 | 78.4% |
| 39 | The Da Vinci Code | Sony | $758.20 | $217.5 | 28.7% | $540.7 | 71.3% |
| 40 | Shrek Forever After | Paramount | $752.60 | $238.7 | 31.7% | $513.9 | 68.3% |
| 42 | The Matrix Reloaded | Warner Bros. | $742.10 | $281.6 | 37.9% | $460.6 | 62.1% |
| 43 | Up | Buena Vista | $731.30 | $293.0 | 40.1% | $438.3 | 59.9% |
| 44 | The Twilight Saga: New Moon | Summit | $709.80 | $296.6 | 41.8% | $413.2 | 58.2% |
| 45 | Transformers | Paramount | $709.70 | $319.2 | 45.0% | $390.5 | 55.0% |
| 47 | Forrest Gump | Summit | $677.40 | $329.7 | 48.7% | $347.7 | 51.3% |
| 48 | The Sixth Sense | Paramount | $672.80 | $293.5 | 43.6% | $379.3 | 56.4% |
| 49 | Kung Fu Panda 2 | Paramount | $663.00 | $165.2 | 24.9% | $497.8 | 75.1% |
| 50 | Ice Age: The Meltdown | Fox | $655.40 | $195.3 | 29.8% | $460.1 | 70.2% |

Source: http://boxofficemojo.com/alltime/world/ (accessed 9 November 2011)

well, since a large portion of global television programming consists of rebroadcasts of American films. Hollywood built American film dominance around the world.

## A BRIEF HISTORY OF THE MUSIC INDUSTRY

Like the movie industry, the recording industry has faced a series of technological, financial, and social pressures that have led to its contemporary form. However, the history of the American recording industry cannot be understood only in terms of recorded music sales. The modern music industry is the result of both sales of recorded music and the emergence of radio as a form of communication, particularly once radio lost control of mass-market entertainments to television. It is therefore necessary to understand how the modern recording industry developed, both in terms of recordings in themselves and in terms of how radio served as a venue to advertise and promote recorded music.

The recording industry is the product of Thomas Edison's invention of a "talking machine" in 1877. (It was Edison's patenting of this machine that brought him the funds to move into the film industry a few years later.) This device used wax cylinders as the recording medium. Speakers or musicians played or shouted into an acoustic horn that scratched marks into the cylinder that could later be sensed by a needle and amplified through another acoustic horn into sounds loud enough to hear. Quality, unsurprisingly, was poor.[27]

Record players began to be marketed to consumers beginning in the 1890s. These early machines included the capacity for owners to record their own music or speech. Given the low quality of these recordings, however, a market quickly developed for prerecorded discs on which highly skilled performers overcame the limitations of the media and created impressive recordings. This preference was reinforced when, in the years prior to World War I, recording discs (as opposed to cylinders) were invented. While these could not be recorded on, they provided sound quality superior to that presented on cylinders. By 1919, almost two hundred companies were selling two million records per year; in 1921, total record sales surged past one hundred million.[28]

As quickly as the phenomenon of recorded music as mass entertainment rose, it very nearly collapsed just as fast. The causes of this collapse were the Great Depression and the emergence of radio as a source of entertainment. Once the Great Depression hit, people had virtually no money to spend on entertainment niceties like recorded music. Record sales dropped dramatically. There were only six million record sales in 1932, for example, more than ninety-four million units below the peak sales of 1921. Indeed, the only bright spot for the recording industry lay in the emergence of a new technology—the jukebox. By 1939, there were 225,000 jukeboxes playing thirteen million records; by 1942, that number had nearly doubled.[29]

Radio's contribution to the near-demise of the recorded music industry was also powerful. Recorded music had little, if any, role in the early days of radio. Instead, live performances, usually of comedy shows, soap operas, or mysteries/dramas, dominated these early radio broadcasts. These live performances were broadcast over one of the true entrepreneurial innovations of the early AV industry: networks. A radio network is a contractual affiliation between a series of stations and a production company to present the production company's programming on the contracted stations. Radio networks shared programming produced by a central production company such as the Columbia Broadcasting System (CBS), the National Broadcasting Company (NBC), or the American Broadcasting Company (ABC). Individual stations within a given network were usually owned independently, but they received much of their programming from the common production company. Thus, independently owned stations did not have to each create hours of programming to fill their airtime; rather, they broadcast programs that were actually produced by another company—the network.

Economic pressures drove the creation of radio networks. Radio stations are expensive to purchase and run. One has to buy the station, get a license, maintain the equipment, hire staff, and develop and present programming. It was, as a practical matter, relatively cheaper and more cost effective to buy and run a second and a third and a fourth radio station than it was to buy and run the first. The relative cost of creating programming would go down for each station if several stations shared costs. Each station's chances of making a profit would go up as a consequence. By 1945, even though most were independently owned, 95 percent of radio stations in the United States were affiliated with a broadcast network.[30]

In order to make their networks profitable, early American radio executives developed an innovative scheme to finance their operations. Unlike movie theaters, where patrons pay an entry fee to see the film, radio is broadcast for free on public airwaves. It can be picked up by anyone with a receiver. The early radio pioneers decided that they could make money from radio by having advertisers pay for the programs. The public would listen free of charge. It would be as if you could get your groceries for free simply for watching a series of advertisements in a grocery store: the purpose of the radio program was to deliver an audience to an advertiser. The higher the number of listeners, the greater the fee the stations could charge for advertising time. Profit was generated from advertisers rather than from ticket buyers.

In exchange for receiving programming from a network producer, local radio stations had to allow the producer to control a certain amount of advertising time on the local station. If the radio station anticipated selling fifteen minutes of advertising in a given hour, for example, it could be forced to cede five minutes of that fifteen-minute block to the producer. The producer, rather than the local station, earned the profit from the five minutes of advertising it booked. The local station earned revenues from the remaining ten. The local station thus forewent some of its potential earned revenue (from the five minutes of advertising time it ceded to the network) in order to avoid the substantial costs associated with creating radio programming.

Between the 1920s and the 1950s, radio drew vast, unprecedented audiences across the United States, almost all of it for live programming. Record sales languished. This changed, however, when television (discussed later in this chapter) took over the general in-home entertainment market in the United States after the end of World War II. As radio lost markets to television, stations began to specialize and develop niche markets otherwise not served by the television networks. Many began to specialize in broadcasting particular forms of music such as jazz, classical, or country. The most important of these markets was rock and roll. Arriving at the same time as a large generation of teenagers known as the baby boomers, rock music linked radio to teen markets in immensely profitable ways. The industry took advantage of a new technology—a 45-rpm record that was smaller and more durable than older 78s—to aggressively market rock music to the baby boom generation. From 1955 to 1957, for example, record sales increased from $277 million to $460 million. This was followed by the shift of rock music to LPs—long-play albums on which performers could explore musical complexities in rock and other genres and could take advantage of the higher fidelity, stereo sound, and audio quality available on FM radio bands. As a consequence, the industry again saw increasing sales. For example, the Beatles' album *Sgt. Pepper's Lonely Hearts Club Band* (1967) sold seven million copies in LP, an unheard-of number for rock music prior to that time.[31] In a stunning reversal from its days as the nemesis of recorded music, radio had become the primary tool for marketing records to the American audience.

As was the case with the film industry, the music heard on these networks was the product of large global corporations. Major producers, usually centered in cities like Los Angeles, Detroit, or Nashville, took responsibility for identifying new talent and marketing it to the broad U.S. market. Alternatively, when independent producers created and marketed new sounds like hip-hop or rock and roll, established labels either purchased the upstart labels or started their own record labels to compete for entertainment dollars. These companies used their skills at recognizing and marketing talented acts both within the United States and across the world. They carried American music to a global audience.

It should be noted that the Americanness of the music these global corporations took around the world was not influenced only by economic considerations of record sales and radio airplays. Like the film industry, the recording industry has faced an array of social pressures that have shaped its character. As music evolved in the early twentieth century, for example, it developed the fast rhythms of Dixieland and the innovative harmonies of jazz. In response, people began dancing differently. No longer did they use the formal patterns and prescribed movements of ballroom dancing. In their place rose free-form dancing, often at a fast pace and mimicking, in various degrees of specificity, sexual contact. Persons of conventional morality were shocked, seeing in this new explicit music and dancing the corruption of Western civilization. Accordingly, they pressured music companies and radio stations to censor or otherwise control the suggestiveness of "new" music. In one particularly humorous example, the Cole Porter song "Let's Put Out the Lights and Go to Bed" was renamed "Let's Put Out the Lights and Go to Sleep" before being aired on radio.[32] More ominously,

Billie Holiday's "Love for Sale" was banned altogether for its allusions to prostitution.

Music producers and distributors have also faced indirect regulatory pressure from the U.S. government. This is the result of the fact that radio (and, as will be discussed, broadcast television) is regulated by the federal government through the auspices of the Federal Communications Commission (FCC). The U.S. government licenses the use of specific frequencies to radio station owners. A radio station owner gets a license from the federal government to broadcast on a specific radio band. Only the licensed radio station is allowed to broadcast on that frequency in a given area known as a market. The license regulates how powerful the radio station may be, thereby limiting its effective range and allowing the same frequency to be used in neighboring markets.

In exchange for the exclusive right to use a specific frequency, which the federal government enforces by seeking out and penalizing any broadcasters who broadcast without a license, station owners must agree to a series of limitations on their freedom to do business. While these limits have varied over time, they have included rules about the number of stations one individual or company is allowed to own and a requirement that a certain amount of programming serve the public interest, like news broadcasts or emergency broadcasts in times of war or other crisis. More important have been regulations governing the moral content of a station's broadcasts. The federal government insisted that, on penalty of losing one's license or facing serious fines, broadcasters had to uphold high moral standards in their programming. Offensive language and controversial speech were thus effectively banned for much of the history of radio. By extension, these limits also worked to limit how scandalous most music might become, since music companies needed their records played on radio to market them.

As a consequence of FCC restrictions, corporations regularly edited the music they distributed for play on the radio. They bleeped or otherwise obscured offensive words and language. Yet the rock and roll explosion in the 1950s and the subsequent music movements of the 1960s offered a strong challenge to the limitations embedded in FCC rules—especially once producers discovered that music about drugs, sex, and rock and roll sold well. More and more performers offered adult, challenging, and even offensive music, ranging from 1970s hits like Blue Oyster Cult's "Don't Fear the Reaper," a song commending the virtues of suicide, to Madonna's 1980s classic "Like a Virgin," which most decidedly does not applaud the virtue of virginity. Lady Gaga offers a similar norm-challenging act today. Such challenges to conventional morality only increased as the music industry fragmented and differentiated into new genres like hip-hop, rap, and Latin music. In order to avoid FCC regulation, music companies regularly released two versions of songs: one for radio and one for the home consumer. A significant gap therefore often emerged between what one might hear on cleaned-up or obscured versions of songs on the radio and what was actually on a given album.

Tipper Gore, wife of then U.S. senator (D-Tennessee) and later U.S. vice president Al Gore, discovered this radio version–home version gap while listening to one of her children's albums in 1985. Shocked by the explicitness of what she heard in the home version in contrast with what she had heard on the radio, Gore worked with a number of allies to form the Parents' Music Resource Center (PMRC). The PMRC asked Congress to find that offensive music was pornographic and should be restricted, at least in sales to children. Like adherents of the Frankfurt School and mass society theory before them, the PMRC claimed that violent, sexually explicit music contributed to the decline of the American family and to the moral decay of society in general. To support their contention, in 1985 they issued a list they called the "Filthy Fifteen," which included songs like Sheena Easton's "Sugar Walls" and Twisted Sister's "We're Not Gonna Take It," which the PMRC claimed were harmful due to their explicit references to sex and violence.[33]

Rather than face congressional sanction, the major record companies adopted a voluntary labeling system in which they placed stickers on albums that contained offensive material. The idea was to forestall regulation by providing parents with important information they could use to exercise informed control over what their children listened to. Subsequently, the giant discount retail chain Walmart announced it would not carry any albums deemed offensive; this led many major producers to create two versions of their products—one for Walmart and the one the performer actually intended to create.

Cumulatively, the technical, economic, and social forces that shaped the development of the American music industry encouraged consolidation among music houses, as well as with movie and television production studios. (The effects of the digital revolution on the recording industry will be addressed later in this chapter.) The major producers had advantages in the areas of money, technical capacity, marketing and licensing, and royalty management. These advantages allowed them to survive when many minor producers failed. The end result was the dominance of American music producers and American musical forms in international musical production and distribution.

As was the case with American movies, there are a number of ways to assess the preeminence of American music in world entertainment. A review of the top-selling albums of all time suggests the dominance of American music, for example. Even considering only certified sales as evidence of success—since there is no way to account for the untold millions or billions of illegal downloads of music in the digital era, a problem to be addressed later in this chapter—American performers are a dominant global music presence. As of November 2011, there were twenty-seven albums that had sold at least fifteen million copies worldwide, and sixteen were the product of undeniably American acts. The Eagles' *Their Greatest Hits* is tied with Michael Jackson's *Thriller* for the number one selling album of all time, at twenty-nine million sales. Other American groups on the list include Billy Joel, Boston, Hootie and the Blowfish, Garth Brooks, and Guns n' Roses. As was the case with the top-selling groups of all time, the top-selling non-American albums were made in genres created by Americans: rock (Pink Floyd's *The Wall*; Led Zeppelin's *Led Zeppelin IV*; the Beatles' *The Beatles*) and country (Canadian Shania Twain's *Come On Over*).[34] These sales numbers were mirrored in the United Kingdom. Of the sixty-three albums that had sold more than two million copies in the UK by 2011, twenty-three were from U.S. acts.[35]

Similar evidence for American music prominence can be found in considering the individual artists and groups in terms of their certified global record sales. The most successful musical act of all time, for example, is not American: it is The Beatles, with 177 million album sales in their history (playing rock music, of course, but expanding the genre along the way). However, the majority of the highest-selling acts of all time are American, starting with number two, Elvis Presley, with 133,500,000 album sales, and extending through number forty-nine, R. Kelly, with 33,500,000 album sales. Thirty-six of the top fifty music acts are Americans; the rest, with the exception of Canadian singer Celine Dion, perform in the rock, hip-hop, and country genres.[36]

Not all music is produced in the United States, of course. Other nations and cultures have distinct musical forms. American preeminence is substantial, not total, and is particularly focused in the rock and country genres. Hip-hop also plays a significant role in global music, although American acts do not sell as well globally as American rock and country performers do. Accordingly, it is to rock and country, and to a lesser extent hip-hop, that one's attention should be turned to assess the way(s) people around the world are attracted, repelled, lured, and horrified by the appearance of contemporary globalization as expressed by the United States. In other words, it is in American rock, country, and hip-hop that American music expresses its values, worldview, and desires to a global audience.

The dominance of American rock, country, and hip-hop is perhaps most evident in the direct linkage of music and television created in 1981 with the formation of the cable network MTV, Music Television. In their endless search for venues in which to promote their products, music companies and artists hit upon the idea of filming videos to accompany the songs that were playing on the radio. These videos were, in effect, mini-movies that linked television and film directors with musical groups to create visually exciting accompaniments to particular songs. The videos served as advertisements for the songs and albums. As a consequence, watching a music video is watching a commercial. The genius of MTV—which is owned by media giant Viacom—is that having watched the videos, which are commercials for songs, artists, and albums (and which music companies paid MTV to show in the first place), viewers would then watch formal, traditional commercials for which the network would be paid just like every other network. This was a moneymaking breakthrough: everything, whether advertisement or video, was paying MTV a fee for airtime.

An idea this profitable was sure to spread, and spread it did. Just ten years after its creation, MTV was available in 201 million households in seventy-seven countries ranging from Australia to Brazil to Hong Kong. MTV Europe grew from 3 million households in 1988 to 14 million in 1991 and then 37 million in 1992.[37] By 1995, almost every country in the world (barring most of Africa and a few countries in South America, along with a scattering of nations elsewhere) had MTV or copycat music television networks.[38] MTV has now spread across the globe.[39] As was noted in chapter 1, MTV has even gone to Saudi Arabia. While the network adapted its playlist to local tastes and preferences, it concurrently provided a platform on which American music was linked to global television audiences across the world.[40]

The combination of radio's market reach to domestic U.S. country, rock and roll, and hip-hop fans, as well as the global megacorporations that came to oversee and market these styles around the world, made American music a globally pervasive music purveyor. MTV then sealed the deal and linked television to music in a global phenomenon. Whether listening to American acts or enjoying music created in forms native to the United States, there is a vast global audience for American music today.

## A BRIEF HISTORY OF THE TELEVISION INDUSTRY

As was the case with both the film and music industries, television has been affected by a series of technological, fiscal, and social developments that have shaped its contemporary role in global entertainment. These forces have also encouraged the growth of major corporations as controlling agents of popular television programming. Notably, as the last of the AV media to be invented, television entered a world in which American pop culture programming was already globally dominant. Accordingly, American television programming did not have to invent a global presence. The concentration of talent in Hollywood, combined with the story-telling prowess of producers capable of satisfying the large, diverse, and wealthy U.S. market, created conditions in which the American television industry would grow to have the same global influence as the American film and music industries. It built on the economic, cultural, and production advantages created by the movie and music industries to grow into a worldwide phenomenon.

Television grew as an entertainment medium only when the technology necessary to send pictures in radio waves and to receive and interpret those signals and convert them into visual images was invented in the 1930s. The first broadcasts began in 1939; by 1940, there were twenty-three television stations broadcasting to approximately ten thousand television sets around the world (mostly in New York and London). These broadcasts were quite primitive, and as a practical matter television was put on hold during World War II. The postwar economic boom in the United States, however, led to the dramatic expansion of the American middle class. This expanded class demanded new forms of entertainment. Television fit the bill, and the number of television sets in the United States grew over 700 percent in just the years 1951–1953.[41]

Early television programming borrowed from radio the practice of having performers present live on stage. In many cases, radio hits simply transferred to television; in others, radio formats crossed over but with different actors. Accordingly, early televisions were filled with soap operas, quiz shows, talk shows, and variety performance shows. New programming was offered every week; almost all of it was broadcast live.

These early broadcasts were usually local. The capacity to offer coast-to-coast broadcasts only developed in 1957. If producers wanted to distribute a program across the nation, they had to film the program and then distribute the resulting kinescopes to other stations for presentation. The kinescopic copy was inevitably quite poor. Only the invention of videotape in 1956 made it possible for distribution of quality programming across the nation: videotape could capture action as it was being performed and then could easily be edited into a final product without first being shown on a television screen. The resulting quality was much higher than that of the kinescope. This made it much easier to create shared programming across networks of television stations.[42]

As television expanded, it adopted not just the genres but also the basic business practices of radio. These included the use of networks to produce and distribute programming and the reliance on advertisers to pay for programming. Individual television stations were usually owned and operated independently, but they received at least half of their programming from central production companies like CBS, NBC, and ABC (among others). In other cases, programming was actually purchased by advertisers and provided to stations independent of the networks.[43] In either case, programming was provided to consumers free of charge in exchange for the network receiving the right to sell advertising on the local station or for the advertiser's exclusive right to have its name and product embedded in the show.

Over time, the costs of producing television programs grew as casts, plots, sets, and special effects became more complex. As the price of making television shows grew, the prospects of being supported by an individual sponsor diminished. Only the networks had access to the array of marketers, advertising executives, promoters, developers, directors, actors, writers, and other components of the television production process to make the production of television programming economically viable. Accordingly, only they had practical ability to continue producing television programs. Networks largely replaced advertisers as developers and distributors of programming in the 1960s.[44]

Three major networks, ABC, CBS, and NBC, dominated the television industry between 1957, when true coast-to-coast network broadcasts began, and the 1970s. These networks offered pre-taped programs to their affiliated stations, although news and sporting events were usually, although not always, shown live. In the 1980s, Fox Television began a broadcast network. Independent stations existed, usually in local areas, and the Public Broadcasting System (PBS) was created by congressional mandate to provide programming independent of the need to sell commercial time. The commercial broadcast networks were dominant, however—a position they would retain so long as television signals were received at home over the airwaves.

Starting in the 1970s, however, cable and satellite technologies developed through which non-network entrepreneurs could make money by collecting the broadcast signals of the networks (and other stations) and sending them packaged together directly into individual homes. Consumers paid a fee to the cable and satellite companies to bring programming directly to their homes, while the cable and satellite companies paid fees to the networks and other producers for the right to package network and other signals for transmission through cable lines or satellite signals. Cable and satellite companies generated the bulk of their revenues from subscriber fees; however, they also demanded advertising time on broadcasters' programs. As a consequence, cable and satellite companies began competing with the networks for advertising dollars. Network broadcast television was forced to compete for revenues in ways it never had before.

The rise of cable and satellite companies and the multiplication of niche channels that followed the increased transmission capacity of these new technologies drew viewers away from traditional broadcast networks and toward cable and satellite programming. Movie, sports, news, and other specialty channels drew increasing shares of the viewing audience. In many cases, these niche channels provided superior service to the traditional broadcasters. At the start of the first Iraq war (1990–1991), for example, the only network with reporters still in Baghdad was the Cable News Network (CNN). By the end of the war, CNN was America's most-watched news network. Similarly, ESPN, a cable network focused on sports, founded in 1979, quickly took a leading position in providing sports programming to viewers. By 2000, viewership of the traditional networks had declined precipitously, and the distinction between "broadcast" and "other" television had substantially blurred.

Yet while the networks' share of the overall television market declined, the reach of American programming grew throughout this period. As a practical matter, all the new networks that emerged to fill the bandwidth available on cable and satellite channels had to begin to produce substantial amounts of programming on their own. HBO, USA, TNT, and other networks each began to create and broadcast their own shows. In turn, these networks licensed their programs to global cable and satellite companies for rebroadcast around the world. For example, the Cambodian website everyday.com.kh reports that if you were watching television in English in Cambodia on November 27, 2011, you could watch an array of shows like *Hawaii Five-O*, *NCIS: Los Angeles*, *Chuck*, *The Amazing Race*, and even CNBC's *Closing Bell*. Networks like Animal Planet, CNBC, CNN, Discovery, ESPN, and HBO were available as well.[45] Similarly, BSkyB, a satellite network wholly owned by Rupert Murdoch's News Corporation, broadcasts a wide array of American programming across Britain and Ireland: Bravo, several Discovery channels, National Geographic, E!, Disney, Syfy, and, of course, several music TV channels.[46]

The rise of alternatives to broadcast television like satellite, cable, and the Internet combined with technological developments like the remote control and the VCR/DVR to change the ways television programs were produced. As the number of channels proliferated, the margin of profit per channel grew quite thin. As was the case with the movie and music industries, it was only the major producers who had sufficient resources and talents for marketing and synergy that could increase the chances for a profit in any individual channel or program. Networks stopped producing their own programming, with the exception of news and sports programming, and instead grew to rely on external producers to create the content the network, cable, and satellite channels later broadcast. This process concentrated the production of television programming in the major studios in and around Hollywood, California.

Social and political forces as well as economic ones have shaped the contemporary television industry, just as they shaped the movie and music industries before it. TV has found itself under repeated attack as a force for social evil and moral chaos. As early as 1949, for example, the *Saturday Review* worried, like so many adherents of the Frankfurt School and mass society theory before it:

> Here, in concept at least, was the most magnificent of all forms of communication. Here was the supreme triumph of invention, the dream of the ages—something that could bring directly into the home a moving image fused with sound—reproducing action, language, and thought without the loss of measurable time. Here was the magic eye that could bring the wonders of entertainment, information and education into the living room. Here was a tool for the making of a more enlightened democracy than the world had ever seen. Yet out of the wizardry of the television tube has come such an assault against the human mind, such a mobilized attack on the imagination, such an invasion against good taste as no other communications medium has known, not excepting the motion picture or radio itself.

Similarly, just five years later (1954), the *New Republic* opined:

> Seeing constant brutality, viciousness and unsocial acts results in hardness, intense selfishness, even in mercilessness, proportionate to the amount of exposure and its play on the native temperament of the child. Some cease to show resentment to insults, to indignities, and even cruelty toward helpless old people, to women and other children.[47]

Notably, these attacks occurred despite the fact that the FCC regulated television broadcasts like it did radio transmissions. Television is broadcast on radio frequencies, and the U.S. government imposes the same conditions of public ownership of the airwaves, monopoly licensing in exchange for protection of markets, and other restrictions on television as it does on radio. Indeed, as was the case for radio, the FCC announced decency standards for television programming similar to those embedded in the Production Code for movies: sexual conduct was to be avoided; individuals were to behave with decency and dignity or, if they did not, were to be the "bad guy" of the story; bad language was not to be used. These restrictions were enforced even when they were inherently absurd, as was the case when the top-rated *I Love Lucy* showed star Lucille Ball's bedroom in one episode (itself a fairly shocking event at the time). The program was forced to show the room as containing only twin beds placed several feet apart—despite the fact that Ball was actually pregnant, her pregnancy was written into the show, and her real-life husband, Desi Arnaz, was her on-screen husband and the program's costar as well. Popular shows of the era, like *Father Knows Best* and *Leave It to Beaver*, likewise reinforced conventional morality as delimited in FCC regulations.

Social changes in the 1950s and 1960s challenged the conventional morality of the time. The desire to broadcast rock performances, in particular, pressured television executives to stretch the boundaries of social acceptability. For example, *American Bandstand* presented popular musicians and bands live on stage as teenagers danced, often provocatively by the standards of the time. Ed Sullivan, a host of a variety show, allowed rock and roll superstar Elvis Presley to appear on his show, though he only televised Presley's performance from the waist up, as Presley's gyrating hips were believed to be too sexually suggestive for the television audience. Over time, a distinction emerged between programming aimed at adults, which was generally broadcast after 9 p.m. Eastern time, and children's programming, which would be shown earlier in the day. Later programs were allowed to be more sexually explicit and adult-themed, although outright nudity was still banned. Language limitations were loosened at the same time, leading one comedian, George Carlin, to offer a routine called "The Seven Dirty Words You Can't Say on TV," lifted directly from the FCC's banned words list.

There has been a recent turn toward stricter FCC enforcement of morals regulations on broadcast television and radio. This resulted from an incident at the Super Bowl on February 1, 2004, in which Justin Timberlake, a pop singer, removed a patch that was covering pop singer Janet Jackson's right breast during the halftime show. This event, which was quite mild compared with much of the programming available even on broadcast television in the later evening, much less on cable or satellite networks, nonetheless caused a substantial outcry from many people across the United States. As a consequence, the FCC launched an investigation of the incident and levied a total of $550,000 in fines on CBS for the violation. The FCC then turned its attention to radio broadcasts: a number of network programs, including several by nationally prominent radio star Howard Stern, were noted for their apparent obscenity and fined.[48] (The FCC fine on CBS was overturned in court in 2011.[49])

The various economic, social, political, and technological forces that have shaped the development of the television industry have combined to both concentrate television-making power in the hands of a few megacorporations and to position American products as dominant in the world market. The television industry combined the business model of radio with the talents of Hollywood's filmmakers to establish its central position in global television. Thus, American television programs dominate the global market. For example, less than ten years after the fall of the Soviet Union, 75 cents of every dollar spent internationally on purchasing television programming went to U.S. companies. The bulk of these 75 cents went to the motion picture and television production studios that dominate the production of television programming. In fact, these studios generated at least 25 percent of their revenues from international programming.[50]

Much of this imported programming has been feature films intended for broadcast on television. One study of European television, for example, showed that 80 percent of program imports were feature films; of these, 53 percent were American. The percentage of American movies shown on European television screens grew from 46 percent to 53 percent between 1988 and 1991. In Norway, 100 percent of films showed on the commercial television station TV Norge during the same three years were American; Sweden's TV3 broadcast American movies 81 percent of the time in the same period. Commercial television stations in France and Italy likewise broadcast American movies at least 73 percent of the time in the same period. Meanwhile, the percentage of domestic movies shown on these same stations in that period declined approximately 10 percent.[51]

Television series have been another area in which American programs have been successfully marketed globally. In Europe, only the United Kingdom produces a majority of its own programming; in general, 83 percent of television series shown in Europe are from elsewhere—particularly the United States and Australia. From 1988 to 1991, American programming was popular even in non-English-speaking European countries. Commercial television stations in West Germany showed imported television series 99 percent of the time during this period, for example. Between 1988 and 1991, imports of American television series grew from 36 percent to 56 percent of total programming across Europe as a whole, while domestically produced European series declined from 37 percent to 16 percent.[52] Similarly, in the mid-1980s, the global TV satellite service Sky Channel filled two-thirds of its broadcast time with American situation comedies and rebroadcasts of American movies. In 1987, Lorimar Studios licensed the nighttime soap opera *Knots Landing* for broadcast in France for $50,000 an episode.[53]

Another way to assess the dominance of American programming on global television screens is to focus on fiction programming in Europe. In 1996, for example, the five major European markets broadcast 50,000 hours of fiction. Of these, only 8.42 percent of programming was produced in Europe, with Germany producing the most fiction. (As noted above, the United Kingdom produces the majority of its own programming, taking into account all genres, including sports and documentaries, but it produced less fiction than Germany did in 1996.) Much of the gap between the 50,000 hours of fiction broadcast in these five major markets and the 4,210 hours produced in Europe was filled by American programming like scripted television shows and rebroadcasts of Hollywood movies.

One particularly popular American television genre that, as one commentator explains, has been "seen across the globe wherever a TV set is to be found," is the soap opera. With their high production values, pleasant visual settings (often involving people and places of great wealth and privilege), fast pace, use of conventional narratives already well established in the audience's minds through Hollywood movies (good versus evil, etc.), and melodramatic style, soap operas are popular around the world. Nighttime American soaps like *Dallas* and *Beverly Hills 90210* have been extremely popular worldwide. American daytime soaps, too, have found a global audience. One commentator notes that in September 1996 he was able to watch *Days of Our Lives*, *The Bold and the Beautiful*, *The Young and the Restless*, and *Santa Barbara* (as well as *Beverly Hills 90210*) while visiting South Africa.[54] The more recent drama/melodrama *The West Wing* has likewise found a substantial international audience, and as was discussed in chapter 1, *House* is now the most popular program in the world. Four American television shows—*The Simpsons* (season 1), *Sex and the City* (complete season 1), the HBO series *Band of Brothers*, and *Seinfeld* (seasons 1 and 2) also make Amazon.com's top twenty-five in DVD sales.[55]

As was the case with movies and music, American television programming drew on the core economic conditions of the United States, its vast and diverse audience, and its comparative political freedom to develop products that could be marketed successfully around the world. It drew on the skills and talents already present in Hollywood to offer both rebroadcasts of American movies and newly produced filmed entertainments to a global audience. It thus became another piece of the U.S. global empire of AV popular culture.

## THE DIGITAL DILEMMA

Notably, the two decades since the fall of the Soviet Union in 1991 have brought new opportunities for American AV cultural products to spread worldwide. The collapse of the regimes of Eastern Europe removed the last effective barriers to the spread of American popular culture into those once-Communist nations. (The world's other great Communist nation, China, survives, of course, and sponsors a number of restrictions on the infusion of American popular culture in contemporary China, as is discussed in chapter 5.) The end of the Cold War once and for all broke the Soviet Union's ability to control or significantly shape the cultural messages its citizens could experience. American popular culture products rushed to fill the void.

Moreover, advances in digital technology made the production and dissemination of movies, television, and especially music remarkably easy over these same twenty years. Movie theaters are resource-intensive, requiring trained staffs to operate and needing formal buildings with appropriate equipment to be useful as cinemas. Television and radio stations are likewise expensive to buy and maintain, and in any case only make economic sense to buy if enough people in your local community have enough money to buy TV and radio sets and are connected to an electricity source they can either coopt for their own or afford to pay for—conditions that are not met in large parts of the world. The advent of cell phone service and wireless broadcasting has largely obvi-ated these expensive opportunity costs, however. It is simply no longer necessary to have enough money to buy and operate a television or radio set (or both) in order to access American programming. Now all you need is a cell phone and Internet access of some form or another. In other words, the spread of American cultural products is no longer subject to the market whims of centralized, prominent actors like state television companies (the BBC, for example). Instead, access to Ameri-can products is, in many countries, no more than a browser click or an app download away from the user's fingertips. At least for those people living in reasonably open societies with Internet access, American mov-ies, music, and television are never more than a click away.

Netflix stands as a useful example of the shift in film and televi-sion distribution. What started as a mail order service in which people listed films and television programs they wished to watch and then received them by mail, only receiving whatever program was next in their queue when they returned the product they were using, changed into an on-demand download service that had thousands of movies and television programs in its databases. Users paid Netflix a flat fee that then covered a mix of hard copy DVDs and access to the digital data-base for streaming downloads directly to consumers' homes. By May 2011, Netflix was responsible for 30 percent of prime time web traffic, as users chose to download their nightly entertainment—both movies and television programs—directly from Netflix's servers rather than wait for it to be delivered as a DVD.[56] Netflix suffered a setback when, in September 2011, it announced plans to split its download and DVD-by-mail services, charging separate fees for each mode of distribution. It was forced to withdraw the proposal three weeks later.[57] The company has subsequently moved aggressively to allow subscribers to download content digitally, offering an unlimited digital download plan for $7.99 a month. It still offers subscribers the alternative of queuing DVDs for mail distribution as well.[58]

Whatever Netflix's business mistakes, the fact remains that it of-fers a fundamental challenge to the business model on which the film and television industries developed. Movies historically generated revenues by selling tickets to enter the theater and watch a film; televi-sion programs made money by delivering an audience to an advertiser. Now, even people legally watching a movie or television show through

Netflix's service need do neither to enjoy the program. (Users of Bit-Torrent and similar programs are typically downloading a television program or movie outside the licensing agreements Netflix has with producers of films and television shows, and so provide no revenue at all to the maker of the programming.) Thus, while television manufacturers have responded to the internetization of entertainment by adding Internet access to their sets to accommodate web-based viewing, it is not clear that the industry has really figured out how to generate sustainable revenues in the digital era. Moreover, as Internet download speeds increase, online film and television piracy may well increase to the levels common in the music industry.

Looked at across the board of AV popular culture, it is clear that digital technology has worked to undermine the means by which American AV pop culture producers make profits on the products they make. This has been particularly true in the music industry. The problem, at least from the point of view of those seeking to make money from the global distribution of films, music, or television is that once these products are digitized, as they have to be to record DVDs or MP3s, they can be transmitted in any digital media. For example, all a DVD really is, in the end, is a tool to carry around encoded digital information conveniently and comparatively safely. If someone can copy or rip the contents of a DVD or otherwise gain access to a digital copy of a movie, it is relatively easy to commit what the industry calls piracy: storing the entertainment in a computer and then distributing it across an increasingly fast Internet to an increasingly connected world. The major short-term limitation on film downloads has been the size of movie files and the speed of users' Internet connections; however, as Internet download speeds increase, this technological limit will likely be less and less restrictive. Crucially, at least from movie producers' points of view, once the film is available on the Internet, the producer's ability to control who sees the movie by forcing the audience to buy a ticket or buy a copy of a DVD is pretty much lost. DVDs might be shared among friends today, of course, and illegal theaters might show a DVD to a large paying audience, but the fact that one person or group has to be in physical possession of the DVD in order to show the film puts a practical limit on how many people can see a film without paying for the privilege. Such limitations are meaningless on the Internet. One copy of a movie can be downloaded and perhaps viewed by millions of people all at the same time, and all for free. The Internet has therefore posed a major challenge to filmmakers as they try to make money in the movie business.

This financial problem has grown exponentially with the seemingly endless number and variety of devices on which filmed or recorded content can be viewed. While it is at least possible to find out about and raid the site of an illegal theater showing bootleg copies of a major motion picture, the development of laptop computers with wireless connections and the spread of devices like the iPod and smartphones have put digital content into the hands of hundreds of millions, if not billions, of people. Whereas only about 700 million people had cell phones in 2000, by 2009 that number had grown to at least 3.6 billion. India added 15.6 million cell phones in March 2009 alone; estimates are that at least 6 billion people will have cell phones by 2013.[59] Admittedly, not all of these devices are smartphones capable of viewing digital material, and the experience of watching a movie on an iPod or iPad screen might not equal that of viewing it in a theater, but the iPod and similar devices travel with the user, are discreet, and can be only expected to grow in use globally. (Apple's iPhone 4, for example, sold 1.7 million units in the first weekend after it was released, and sold more than 3 million units in its first month on the market.[60]) Such ubiquity makes enforcement of copyright and other laws restricting the right to view digital content essentially impossible to enforce.

The challenge to the profitability of American movies, music, and television offered by the digitization of AV pop culture hit the recorded music industry first and hardest, because music files are relatively small and thus easy to download across the Internet. Where once consumers went to a record store and purchased a 78, a 45, a cassette tape, or a CD, much music is captured online today. There were more than one billion legal music downloads in 2008, an increase of 27 percent from 2007.[61] New businesses like Apple's iTunes emerged as popular places for customers to purchase music legally, even as numerous sites where users can pirate music for free continue to operate. In any case, the traditional means by which music companies made money, selling music to consumers, is under severe challenge in this electronic age.

MP3s and other digital recordings are easy to export around the globe, whether they are downloaded into private digital music players or into another person's computer. This has made them particularly vulnerable to piracy. Music sharing sites like Napster and Kazaa offered large numbers of people the opportunity to download music from the Internet for free and to upload their music for others to take. The Recording Industry Association of America estimates that some 30 billion songs were illegally downloaded between 2004 and 2009 alone; legal music purchases have declined 47 percent since 1999—the year Napster was created—from $14.6 billion to $7.7 billion. It further reports that only 37 percent of music acquired in the United States was paid for, while consumers illegally download between $7 billion and $20 billion worth of music annually.[62] The best-selling album of 2008, rapper Lil Wayne's *Tha Carter III*, sold only 2.87 million albums, making it the first album in the media-reporting firm SoundScan's seventeen-year history to be the highest-selling U.S. album of the year with fewer than 3 million album sales. In 2008, 361 million CDs were sold in the United States, a decline of 20 percent from 2007.[63] Total revenue generated from music sales in the United States declined from $14.6 billion in 1999 to just $6.3 billion in 2009.[64]

The digital era has had similar effects on the film industry. Among other things, it has led to the dramatic reduction in movie sales. DVD sales were down 9 percent in the third quarter of 2008 compared with the third quarter of 2007, for example. In a survey of likely purchases, people in the key advertiser demographic of 25–34 years old indicated that the first expense they would cut back on in an economic downturn was movie tickets; the last thing they would cut was their broadband Internet connection. And while the experience of watching a film on an iPod might not come close to watching a movie in the theater or even on a high-quality television, Apple's iTunes download site sold $1 million worth of downloads of the big action-adventure hit movie *Iron Man* in the first week it became available online.[65] Notably, e-books are now pirated as well.[66]

Pressures such as these led content makers in the film, music, and television industries to promote two pieces of legislation in the U.S. Congress in the fall of 2011. SOPA—the Stop Online Piracy Act—was introduced in the House of Representatives, while a similar bill, the Protect Intellectual Property Act (PIPA), was offered in the Senate. These bills were ostensibly aimed at cutting off third-party sites that hosted illegally downloaded content or served as link points for accessing illegal downloads. Under the proposed legislation, U.S. authorities would be empowered to shut down any web service that provided access to illegal downloads of copyrighted music, movies, or television programs. Persons running such websites would be subject to arrest, fines, and as many as five years in prison for their role in hosting and disseminating pirated content.

While the benefits of these proposed laws to major film, television, and music producers should be obvious—entertainment companies would find an ally in the U.S. government in their war to stop illegal downloads of their products—the legislation faced substantial opposition from what might be termed the "e-world." Companies like Google and Yahoo worried that they and their officers would be held liable if a user posted illegally downloaded content to servers the Internet giants operated. They feared that if you or I found a copy of the newest episode of a favorite television program online on a BitTorrent site and then reposted it on YouTube, Google employees might go to jail and Google the company might face enormous fines—all for actions that Google itself did not undertake. They and many other Internet companies and activists supported an online petition campaign to stop SOPA and PIPA in their tracks.

Ultimately, SOPA and PIPA were put on the shelf in the aftermath of the Internet campaign against them, and after President Obama indicated he would veto SOPA if it were to come to his desk. The issues of piracy and control of downloaded content that drove the creation of SOPA and PIPA have not gone away, however. As a practical matter, the AV industries are likely on the cusp of another significant change driven by the nature of their economics. Smaller producers, whether in the United States or elsewhere, will likely have a harder time surviving the loss of ticket and DVD sales. This is true, ironically, at the exact same time that the spread of laptops, smartphones, and other handheld electronic devices makes it easier for more people worldwide to view the movies made by the American pop culture machine.

In the end, even as MP3s, digital technology, music-sharing websites, and services like Netflix have hurt corporate profits, they have enhanced the spread of American popular culture worldwide. Untold billions of downloads have occurred both legally and illegally in the decade since music sharing became common. While access to the Internet varies widely across the globe, almost anyone who can access it can download American AV popular culture—bringing American products, values, attitudes, behavioral norms, and culture along with films, television programs, and music. And while there is little doubt that the particular companies involved in the production and distribution of global AV entertainment will change as some negotiate the challenges of the Internet era while others fail, American producers, as a result of their size and the global transparency of the products they create, are uniquely poised to exploit the global commercial opportunities of the new period.

## CONCLUSION

As a consequence of the business, technological, and social factors noted throughout this chapter, the production of mass popular culture has always been centered in the United States, even as Americans have reached out to the rest of the world for ideas, money, and markets. In addition, much, if not most, of the music, films, and television programming generated by the major popular culture corporations carries an American label regardless of the nation of origin of the company that owns it. American movies, music, and television programming have, as a consequence, become the dominant forms of AV entertainment worldwide.

## NOTES

1. CJR, "Who Owns What: Sony Corporation," http://www.cjr.org/resources/?c-sony (accessed 1 December 2011).

2. CJR, "Who Owns What: Time Warner Company," http://www.cjr.org/resources/?c-timewarner (accessed 3 December 2011).

3. CJR, "Who Owns What: The Walt Disney Company," http://www.cjr.org/resources/?c-disney (accessed 3 December 2011).

4. Matthew Garrahan and Courtney Weaver, "Disney Expands Free TV Channel to Russia," http://www.ft.com/intl/cms/s/0/95a09354-00a4-11e1-930b-00144feabdc0.html#axzz1fXbiNSBr (accessed 3 December 2011).

5. CJR, "Who Owns What: Viacom, Inc.," http://www.cjr.org/resources/?c-viacom (accessed 4 December 2011).

6. Matt Russell, "A Short History of *Star Trek*," http://www.trekdoc.com/database/fanfeed/43.htm (accessed 1 March 2012).

7. CJR, "Who Owns What: CBS," http://www.cjr.org/resources/?c-cbs (accessed 4 December 2011).

8. CJR, "Who Owns What: News Corporation," http://www.cjr.org/resources/?c-newscorp (accessed 4 December 2011).

9. CJR, "Who Owns What: Vivendi S.A.," http://www.cjr.org/resources/?c-vivendi (accessed 4 May 2012).

10. CJR, "Who Owns What: General Electric," http://www.cjr.org/resources/?c-ge (accessed 4 December 2011).

11. Paul Starr, *The Creation of the Media: Political Origins of Modern Communications* (New York: Basic Books, 2004), 23–46.

12. Starr, *Creation*, 47–86.

13. Starr, *Creation*, 267–402; see also Robert C. Toll, *The Entertainment Machine: American Show Business in the Twentieth Century* (New York: Oxford University Press, 1982).

14. Scott R. Olson, "Hollywood Planet: Global Media and the Competitive Advantage of Narrative Transparency," in *The Television Studies Reader,* ed. Robert C. Allen and Annette Hill (New York: Routledge, 2004), 111–29.

15. Toll, *Entertainment Machine*, 19–30; see also Starr, *Creation*, 295–326.

16. Richard Maltby, *Hollywood Cinema* (Malden, Mass.: Blackwell, 2003), 126.

17. Maltby, *Hollywood Cinema*, 29–30.

18. Maltby, *Hollywood Cinema*, 128–76.

19. All these quotes are from Stanley J. Baran and Dennis K. Davis, *Mass Communication Theory: Foundations, Ferment, and Future* (Belmont, Calif.: Wadsworth, 1995), 42.

20. Maltby, *Hollywood Cinema*, 60–63, 593–97; Starr, *Creation*, 318; Richard Maltby, *Harmless Entertainment: Hollywood and the Ideology of Consensus* (Metuchen, N.J.: Scarecrow Press, 1983), 97–102; Robert Sklar, *Film: An International History of the Medium* (New York: Abrams, 1993), 96–125.

21. Maltby, *Hollywood Cinema*, 177–79.

22. "Yearly Box Office Index," http://boxofficemojo.com/intl/yearly/?page=country&p=.htm (accessed 9 November 2011).

23. Benjamin R. Barber, *Jihad vs. McWorld: How Globalism and Tribalism Are Reshaping the World* (New York: Ballantine Books, 1996), 92–93.

24. "Bigger Abroad," *The Economist*, 17 February 2011, http://www.economist.com/node/18178291 (accessed 16 September 2011).

25. Lauren A. E. Schuker, "Plot Change: Foreign Forces Transform Hollywood Films," *Wall Street Journal*, 2 August 2010.

26. Chris Boylan, "Amazon.com Announces Top-Selling DVDs of All Time," http://www.bigpicturebigsound.com/article_535.shtml (accessed 21 November 2011).

27. Toll, *Entertainment Machine*, 46–47.

28. Toll, *Entertainment Machine*, 48.

29. Toll, *Entertainment Machine*, 48–59.

30. Starr, *Creation*, 381.

31. Toll, *Entertainment Machine*, 70–74.

32. Starr, *Creation*, 368.

33. Darrick Lee, "Parental Advisory Warning Labels Steeped in Controversy," *Hush Your Mouth!*, Spring/Summer 2003, http://www.hushyourmouth.com/parental--advisory--labels.htm (accessed 1 March 2012).

34. Recording Industry Association of America, "Top 100 Albums," http://www.riaa.com/goldandplatinum.php?content_selector=top-100-albums (accessed 23 November 2011).

35. EveryHit.com, "Record Breakers and Trivia: Albums," http://www.everyhit.co.uk/recordalb.html (accessed 23 November 2011).

36. Recording Industry Association of America, "Top Selling Artists," http://www.riaa.com/goldandplatinum.php?content_selector=top-selling-artists (accessed 23 November 2011).

37. Corinna Sturmer, "MTV's Europe: An Imaginary Continent," in *Channels of Resistance: Global Television and Local Empowerment*, ed. Tony Dowmunt (London: BFI Publishing, 1993), 51–52.

38. Barber, *Jihad vs. McWorld*, 105–7.

39. Viacom, "Our Brands: Global Reach," http://www.viacom.com/ourbrands/globalreach/Pages/default.aspx (accessed 23 November 2011).

40. Jack Banks, "MTV and the Globalization of Popular Culture," *International Communication Gazette* 59, no. 1 (1997): 43–60.

41. Toll, *Entertainment Machine*, 60–61.

42. Toll, *Entertainment Machine*, 61–65.

43. Toll, *Entertainment Machine*, 66.

44. Toll, *Entertainment Machine*, 66–67.

45. http://www.everyday.com.kh/dir/tvguide/asp/tv_search.asp?page=2&s_keyword=&s_channel=&s_day=27&s_month=11&s_time= (accessed 26 November 2011).

46. Sky TV, "TV Guide and TV Listings," http://tv.sky.com/tvlistings (accessed 9 January 2009).

47. Both quotes are from Baran and Davis, *Mass Communication Theory*, 42–43.

48. Corey Deitz, "FCC Fines Howard Stern, Two or More Clear Channels Stations, Revises Bono Ruling," About.com: Radio, 19 March 2004, http://radio.about.com/cs/latestradionews/a/aa031904a.htm (accessed 1 March 2012).

49. "Court Tosses Out CBS's Superbowl Indecency Fine," http://www.pbs.org/newshour/updates/media/july-dec08/fcc_07-21.html (accessed 26 November 2011).

50. Kerry Seagrave, *American Television Abroad: Hollywood's Attempt to Dominate World Television* (Jefferson, N.C.: McFarland, 1998), 1.

51. Julian Petley and Gabriella Romano, "After the Deluge: Public Service Television in Western Europe," in *Channels of Resistance: Global Television and Local Empowerment*, ed. Tony Dowmunt (London: BFI Publishing, 1993), 31.

52. Petley and Romano, "After the Deluge," 31–32.

53. Colin Hoskins and Stuart McFayden, "The U.S. Competitive Advantage in the Global Television Market: Is It Sustainable in the New Broadcasting Environment?," http://www.cjc-online.ca/index.php/journal/article/viewArticle/602/508 (accessed 23 November 2011).

54. Petley and Romano, "After the Deluge," 50–95.

55. Chris Boylan, "Amazon.com Announces Top-Selling DVDs of All Time," http://www.bigpicturebigsound.com/article_535.shtml (accessed 21 November 2011).

56. Cecilia Kang, "Netflix Biggest Driver of U.S. Internet Traffic, Puts Spotlight on Broadband Pricing," http://www.washingtonpost.com/blogs/post tech/post/netflix-biggest-driver-of-us-internet-traffic-puts-spotlight-on-broad band-pricing/2011/05/16/AFg3yg5G_blog.html (accessed 1 December 2011).

57. Tom Loftus, "Netflix: Qwikster Is No More," http://blogs.wsj.com/digits/2011/10/10/netflix-qwikster-is-no-more/ (accessed 1 December 2011).

58. Netflix, "How It Works," https://signup.netflix.com/HowItWorks (accessed 4 May 2012).

59. "Mobile Marvels," *The Economist*, 24 September 2011, http://www.economist.com/node/14483896 (accessed 5 December 2011).

60. Chris Ziegler, "iPhone 4 Sales: 3 Million and Counting, 1.7 Percent Returned," http://www.engadget.com/2010/07/16/iphone-4-sales-3-million-and-counting/ (accessed 5 December 2011).

61. Ben Sisario, "Music Sales Fell in 2008, but Climbed on the Web," *New York Times*, 1 January 2009, http://www.nytimes.com/2009/01/01/arts/music/01indu.html (accessed 1 March 2012).

62. http://www.riaa.com/faq.php (accessed 5 December 2011).

63. Sisario, "Music Sales."

64. David Goldman, "Music's Lost Decade: Sales Cut in Half," http://money.cnn.com/2010/02/02/news/companies/napster_music_industry/ (accessed 1 December 2011).

65. Brooks Barnes, "For a Thrifty Audience, Buying DVDs Is So 2004," *New York Times*, 23 November 2008, http://www.nytimes.com/2008/11/23/business/23steal.html (accessed 1 March 2012).

66. Eduardo Porter, "The Perpetual War: Pirates and Creators," *New York Times*, 4 February 2011, http://www.nytimes.com/2012/02/05/opinion/sunday/perpetual-war-digital-pirates-and-creators.html?_r=1 (accessed 9 February 2012).

# CHAPTER 4

## THE AMERICAN GLOBAL CULTURAL BRAND

While American movies, music, and television programs are important parts of the U.S. global pop culture, they are not the whole of it. The values, ideals, mores, attitudes, behaviors, norms, and rituals that embody life in the United States can be found embedded in a host of other artifacts. Consumer goods and other values combine with the products of the audiovisual pop culture industry to create a seemingly seamless, integrated American popular culture that can be found almost everywhere in the world.

This chapter examines some of the other features of globalized American pop culture. Whether the product in question is a car, a restaurant, clothing, or a sport, American brands, styles, and even identities have had a profound impact on markets, values, and attitudes across the planet. Moreover, the relatively new phenomenon of social networking adds layers of complexity and subtlety to both the marketing and the branding of pop culture artifacts. Understanding the impact of American popular culture on the process of globalization necessarily entails exploring at least some of the other ways American pop culture crosses national and cultural boundaries. This chapter offers a partial look at this multifaceted phenomenon.

## FRANCHISING AMERICA

One factor crucial to the global expansion of American popular culture across the globe has been a commercial concept known as the franchise. A franchise is a contractual relationship between a company that controls a brand label for a good or service and private individuals and companies that buy the right to use the brand's name and products but otherwise operate the business on their own. Such arrangements have proved to be useful, flexible means for corporations to spread their brands at minimal risk to their bottom lines. After all, when a company owns a store—which does happen, even in some franchised businesses—the company assumes the risks associated with purchasing or leasing business space, hiring staff, marketing and building a market, and other matters. If a company-owned store fails, it costs the company a substantial amount of money. By contrast, in a franchise arrangement, the franchisee accepts most of this risk. As a consequence, franchisers can offer franchise opportunities in places and markets that might be too uncertain for the company to invest in otherwise. The franchise brand can therefore spread more quickly and into otherwise unreachable markets more easily than could an unfranchised company.

Franchises have a number of advantages that have encouraged their use. Some of these are practical and some are matters of loyalty and brand identity. From a franchisee's point of view, for example, buying a franchise can significantly reduce the cost and complexity of starting a business. One does not need to establish contracts with local vendors to provide things like hamburger to a restaurant; instead, the franchiser has preexisting networks of vendors the new franchisee can tap into to get the goods needed to run the business. In addition, franchisers usually have management-training programs so that new franchisees can learn how to recruit and manage their employees. The franchiser is also likely to have a complex set of rules and regulations defining workers' rights and responsibilities—a fact that means that franchisees do not have to develop rules and policies on their own. Even rules governing the layout of floor space simplify the task of opening and managing a new business. By buying a franchise, the new owner gives up some freedom to run things as he or she might wish but also simplifies running the business by relying on the skills and expertise of the franchiser.

Another major benefit of the franchise derives from the concept of economies of scale. Franchisers typically buy large volumes of goods and services from vendors. They are able to negotiate price reductions from these vendors that smaller purchasers (who are often local, individually owned businesses) are not able to negotiate: vendors accept lower prices for bulk sales in order to get the contract for the major sale. Franchisers pass these cost reductions on to their franchisees, meaning that the franchisee can often provide a good or a service to the customer at a lower price than an independent business can. If necessary, then, franchisees can beat independent businesses on price, enhancing their market competitiveness.

Franchises also provide regularity and predictability to both franchisees and consumers. Colas from the same franchise taste pretty much the same wherever they are concocted, just as the hamburgers taste the same, just as the coffee tastes the same. Consumers can be pretty sure that they will get a predictable and safe product from any of a chain's stores, just as franchise owners can be pretty sure that competing franchises will not be opened in the area—at least not competing franchises from the same company. This uniformity may strike some people as unfortunate, since it often entails the destruction of local businesses unable to compete with the franchise's economies of scale, but given a choice, consumers seem to flock to franchise businesses instead of local ones. Predictability and regularity are powerful market forces.

Perhaps the biggest benefit to buying a franchise is not managerial at all. Instead, it is perceptual. Franchisers invest substantial amounts of money establishing their brand identities. The most important part of the process of building brand identity is advertising. Franchisers spend a great deal of money advertising their product's label to a broad audience. This advertising both builds brand awareness and creates a public image for the franchiser's goods and services. For example, Ford, the automobile manufacturer, once offered a campaign centered on the notion that "quality is job one," suggesting that if consumers wanted safe and reliable cars they should buy Fords. Starbucks' advertising suggests it is not just a coffee shop but a destination for those who have discriminating taste and demand superior coffee. McDonald's offers decent food served quickly in a way that is supposed to mimic the feeling of home. And Coca-Cola ties itself to wholesome imagery, once promising that it would "like to buy the world a Coke, and keep it company."

This brand identity-making is not an accident. Franchisers establish brand identities to create and maintain markets for their products. One goes to Starbucks not simply because of the coffee; one goes to Starbucks to be seen as someone who goes to Starbucks. Starbucks-goers form a subculture with their own rituals and norms—in this case organized around elaborate processes for ordering cups of coffee. Nike buyers "just do it." Mountain Dew drinkers "do the Dew." "Nothing," the model-turned-actress Brooke Shields once declared, "comes between me and my Calvins" (a brand of blue jeans).

Franchisers augment this subcultural identity-making by physically labeling their customers and turning consumers into walking (and driving) advertisements for their products. Coffee cups can be emblazoned with the brand label, as can shopping bags. Automobiles and many brands of clothing come with labels that advertise the product's maker—and label the driver/wearer/user as someone who uses that company's goods and services. Some consumers respond to this labeling and identification by buying gift items emblazoned with the product's labels. Brand identity is a central feature of creating and maintaining markets for a franchiser's products.

Buying a franchise therefore means buying a brand identity and its associated market. Franchisees are largely freed of the need to convince consumers to come to their store. Instead, franchisees merely have to inform consumers about the location of their stores in order to give customers who appreciate the brand's identity the chance to shop for that store's products—and to be seen to shop for those goods and services.

Through franchising, consumers across the world have become aware of the brand identities of American clothing, restaurants, vehicles, sports, and innumerable other things. Brand identity can combine with price advantages to make American goods popular with foreign consumers, and of course American tourists appreciate the predictability of franchise brands. People across the globe seem willing to pay to associate themselves with American brands of clothing and food and other products. America has become, at least in part, a global franchise.

## A BRIEF HISTORY OF THE FRANCHISE

Franchising began in Europe. It began as a way to link taverns to specific types of beer: at franchised pubs, only beer of a particular brand would be sold. However, franchising never became as important in Europe as it did in the United States. Whether for reasons of an entrepreneur-friendly culture or the vast geographic size of the United States, franchising began in America in the 1800s and quickly expanded. It took off after World War II when the automobile came to dominate American life.[1]

The earliest American franchises were in manufactured goods. As early as the 1850s, suppliers like Isaac Singer and the makers of the McCormick Harvesting Machine offered sewing machines and tractors to franchisees, who sold these products out of their stores. The franchiser, then, did not own the store in which the franchiser's goods were sold. Instead, the franchiser sold the goods to the franchisee. The franchisee then made a profit (or tried to) by marking up the price of the item, offering service, and perhaps earning incentive payments from the franchiser if the company sold a large number of units.

While Singer's first attempts at a franchise ultimately failed, the Singer model was adopted by the automobile industry as it grew. The first automobile franchise was granted in 1898, just a decade or so after the first recognizably modern car had been invented. Auto franchises allowed dealers to establish businesses at which to sell and service vehicles purchased from the manufacturer at a discount. This arrangement remains the way most cars are sold today.

The franchising concept branched out into food and services starting in the 1880s. The first truly successful franchise of a food product was Coca-Cola, the invention of an Atlanta, Georgia, druggist named John S. Pemberton. Pemberton, who sold the formula for his concoction before his death in 1888, mixed kola root, caffeine, and coca extract into a sweet, soothing formula. The person who bought the secret formula (which remains secret to this day), Asa Candler, created a franchising deal in which the Coca-Cola Company sold premixed syrup base to franchisees. (Coca was eventually removed as an ingredient of the formula.) The franchisees then added water, bottled the soda, and marketed it in their areas of operation. In time, as is discussed later in this chapter, Coca-Cola, aka Coke, would be bottled and drunk around the world—always with the same base syrup shipped from the Coca-Cola Company.

Restaurants were added to the list of goods and services that were franchised early in the twentieth century. After Roy Allen bought the formula for a new drink called root beer from an Arizona druggist in 1919, he and his partner, Frank Wright, founded the A&W restaurant franchise in 1922. A few years later Harland Sanders invented a flavor packet that he added to the fried chicken he had learned to cook quickly at the restaurant he ran at his gas station and motel complex in Corbin, Kentucky. He began selling the flavor packets and licensing his quick-cook technology to other entrepreneurs in 1930. While that business ultimately failed, his model became the foundation for the Kentucky Fried Chicken (KFC) restaurant chain. In the same period, Howard Johnson, a pharmacist from Quincy, Massachusetts, began to sell ice cream and a small selection of other items in his store; he franchised the concept in 1935. In time both the menu and the ice cream choices expanded, and distinctive, orange-roofed Howard Johnson's restaurants spread across the United States.

The emergence of the automobile as the major mode of American transportation after World War II provided the opportunity for massive expansions in franchising across the United States. Americans began traveling on wide, well-built highways in comfortable cars. They also moved to suburbs with their attendant large yards and commuter lifestyles. Travelers sought reliable, consistent places in which to eat and spend the night; car owners desired the security of knowing they could get their cars serviced at reliable, reputable chains across the United States; and consumers with money to spend pursued whatever fashion, music, or fad was hot at the moment. (One of Harland "Colonel" Sanders's innovations was to put a facsimile of one of the rooms of his motel inside his restaurant so that potential guests could see the quality of his rooms. Women wishing to use the restroom in his restaurant had to actually enter the display room in order to reach their destination.) Franchised restaurants, hotels, automobile service chains, and clothing stores rushed in to fill this market. Chains like McDonald's, Kentucky Fried Chicken, Holiday Inn, and Western Auto grew dramatically.

Table 4.1 summarizes the franchises that have at least one thousand locations outside the United States. Fast-food restaurants are disproportionately represented, although service industries like real estate sales, tax preparation, and janitorial services also make the list. The chain of 7-Eleven convenience stores is by far and away the largest international chain; however, McDonald's remains the sales champion among global franchises. Subway, notably, now has more restaurants than McDonald's overall, but McDonald's has more than a $60 billion advantage in global sales. In any case, it is clear that the American way of eating is spreading around the world in ever-expanding networks of franchises.

Fast food, services, and convenience stores are of course not the only global franchises for American products, goods, and services. Ford and

**Table 4.1. Top Global Franchises**

| Rank | Franchise | U.S. locations | International locations | Total locations | Global sales (M $) |
|------|-----------|----------------|-------------------------|-----------------|--------------------|
| 1 | McDonald's | 14,027 | 18,710 | 32,737 | 77,380 |
| 2 | 7-Eleven | 6,137 | 33,345 | 39,482 | 63,000 |
| 3 | KFC | 5,055 | 11,798 | 16,583 | 19,400 |
| 4 | Subway | 23,850 | 10,109 | 33,959 | 15,200 |
| 5 | Burger King | 7,523 | 4,998 | 12,251 | 14,800 |
| 7 | Circle K | 3,367 | 4,056 | 7,423 | 12,500 |
| 8 | Pizza Hut | 7,542 | 5,890 | 13,432 | 10,200 |
| 11 | Hertz | 4,942 | 3,576 | 8,518 | 7,600 |
| 15 | RE/MAX | 3,411 | 2,873 | 6,284 | 6,625* |
| 16 | Domino's Pizza | 4,929 | 4,422 | 9,351 | 6,268* |
| 17 | Dunkin' Donuts | 6,772 | 2,988 | 9,760 | 6,004 |
| 18 | Tim Hortons | 602 | 3,424 | 4,026 | 5,625 |
| 27 | H&R Block | 11,506 | 1,643 | 13,149 | 3,874* |
| 31 | ampm (BP) | 1,225 | 1,592 | 2,817 | 3,415 |
| 38 | Dairy Queen | 4,514 | 1,384 | 5,898 | 2,750 |
| 49 | GNC | 3,651 | 1,606 | 5,257 | 2,050* |
| 56 | Century 21 | 3,000 | 5,000 | 8,000 | 1,800* |
| 58 | ServiceMaster | 3,021 | 1,804 | 4,825 | 1,791* |
| 61 | Snap-on Tools | 3,464 | 1,350 | 4,814 | 1,666 |
| 62 | Baskin-Robbins | 2,547 | 3,886 | 6,433 | 1,653 |
| 81 | Curves | 4,956 | 3,076 | 8,032 | 1,000 |
| 110 | Jani-King | 9,245 | 2,209 | 11,454 | 647* |
| 111 | ERA Real Estate | 695 | 1,852 | 2,547 | 641* |

* Revenues estimated.

Source: 2011 Franchise Times, "Top 200 Franchise Systems," http://www.franchisetimes.com/content/page.php?page=00141(accessed 26 January 2012)

General Motors sell millions of cars globally, for example. (Chrysler, the third major American car manufacturer, has recently been taken over by Italian manufacturer Fiat.) Even in what have been relatively hard times in the American automobile industry, Ford sold more than two million vehicles outside North America in 2010.[2] General Motors, long the world's largest car company until the recent global slowdown in auto sales, controls the Cadillac, Chevrolet, Buick, Opel, Vauxhall, and Holden brands. It sold more than five million automobiles in areas outside North America in 2010. This included 1.3 million vehicles in Europe, and some 800,000 in Africa, Latin America, and the Middle East. It sold almost 3.4 million vehicles in Asia, including 2.26 million in China alone.[3] Buick is particularly popular in China.

Other aspects of American cultural life have also expanded across the world in recent years. The megaretailer Walmart has a global presence now, and it influences both how products are created and how they are sold to people around the world. For example, Walmart has 352 stores in China, and its focus on the quality of its products is pressuring Chinese producers and vendors to increase the quality of the goods and services they provide to Chinese consumers.[4] The National Football League (NFL) now plays a regular season game in London every year. The National Basketball Association (NBA) is aggressively seeking to expand in global markets; players like the now-retired Chinese-born Yao Ming provided the league with entrée into that vast nation.

Not all American goods and services are marketed globally by franchises, of course. Some companies own the stores in which they sell their products globally, and other distinctively American items like blue jeans have developed a global presence separate from the original manufacturers' control. Starbucks, for example, does not offer a traditional franchise to its operators. Instead, it owns most of its stores, but it licenses some independent businesspersons to run particular stores on its behalf. Such arrangements have made it possible, as of October 2011, for Starbucks to operate 17,003 stores in fifty-eight countries worldwide.[5]

Whether franchised or not, brands like McDonald's, Coca-Cola, Starbucks, and 7-Eleven carry an American identity and an American set of cultural values and practices to the larger world. They are as embedded in American culture as movies, music, and television programming are. They offer entangling threads in which American pop culture spins into global prominence.

## AMERICAN BRANDS, GLOBAL PRESENCE

This section of chapter 4 explores the ways in which specific American brands, franchises, and cultural forms have been integrated into global life. In particular, it offers brief histories of Coca-Cola, McDonald's, blue jeans, and the NFL as case studies of the many ways American pop culture has gone worldwide. These companies and products offer insight into brands that have been long established as global forces (Coke, McDonald's, blue jeans) and those that are seeking to expand their worldwide influence (the NFL). Their international prominence offers evidence of the power of American popular culture on a global scale.

Note that the fact that this section focuses on these companies and products should not lead anyone to the conclusion that they stand as *the* examples of American pop culture corporate globalization. The discussion offered here of how these companies and products have grown to global prominence is intended to explore the ways in which American pop culture has gone global. It is not an exhaustive list of those corporations that have spread across the planet. Indeed, both Coca-Cola and McDonald's are but branches of a complex tree of fast-food and beverage companies with a global scope, and American sports like baseball have had a global following for a century or more. The analyses offered here are presented as a way to explore the ways American brands became global. While each is presented individually, they and the other forces of American pop culture globalization have a collective impact on the people who use American products and integrate them into their lives.

### A BRIEF GLOBAL CULTURAL HISTORY OF COCA-COLA

The Coca-Cola label has been called the most profitable brand in world history. Interbrand, an international consulting firm, lists the international trademarks that are understood to have generated the highest economic returns for their owners. Only those that generate more than one-third of their sales outside the United States are considered. For

2010, Interbrand estimated the Coke brand to be worth $70 billion, far outpacing the next biggest soda giant, Pepsi, at $14 billion. Coca-Cola exceeded the brand value of the second-place company, IBM, by $5.5 billion.[6] It is a global powerhouse.

This is quite a change for a company that started as a store-mixed, coca-extract-laced drink developed to supplement sales at an Atlanta, Georgia, pharmacy. John S. Pemberton, an Atlanta pharmacist, developed the drink in May 1886 and sold it from a local pharmacy. Pemberton sold the rights to his drink to several people before his death in 1888; by 1891 Asa Candler bought back all the rights Pemberton had sold. This cost Candler $2,300. Candler and his brother John joined with several other local businessmen to incorporate the Coca-Cola Company in 1892. The company's distinctive, script-based logo was registered as an official trademark in 1893.[7] It has gone on to the status of global icon.

Coca-Cola is a mix of a secret syrup, sugar, and carbonated water. The key to its success is its syrup, which has been manufactured on a large scale since 1894. In the company's early years, the syrup was shipped to pharmacies and other stores. These stores used so-called "soda jerks"—so named because they pulled the large handles that controlled the flow of the syrup and water like draft beer is dispensed in bars today—to mix the sodas on the spot. In 1894, a Vicksburg, Mississippi, businessman named Joseph Biedenharn decided that he would bottle Coca-Cola so that his customers could store the concoction at home or work rather than needing to come to the store for a soda. Bottled Coca-Cola has been available ever since.

Nationwide franchising began in 1899. A group of Chattanooga, Tennessee, businessmen secured the rights to bottle Coca-Cola across the United States that year. However, they quickly discovered that they could not raise enough capital to build bottling plants around the United States to serve the national demand for the product. They identified bottling partners across the country and created zones of operation guaranteeing each control of a specific territory. Over a thousand bottling plants were established across the United States in the next twenty years.

Coca-Cola's growth was international in these years, although not to the degree it would later enjoy. Asa Candler's oldest son took a batch of syrup with him on a trip to England in 1900, for example, and the company received an order for five gallons of the concoction from the UK later that year. The company had more success in Latin America and American territories in the Far East. Bottling plants opened in Cuba, Panama, Puerto Rico, the Philippines, and Guam in the early years of the twentieth century. Plants also opened in Canada and France by 1920. In 1926, Coca-Cola established an international marketing unit, and in 1928, the company shipped one thousand cases of the soda to the Olympic Games in Amsterdam. This began a long association between the company and the world's premiere sporting event. The soda was bottled in forty-four countries by the late 1930s. That number would double through the 1960s.

In a striking example of the cultural relevance and significance Coca-Cola had achieved by the middle of the twentieth century, Coca-Cola became part of the U.S. war effort during World War II. While in North Africa in 1943, for example, General Dwight Eisenhower's headquarters sent a message to the company asking it to ship enough material to build ten bottling plants. It also requested that three million bottles of the soda be shipped to the front immediately, along with supplies needed to fill a quota of six million bottles a month.

The Coca-Cola Company also made a commitment to provide five-cent bottles of Coke to all servicemen regardless of what it cost the company to produce the drink. In all, Coca-Cola shipped materials for sixty-four bottling plants around the world, including to far-flung outposts like New Guinea. Military personnel drank some five billion bottles of soda during the war—a number that does not include soda and automatic fountain dispensaries. By the end of the war, a generation of Americans, and for that matter a generation of people touched by American military operations around the world, had been introduced or otherwise exposed to Coca-Cola.

While Coca-Cola was the dominant soda brand in the United States in the postwar period, competition from its main rival, Pepsi, induced the company to make what, in retrospect, was one of the biggest marketing and branding mistakes of all time. Concerned that Pepsi's sweeter formula was stealing market share from its products, Coca-Cola executives initiated plans to replace traditional Coca-Cola with a new formula labeled, simply enough, New Coke. The new formula had won numerous blind taste tests against both the old formula of Coca-Cola and Pepsi as well, and in 1985, company leaders decided that it was time to launch a new chapter in the product's history. "Old" Coke ceased production and New Coke was presented as "the" Coca-Cola.

To say the new product flopped would be kind. Executives received hate mail about the new flavor even as consumer lobbying groups formed to boycott the new drink and demand the return of "real" Coke—all in days before the Internet made such communications comparatively easy. Company claims that sales were good and the new formula was popular were met with howls of derision. National news broadcasts covered the marketing disaster. When news leaked that the original Coca-Cola was to return to store shelves in July 1985, barely three months after New Coke was presented to the world as "Coke," then–U.S. senator David Pryor (D-Arkansas) announced on the floor of the Senate that the news "was a meaningful moment in American history."[8] "Old" Coke, renamed "Classic," was marketed alongside New Coke until New Coke was pulled from the market entirely. (It should be noted that by the end of 1985, Coca-Cola's market share had grown dramatically, leading some to conclude that the introduction of New Coke was a cunning advertising strategy. The company has always denied this.) In January 2009, the company announced that Coca-Cola Classic would drop the "Classic" from its name. (Notably, the word "Classic" on the label had been reduced in size several times in the twenty years between New Coke's rise and the decision to remove "Classic" from the soda's package.) Coke would be just Coke again.

At the heart of this disaster was the failure to appreciate the iconic position Coca-Cola had come to hold in American society. Coca-Cola had worked hard to make itself a brand affiliated with the notion of America itself. Changes to the brand meant change to the emotional connection many consumers felt toward not just the soda but also the idea of the soda's existence as a cultural touchstone. To drink Coke was to be an American, and if Coke could change then so could America—and not in a good way. Changing to New Coke was a betrayal of the brand identity that Coca-Cola had worked hard to create.

Notably, Coca-Cola faced a similar, if less intense, controversy during Christmas season 2011. The company decided to change the color of its cans from red to white during the Christmas holidays to honor polar bears and to raise awareness of the loss of Arctic habitat for the bears and other regional wildlife. The campaign caused confusion among some drinkers who thought they were buying Diet Coke, which is sold in silver cans, and got "real" Coke instead. But others were outraged that Coke had abandoned its iconic red color. Coca-Cola, it seems, had to be offered for sale only in red to be "real" Coca-Cola.

Notably, the popular sense that Coca-Cola had an iconic, cultural identity that ought not be violated by silly issues like marketing and flavor was in many ways itself a result of Coke's efforts to turn itself into a quintessentially American product. From its early decision to use the script-lettered Coca-Cola label (drawn by John S. Pemberton's partner and bookkeeper, Frank Robinson), the company showed remarkable creativity and success in branding its product. In 1916, for example, the company created the iconic Coke contour bottle as a tool to ensure consumers were getting—and choosing—Coca-Cola instead of a competitor's products. (This shape was granted a trademark by the U.S. Patent Office in 1977.) In 1929, the company introduced a distinctive fountain glass to be used in pharmacies, restaurants, and other venues that served Coke products; this glass is still used in many restaurants and can be purchased for home use as well. In 1933, the company introduced the automatic fountain dispenser at the Chicago World's Fair. This device allowed consumers to pour their own sodas as the water and syrup were mixed in the dispenser rather than by a soda jerk. It made it possible for millions more drinks to be dispensed than ever could be before.

Coke also invented Santa Claus. Or, put another way, it was Coca-Cola's marketers who helped establish the now-classic vision of Kris Kringle as a jolly fat man with a white beard dressed in red from top to bottom. Coca-Cola co-opted Santa's image in an effort to get people to drink soda in the winter, and in the process created the modern image of Santa Claus. Prior to 1931, when a series of magazine ads for Coca-Cola featuring Santa Claus first hit American magazines, Father Christmas had been portrayed in an array of ways. In some cases he was seen as an elf; in others as a tall, thin, somewhat austere man. (This image remains popular in some parts of the world.) At times he wore a clerical robe, and at other times he was dressed in the furs of a Norse hunter. When cartoonist Thomas Nast drew Santa in the U.S. Civil War era, the character's clothes were tan, although in time Nast changed them to red.

Consumers became so obsessed with the images Coke produced that they actually scanned each year's drawings for changes. One year, when Santa appeared without a wedding ring, people wrote in wondering about Mrs. Claus. Another year readers asked why Santa's belt was on backwards. An icon was thus made, courtesy of Coca-Cola.

What was true for Santa Claus was true for a stunning array of consumer collectibles as well. It is possible to collect a vast amount of Coca-Cola labeled products, ranging from trays and bottles and bottle caps to advertising, games, smoking paraphernalia, and company gifts.[9] If it has a logo on it, it is a potential collectible; if it is older and genuine, it is likely to have substantial economic value. But of course economic value is not the only reason people collect: surrounding oneself in Coca-Cola labeled products links one to the brand and the values it expresses. Many people collect Coca-Cola for its distinctive colors and logos rather than its potential sales value. It is a subculture.

It is also a global symbol. At least two international movies have put Coca-Cola paraphernalia at the center of their films. The 1980 cult hit *The Gods Must Be Crazy* makes the brand's distinctive glass bottle the point of dramatic tension around which the movie hinges, for example. When a Coke bottle falls from a passing airplane into the hands of a tribe of hunter-gatherers in the Kalahari desert in southern Africa, the tribe's people find it useful for grinding food and other matters until, in a fit of jealousy, one tribesperson hits another over the head with the bottle. One member, Xi, decides that the gods were crazy to give them the bottle and goes on a quest to return it to its rightful owners. Along the way, viewers get a travelogue of life in the modern world as seen through the eyes of one tribesman—and his Coke bottle.

Another film, *The Cup*, a cult hit from 1999, is less focused on Coke, but uses one of its iconic symbols, its distinctively colored aluminum can, as an evocative introduction to the film. The movie is set in a Buddhist monastery in India filled with young monks obsessed by the World Cup soccer tournament. It chronicles their efforts to rent a satellite dish and television so they can watch the competition despite the supposed asceticism of life in a monastery. The film opens with a scene of young monks using a Coke can as a soccer ball in their courtyard. An older monk interrupts to take the can to his master; we see that the master has used many such cans to create oil lamps in his study. Coke is quite literally everywhere—and quite literally recognizable around the world.

Along with its iconography, Coca-Cola has become a force of economic globalization. At one level, this is the result of the substantial economic impact Coca-Cola has around the world. The opening of bottling plants brings an array of other jobs and services to the communities that house them. Coca-Cola bottling facilities rely on local water and local sweeteners to mix with the base syrup, meaning that local bottlers have to establish relationships with local providers for these services. Bottles, whether plastic or glass or aluminum, have to be produced locally, delivered to the plant and used to store the soda. Trucking firms have to hire drivers to deliver the product to the many venues in which it is sold. Then, in a process known as the multiplier effect, the employees of the trucking company and the water provider and the sweetener company and the employees of the bottling plant and the places that sell Coke all have money to spend on new goods and services. People with money in their pocket tend to go to restaurants and movies and buy cars and better televisions—or televisions in the first place. In turn, this financial boon causes other businesses to hire workers as restaurant servers and car sales staff and television repair people. Bringing a large business like a Coca-Cola bottling facility to a new area is expected to promote economic growth broadly throughout the community.

Yet Coke is not always perceived as a good force in global affairs. In part this is because the reality of local economic development is never as clearly beneficial as the process described above. Corrupt officials and their cronies do better than they ought to from the deals the company strikes in the local area, and many people do not see the economic benefit that is expected under the logic of the multiplier effect. There are also concerns that as local suppliers of water, sweeteners, and bottles and distribution networks expand to meet the company's demands, they replace rain forests and other natural areas with sugar fields and build roads across previously undisturbed countryside, displacing endangered animals and plants in the process. The diversion of large amounts of water from their natural sources to satisfy the demand for soda can likewise harm the local environment.

Many people also wonder if addicting the planet to sweetened, caffeinated beverages in a world of limited resources and growing obesity is really a very good idea from a public health perspective. Indeed, since sodas are American beverages, the criticism arises that American soda manufacturers are contributing to making the world obese, all while destroying the local culture, flavors, and styles of consumption innate to other cultures. For some, then, Coke is a symbol of cultural degradation rather than a tool of global economic development.

One other critique has been aimed at Coke: its alleged role in repressing global labor movements, particularly in Colombia. Organizers of the "Killer Coke" campaign argue that Coca-Cola officials have been complicit in or have actually caused the murders and/or kidnappings of numerous labor organizers at Coke bottling plants in Colombia.[10] Coca-Cola, then, is seen to be a central player in the efforts of global megacorporations to dominate the worldwide labor market by keeping costs low and profits high. The company of course denies these claims.

Regardless of one's position on the economic or moral significance of the Coca-Cola Company, it is clear nonetheless that it is an iconic representative of American pop culture across the globe. Its products, its logos, its values, and its brand identity have found a worldwide market and a worldwide audience. It is hard to imagine going pretty much anywhere on the planet that is inhabited by people who have ever had contact with groups from the outside world without expecting to be able to buy a Coke or a similar product when visiting. Indeed, it seems probable that one could visit a tribe or group that has pretty much been left alone by the outside world and find, quite by chance, someone wearing a Coca-Cola T-shirt or, à la *The Gods Must Be Crazy*, using a Coke bottle as a tool. It is a global symbol of American popular culture.

## A Brief Global Cultural History of McDonald's

McDonald's is, like Coca-Cola, a global powerhouse. It is, first of all, ubiquitous. There are McDonald's restaurants all over the world. They serve as a haven for American tourists, of course—many a weary traveler has eaten at a McDonald's elsewhere, even if they rarely eat at McDonald's at home. But McDonald's attracts customers all over the world. When McDonald's opened stores in Moscow and Beijing, the lines of local people waiting for service stretched for blocks. Its 32,737 stores seem to be quite literally everywhere.

In addition, McDonald's stands as a powerful symbol of American cultural globalization. Its symbolic golden arches logo is as distinctive as the American flag. Its restaurants grew in concert with the American love of the automobile, a fact reflected in the presence of drive-through lanes at many of its stores. What could be more American than to not have to get out of one's car even to eat? McDonald's is thus both an indicator of globalization and evidence of the American cultural way of life.

The success of McDonald's was grounded on a simple idea: providing desirable food and drink at low cost, fast. This was by no means a new idea: Ray Kroc, the creator of McDonald's as a nationwide chain, discovered the technique when he visited a group of restaurants in Los Angeles, California, to which he had sold a large number of Mixmaster automatic milkshake machines. Kroc was the national salesman for these machines, which could make five milkshakes at the same time. He could not understand why some of the Los Angeles restaurants needed as many as eight of these machines in a single store. On visiting this mini-chain, called McDonald's, Kroc was impressed with the production-line nature of the store's operations—and also with the line of customers who waited outside the restaurants' doors from the moment they opened until the moment they closed. The stores sold hamburgers for 15 cents; cheese was 4 cents extra. In 1954, at the age of 52, Kroc bought into the McDonald's partnership and in 1955 began franchising its stores nationwide. The first modern McDonald's opened in Des Plaines, Illinois, on April 15, 1955. It stands as a museum today.[11]

Not only was the idea not new to Ray Kroc, it wasn't new in the United States. Chains like Burger King, Carl's Jr., In-N-Out Burger, Krystal, Steak 'n Shake, White Castle, and Burger Chef all sold hamburgers before Kroc franchised his first McDonald's.[12] There were, moreover, competitive chains selling chicken, sandwiches, and ice cream across America in those years, along with an array of more formal, sit-down, full-service restaurants catering to the ever wealthier and ever more mobile American market. However, through a combination of factors like picking good sites for stores, systematizing operations across all restaurants, and effective marketing, McDonald's caught on with American consumers quite quickly. By 1958, there were 34 McDonald's restaurants in the United States; 67 more opened the next year, for a total of 101. Sales escalated accordingly: in 1963, the company sold its one-billionth hamburger, and in 1968 it opened its one-thousandth store. In 1972 the company had $1 billion in sales, and by 1976 the company passed $3 billion in sales—and twenty billion in total hamburger sales.

McDonald's updated its product offerings regularly in order to attract repeat business and entice new customers into its restaurants. It added the Filet-O-Fish sandwich to its national line in 1965 after a Cincinnati, Ohio, franchisee noted that he was losing a great deal of business on Fridays, when Catholics were supposed to avoid eating meat. Kroc initially rejected the idea of a fish sandwich for the restaurant, but he was persuaded when the local owner developed a sandwich on his own and proved that it sold well. Local pressures likewise inspired the Big Mac: a Pittsburgh, Pennsylvania, storeowner discovered that local steel mill workers weren't satisfied with the size of a single burger. The Big Mac was added to the McDonald's menu in 1968. McDonald's developed the Egg McMuffin breakfast sandwich in 1973 and expanded to offer a full breakfast menu in 1977. By 1987, 25 percent of all breakfasts eaten outside the home in the United States were eaten at McDonald's. In time, products like the Happy Meal for children, Chicken McNuggets, and salads were added to the franchise's lineup. While not all of these product innovations succeeded—the McLean burger, with less fat, was a notable failure—they continued to draw consumers to the restaurants.

McDonald's greatest product accomplishment may well have been the french fry. The original McDonald's restaurants in Los Angeles made fresh fries daily. They were a big hit. However, when Kroc tried to duplicate this item in the franchise, the results were failures: potato storage took a large amount of floor space in each facility, and potatoes had to be dried under a fan to become starchy enough to withstand washing and frying. A McDonald's potato supplier, Jack Simplot, invented a technique to cut, freeze, and prepare fries at his facilities. These could be shipped directly to the restaurants, where they could then be fried. This process saved space in the stores—and guaranteed product uniformity throughout the McDonald's chain.

Other innovations made McDonald's a destination restaurant with strong brand identity. The chain moved from its "Speedee man" mascot to a circus clown–like character, Ronald McDonald, in 1963. Ronald McDonald would become the instantly recognizable face of the franchise and would also become the character and face of Ronald McDonald House Charities, which provides places for the parents and loved ones of children with cancer to stay during their children's treatment. Eating at McDonald's could thereafter be justified as an act of charity, not just self-indulgence.

McDonald's offered other innovations to attract customers. In 1971, it opened its first McDonald's Playland, a play area for children common in many roadside McDonald's restaurants. It became heavily involved in movie cross promotions, regularly providing figurines based on popular films as part of Happy Meals and thereby drawing in more children and their families. And while the company did not invent the idea of a drive-through lane for its restaurants, it added them in 1975. The drive-through would eventually account for more than half of all McDonald's sales across the franchise.

At least one other aspect of McDonald's success deserves attention: its linkage of architecture and advertising. McDonald's integrated its distinctive golden arches logo into the actual architecture of its early restaurants. In time, the arches were moved from the building to the restaurant's sign, with the arches linked together to form an instantly recognizable "M" at the beginning of McDonald's. Intrade now ranks the McDonald's brand as the sixth most valuable in the world, worth $33.6 billion in 2010.[13]

After first establishing restaurants across the United States and Canada, McDonald's went global in the 1970s. Starting in Costa Rica, the company opened stores in Germany, Holland, Australia, and Japan in the early years of the decade. The five-thousandth store the chain opened was in Japan, in 1978.

While expansion continued throughout the 1980s, it was the fall of the Berlin Wall and the end of the Cold War that really made McDonald's a ubiquitous global presence. It operated in fifty-eight foreign countries with more than 3,600 restaurants in the early 1990s; it only opened its ten-thousandth store in April 1988, thirty-three years after it was first franchised. Since then, its growth has been explosive. It only took the company eight more years, until 1996, to add another ten thousand stores to its portfolio, for a total of twenty thousand in 1996. By the end of 1997, the chain was opening two thousand new restaurants a year. That works out to an equivalent of one every five hours.

International growth drove much of this increase. The chain added over 7,400 new stores overseas in the years 1991–1998. It had franchises in 114 countries in that time. It entered the Middle East (Israel) in 1993; it entered India in 1996. It developed the McSki-thru in Lind-vallen, Sweden, that same year. When a McDonald's opened in Kuwait City, Kuwait, in 1994, the line at the drive-through was seven miles long. This growth led to a shift in the sources of McDonald's revenues: in 1992, the company generated 60 percent of its sales in the United States, but by 1997 that percentage had fallen to 42.5.

The opening of two stores, one in the heart of the former Soviet Union in Moscow, and the other in Beijing, China, near Tiananmen Square, stand as particularly striking examples of the global growth of McDonald's. The openings of these two stores were highly symbolic acts that seemed to confirm political theorist Francis Fukuyama's claim that the fall of the Soviet Union meant the "end of history," the end of great global ideological struggles. American-style liberal capitalist democracy had won.[14] Indeed, the Moscow McDonald's, opened in 1990, quickly became the city's biggest attraction, serving 27,000 customers a day.[15] Some of them waited for hours to be served. The situation in Beijing was if anything more dramatic: opened on August 23, 1992, the Beijing McDonald's served 40,000 people its first day. [16] (In July 2011 the company was opening a restaurant in China every other day, and expected to open one per day for the next three to four years.[17])

One reason McDonald's has been so successful is its adaptability. Company stores and franchisees have been careful to shape their products in ways that meet the needs and expectations of the local communities they serve. It has had its restaurants inspected as kosher for Jewish customers and as halal, the equivalent standard for Muslims. It has changed the composition of its fry oil, which once was based on beef fat, to accommodate the religious requirements of India's Hindu population. (Problems achieving this standard will be addressed below.) The company also adapts its menus to meet the expectations of its local consumers. It is possible to buy beer in McDonald's restaurants in Germany, for example.

The adaptability of McDonald's is reflected in a series of studies compiled by James Watson in his book *Golden Arches East: McDonald's in East Asia*. The restaurant offers espresso and cold pasta in Italy; chilled yogurt drinks in Turkey; teriyaki hamburgers in Japan, Taiwan, and Hong Kong; a grilled salmon sandwich called the McLak in Norway; and McSpaghetti in the Philippines. It offers the McHuevo in

Uruguay. Waiters in Rio de Janeiro serve Big Macs with champagne at candlelit restaurants. McDonald's restaurants in Caracas, Venezuela, have had hostesses seat customers, place orders, and bring customers their meals. It has thus integrated itself as a provider of local cuisines around the world.[18]

McDonald's has also shaped Asian cultures in several ways. Some of these ways are quite predictable, while others are less so. For example, the restaurants are common hangouts for young people, serving as a place where teenagers can escape the relative strictures of life at home. The restaurants have at times been turned into leisure centers and after-school meeting places. Unsurprisingly, french fries have become a staple part of younger people's diets across Asia—fries are in fact the most globally consumed item in the McDonald's line.[19]

But such fairly predictable changes do not fully describe the many ways in which the chain's restaurants have influenced Asian culture. Many Asian women apparently find McDonald's a safe place to relax and avoid aggressive, often sexual, harassment. Additionally, McDonald's has made birthday parties a central feature of life in parts of East Asia: in Hong Kong, for example, it was historically the practice to record dates of birth only for use later in life, like checking horoscopes of prospective marriage partners, but to make little of annual birthdays. McDonald's made birthday parties a central part of its marketing, thereby placing a premium on families knowing and celebrating—and being seen to celebrate—their children's birthdays. On another front, it was once very rare for people to eat with their hands in Japan. The spread of McDonald's and other fast-food restaurants has made this both more common and more acceptable.[20]

McDonald's has also shaped consumer culture. Even something as seemingly common as standing in a line to wait one's turn to order from a preset and limited menu is in fact a cultural adaptation. As McDonald's restaurants opened, their employees and advertising had to teach potential customers how to behave. For example, employees at the Moscow McDonald's moved up and down the line explaining that at McDonald's smiles were an expected part of the service and should not be confused with threats or a form of mockery, which were what smiles were previously seen to indicate in Russia. Even cleanliness standards changed under pressure from McDonald's: the restaurant has strict standards for hygiene in its kitchens and its restrooms, and competitors were forced to change their practices as consumers grew accustomed to the McDonald's way of doing business.[21]

As was true of Coca-Cola, the global scope and significance of McDonald's has led to serious criticisms of the company as a global entity. International concerns about increasing global obesity have focused on the chain's offerings; American documentarian Morgan Spurlock filmed *Supersize Me*, named after the restaurant's "supersized" drink and fries offerings, to chronicle his experiences eating only McDonald's for thirty consecutive days. His doctor forced him to quit before the thirty days were up because of the severe impact that its high-fat, high-calorie offerings were having on his health. (McDonald's subsequently eliminated its supersize menu.) Eric Schlosser offered a broader indictment of fast-food restaurants and the lifestyles that developed to accommodate them in his 2001 book, *Fast Food Nation: The Dark Side of the American Meal*.[22]

Lifestyle changes like those seen across East Asia provoke further worries on the part of many commentators and analysts. McDonald's has changed various consumer cultures, eating styles, and social relationships. As was discussed in chapter 1, such changes inevitably engender substantial resistance, fear, uncertainty, and even anger. People worry that local cultural products will be replaced by those offered by the global corporation, even as they see local business practices and relationships changed to meet the needs of the global, transnational company. They also worry about the fact that their children spend their time in new places, making new contacts, and perhaps most worryingly adopting new styles and cultural behaviors—like eating lots of french fries or learning English from a McDonald's menu board. Such changes can—or can be seen to—cause a wide range of cultural changes that work as a subtle form of cultural imperialism. Local cultures might be displaced in favor of a global, consumerist, effectively American one.

McDonald's has also not always lived up to its dietary commitments. On entering the Indian market, for example, the chain promised that no beef fat would be used in the oil in which its fries were cooked. This promise was made to meet the dietary restrictions of Hindus, for whom cows are sacred and beef is forbidden. However, McDonald's continued to add a small amount of beef fat to its fry oil mixture in order to assure the desired taste for the fries. The company was forced to change its oil formula when this practice was discovered and it lost a lawsuit. The incident left many people with concerns about whether the restaurant would live up to its other dietary promises.

Like Coca-Cola, McDonald's has also faced an array of criticisms from environmentalists. McDonald's is a hamburger restaurant, after all, meaning that its growth necessitates an increase in the amount of beef available to feed its customers. This is quite separate from the chain's reliance on vast amounts of chicken, potatoes, and other crops it needs to produce its food. Beef production is particularly troubling to many environmentalists because it takes a large amount of grain to feed cows to the point they gain enough weight to take to slaughter. Growing large amounts of grain, in turn, requires both that new land be brought into production and that large amounts of chemicals be used to fertilize crops and protect them from infestation and disease. Rain forests and other delicate ecosystems have been destroyed to serve the planet's growing demand for beef, sparking concerns that humans are both driving some species to extinction and promoting global warming to satisfy their fast-food desires. McDonald's is not the only source of this pressure, of course, but it is the largest and most globally recognizable symbol of the global love affair with beef. It therefore takes a leading role in debates about human-caused environmental degradation and species extinction worldwide. Its demand for cheap chicken causes similar questions to be raised in terms of the mass-production chicken farms needed to satisfy its requirements.

In just fifty-four years, McDonald's has gone from a small number of restaurants offering quick meals at low prices to the symbol of global fast food. (As an aside, the restaurant only sells Coca-Cola soft drinks at its stores, further linking these two brands as planetary forces.) Today it has stores in 119 countries across six continents. It has annual revenues over $24 billion.[23] It is a global symbol of America and a major force in contemporary globalization.

## A BRIEF GLOBAL CULTURAL HISTORY OF BLUE JEANS

It is not strictly correct to say that Levi Strauss, a German-born entrepreneur who moved to San Francisco during the Gold Rush that hit California after gold was discovered there in 1848, invented blue jeans. A thick, heavy cotton called denim preexisted Strauss's use of it, as did the color, a type of blue named after the Italian city of Genoa, which was later translated as "jeans." Indeed, Strauss went to California with the intent of selling tents and other supplies to the miners. When that plan failed, Strauss discovered that the miners complained that their cotton clothes wouldn't stand up to the rigors of mining. He went into business with Jacob Davis, a local tailor who hit upon the idea of adding copper rivets to the pockets and other weak points of the denim pants he made. Thus Levi's blue jeans were born.[24]

Blue jeans quickly became a standard item for American workers. Cowboys wore them as they rode. Farmers wore them as they planted and reaped. Workmen relied on their sturdiness as they laid pipes, built roads, and worked in factories. Manufacturers produced women's sizes in World War II to accommodate the many women who moved into the war production work force. Jeans were reliable. They also signaled the wearer's status as working class.

Notably, the nascent film industry helped bring jeans into global consciousness. Cowboys were seen to wear jeans in generations of early movie westerns. This established blue jeans as quintessentially American clothing. Whether good guys or bad guys, cowboys were American, and so were jeans.

Blue jeans began to move out of the world of work in the 1950s. Blue jeans were adopted by beatnik poets and cultural nonconformists as expressions of their rejection of mainstream culture, which they thought was symbolized by the grey flannel suit that characterized the "organization man" who went to work in a big, anonymous office building to sell insurance or do some other apparently boring and conformist job. Beats and "bad boys," symbolized by actors like James Dean and Marlon Brando and movies like *Rebel without a Cause* and *The Wild Bunch*, expressed their refusal to conform to dominant norms and values by wearing tight jeans rolled up at the ankles, often matched with black leather jackets and white T-shirts with cigarette packs rolled up in the sleeves. Likewise, Elvis Presley challenged the sexual mores of the times as he wore denim pants while performing hits like "Jailhouse Rock." Jeans were a way for wearers to publicly declare their unwillingness to comply with the values of McCarthyite, Cold War America.

Like most cultures facing challenge, 1950s America fought back against the threat it perceived was posed by the growing number of apparent deviants across society wearing blue jeans. Dress codes were instituted and aggressively enforced in schools; not only were jeans banned, but women were often denied the right to wear pants at all. Police treated bands of jeans-wearing youths as likely criminals and sought to break up any group as quickly as possible. Mainstream movies and television shows reinforced traditional morality by showing teenagers in conformist clothing behaving as their parents wanted them to. Wearing jeans was a political act with political consequences.

The 1960s shattered whatever efforts mainstream America had undertaken to limit the cultural spread of blue jeans. The social and political protestors of the decade wore blue jeans to signal their rejection of conventional American values. In part, this was a result of the attempts to control jeans wearing in the 1950s; wearing blue jeans after society tried to stamp them out was a clear declaration of resistance. Moreover, the fact that the pants were made out of denim cotton provided another statement of difference. Fashion in the 1950s had emphasized artificial fabrics like easy-to-clean polyester. Cotton was natural—the antithesis of the corporate-dominated, anti-nature ethos of the organization man. Jeans became as much a symbol of the counterculture and student activist movements of the period as did long hair, drug use, the sexual revolution, and what is today referred to as "classic" rock.

In addition, styles of jeans proliferated, as bell-bottoms and other loose-fitting types offered young radicals a fashion-based way to reject the uptight, constrained values of their parents' generation—values that were mirrored in tight-fitting and aggressively structured clothes, even jeans, of the previous decade. Wearers decorated their jeans with beads, peace symbols, antiwar messages, marijuana leaves, and a seemingly endless number of symbols of their political, social, moral, and cultural sensibilities.

By the end of the decade, jeans were ubiquitous in the United States—especially among students. A decade that had begun with students wearing coats and ties, or at least khakis and button-down shirts, to their college classes ended with students in blue jeans, even if they did not intend to make a political statement. As a consequence, U.S. jeans sales doubled nationally in the three years from 1962 to 1965. They quintupled again from 1965 to 1970.[25]

The 1970s saw jeans embedded across American pop culture. The upscale department store chain Neiman Marcus gave Levi Strauss & Co. its Distinguished Service in Fashion Award in 1973. The American Fashion Critics gave the company a special award for making "a fundamental American fashion that . . . now influences the world." The now-defunct American Motors Corporation, maker of the Gremlin and Hornet car lines, contracted with Levi Strauss to provide blue denim fabric for the interiors of its two automobiles. Denim was believed to signal both patriotism (an ironic reversal of the values of the 1960s counterculture activists) and optimism to consumers. These decisions were confirmed by 1977, when over 500 million pairs of jeans were sold in the United States alone. This was more than double the U.S. population.[26]

The 1970s also saw the emergence of upscale, expensive designer jeans. Fashion powerhouses like Calvin Klein, Givenchy, and Oscar de la Renta produced expensive jeans as fashion statements. Calvin Klein sold 125,000 pairs of these costly pants every week in 1979.[27] Jeans had evolved from workman's staple to fashion essential.

Along the way, blue jeans became a global standard of fashion. Several different measures of their global popularity can be offered, but a particularly striking one derives from a study of consumer awareness of American brands in the Soviet Union. A 1989 survey of college students at Kharkov State University in Ukraine found that English-speaking students knew of a wide range of American brand names, including blue-jean companies. The students also recognized American automobile, cigarette, and soft drink brands.[28] (Jeans were heavily traded on the black market in the Soviet Union in this period.)

Other measures of the global success of blue jeans can be offered as well. One study found that in 2011 the average consumer worldwide owned seven pairs of jeans.[29] The average man owned six pairs, while the average woman owned seven.[30] Seventy-five percent of consumers reported that they "loved" or "enjoyed" wearing denim; 75 percent of women and 72 percent of men reported preferring to wear denim jeans to other casual pants.[31]

One of the more striking features of this global growth is that jeans sales are less dependent on franchised networks of suppliers than is the case with restaurants or soft drinks. While major producers like Levi Strauss, Wrangler, and Guess exist, blue jeans have been adapted and produced across the globe. In some cases, this production is explicit piracy, meaning that established brand labels are simply sewed directly on to pants made in factories and workshops not affiliated with the companies in any way. In many cases, however, the making of blue jeans is simply another domestic industry. It is possible to buy locally produced blue jeans in many places around the world; as one example, I found numerous denim shops in the Grand Bazaar in the heart of Istanbul, Turkey. Jeans are a transparent product, in Olson's phrase[32]: they emerged from the American cultural milieu but offered images of comfort, freedom, and even nonconformist rebellion that resonated with customers worldwide. As a consequence, it is possible to see people wearing jeans virtually anywhere on the planet regardless of, or perhaps in addition to, whatever the native standards of clothing might be.

As with Coca-Cola and McDonald's, any product that has global impact also generates social and economic concerns. The same is true for blue jeans, although in the absence of a leading, central, corporate face on which to focus concerns, the issues raised in regards to blue jeans and the blue-jean industry are more diffuse and indirect than were those aimed at Coke and McDonald's.

One set of complaints is aimed at the creeping casualism embedded in the very notion of wearing blue jeans. Fears that jeans cause cultural change have been common in both industrial democracies and emerging societies around the world. Numerous commentators have opined that blue jeans represent a threat to proper dress codes in the office, in schools, and even in ordinary public life. Blue jeans are seen to tempt people away from proper conduct precisely because they are comfortable and convenient: their casual use is believed to promote lack of care in relation to one's job, one's studies, and one's interaction with other human beings. Such concerns are particularly noteworthy in "new" areas of jeans' global expansion. Whether the style is infiltrating the boardroom or rural Asia, concerns are raised that the norms, values, ideals, and rituals associated with normal life in these cultural enclaves are likely to be changed under the casualism that emerges when blue jeans are common.

Another focus of concern in the globalization of blue jeans has been the politics of cotton. Cotton is a globally traded product that has the potential to be a major export in many developing countries. It is also, of course, the source of denim, the foundation material for blue jeans. Building on the notion of comparative advantage discussed in chapter 1, many countries around the world have excellent growing conditions for cotton. They also have low labor costs, meaning that cotton can be grown there relatively inexpensively. According to the theory of comparative advantage, these countries ought to dominate the global trade in cotton. These nations could then use any profits generated from growing cotton to support their national development, and consumers around the planet could enjoy high-quality cotton products at low prices. The United States, however, has a well-developed cotton industry that is not globally competitive under current trade conditions, but has substantial influence in Congress and the rest of the U.S. political system. U.S. cotton farmers have used their political clout to gain national subsidies for their products, in effect using U.S. taxpayer dollars to subsidize the real price of U.S. cotton on global markets. American taxpayers pay some of their taxes to U.S. cotton producers so that these producers can sell cotton for the same price as international producers can.

This practice violates the theory of free trade in several ways. For example, it raises the actual cost of cotton goods for American consumers, since they are actually paying taxes to buy jeans at the same cost that they could buy jeans made with cotton produced by international farmers without any tax subsidy. It also means that international producers do not have the opportunity to invest their profits into local economies, thereby stimulating local demand for goods and services—including goods and services of U.S. companies and brands.

Regardless of the policy recommendations embedded in the theory of free trade and comparative advantage, U.S. cotton farmers use their political power to maintain the tax subsidies their products receive. This in turn causes significant challenges for advocates of free trade, especially when new international trade agreements are negotiated. Recent trade negotiations have been complicated by the desires of many countries to protect their politically powerful yet uncompetitive industries; one particularly contentious set of issues has been the international trade in cotton. The popularity of blue jeans is by no means the whole cause of growth in cotton farming globally, but it is a central market for the cotton industry. Blue jeans are, as a consequence, indirectly at the center of global trade fights today.

There have been environmental complaints about blue jeans as well. Cotton fields might occupy lands that could be used for growing food. Alternatively, cotton fields might replace vital habitats for native species. Concerns have also arisen about the dyes used to make jeans blue or other colors, or the techniques like acid washing used to weather jeans into fashionable looks. Chemicals can leach into—or be dumped into—local water supplies. Workers exposed to toxic fumes have experienced serious health consequences. And of course, the simple act of transporting cotton and cotton goods to markets around the world entails burning fossil fuels in trucks, trains, and ships. Global trade may well encourage global warming.

At least one other concern about the blue-jean industry deserves attention: how they are made. Most blue jeans are made in factories in the developing world, many of which are what is typically described as "sweatshops." This complaint is by no means unique to the blue-jean industry: most apparel is made in factories in places without the same standards for worker health, safety, comfort, and decent treatment that are common, if not universal, in countries across North America, Europe, and Japan. The low wages paid in many such factories stand in stark contrast to the hundreds of dollars some customers pay for so-called designer jeans (or shoes, or jackets, or other apparel items). One of the consequences of low-priced clothing is exploitative labor standards in the parts of the world that actually make the jeans worn by people elsewhere.

As was the case with the analysis of the global/cultural position of Coca-Cola and McDonald's offered earlier, whether one thinks that blue jeans are wonderful or that blue jeans are a profound symbol of globalization gone wrong, it is clear that what started as a technical solution to the problem miners had getting clothing strong enough to stand up to the demands they placed on it has become a central force in economic and cultural globalization. Blue jeans are an American phenomenon that has become a global one—and also a local one at the same time. They express rebellion, Western individualism, and personal freedom even as they are marketed by global megacorporations to an increasingly interconnected world. This convergence of economics and culture is a central feature of globalization today.

## THE EMERGING GLOBAL CULTURAL HISTORY OF THE NFL

Unlike Coca-Cola, McDonald's, and blue jeans, the National Football League (NFL) has not achieved anything like an iconic global status. American-born sports like baseball and basketball do have an international presence; Iran, for example, has a professional basketball league.

And while Canada has its own national football league, populated mostly by expatriate Americans, far and away the most popular sport in the world is soccer—which is known in most of the world as "football." Global commentators on sports usually have to make an explicit comment that they are referring to "American" football when describing the American game—otherwise their audience would assume the comment was about soccer. Likewise, inside the United States it almost never occurs to anyone who hears the word *football* that one might be speaking about soccer. (This book uses the American terms for these two sports for the sake of simplicity.) Thus, while the world drinks American drinks and eats American foods and wears American clothing (all while watching American movies and television shows and listening to American music), it does not, for the most part, play American football.

Despite the gap that exists between American sports and the global audience, the NFL has begun extensive efforts to take their sport worldwide. League leaders have recognized that the world exists and it has money. They are trying to replicate the success of companies like Coca-Cola, McDonald's, and Levi Strauss in making their products an essential part of global life.

Notably, the NFL is organized on a version of the franchise principle. Power in the league really lies in the hands of each team's owner. Owners (who may be one person or a consortium of owners) enter into contractual relationships with each other to follow agreed-on bylaws governing schedules, rules, labor practices, and cost- and profit-sharing plans. The owners have created a central governing board to enforce rules and adjudicate disputes that can arise among themselves. This differs from the case of both Coca-Cola and McDonald's, in which a central company licenses and administers franchisees, but it has proved a successful model for increasing the size of profits for the NFL. The owners' association reserves the right to approve or reject new owners and new franchises, as other franchise operations do.

As a sport, football emerged in the mid-nineteenth century on American college campuses. Derived from rugby, early football games lacked features like the forward pass that are common in the game today. The first set of rules governing football was negotiated by a consortium of universities in the American Northeast in 1876; over the next decade, many of the rules that define modern football, such as eleven-man teams, four downs per possession, and the requirement that the ball needed to be moved several yards (at first five, then later ten) in order to start a new sequence of downs, were developed.[33]

While this early version of football was popular, especially on college campuses, it was also dangerously violent. Players ran into each other at high speed with little or no protective clothing or equipment, and formations developed that placed opposing players at high risk. Most notorious of these was the "flying wedge," in which players linked their arms together and charged into the opponent's ranks. Eighteen players died in 1905 alone.[34]

In order to protect the sport from its own violence, U.S. president Theodore Roosevelt asked football's governing body to create new rules to reduce the death and injury count. Innovations like the forward pass and the creation of a neutral zone separating teams by a yard before initiating each play were integrated to try to reduce the game's violence. When these innovations failed to prevent further deaths, teams were required to increase the padding and protection offered by their uniforms. Interlocking formations were also banned. The sport flourished.

Professional football developed in the early part of the twentieth century. The first player paid to perform was William Heffelinger, who earned $500 in 1892. The first game between two professional teams occurred in 1915. The first professional football league was established in 1920, with Olympian and semiprofessional player Jim Thorpe as its president. The league changed its name to the National Football League in 1921. The league had eleven teams spread across the Midwest, often in relatively small towns. Today's Chicago Bears, for example, started life in 1920 as the Decatur Staleys in Decatur, Illinois. They moved to Chicago in 1921 and became the Chicago Bears in 1922.[35]

College football dominated fans' attention until World War II. After the war, professional football began to appear on American television screens, and the professional game, which was faster paced and higher scoring than the college version, grew in popularity. Stars like Johnny Unitas, Bart Starr, Paul Hornung, and Frank Gifford wowed audiences with their skills, and American marketers linked those stars with various products for advertising and promotional purposes. (Ironically, it was common at the time for athletes to advertise cigarettes on the grounds that one brand or another was particularly good for calming the lungs and increasing performance.)

Professional football emerged in its contemporary form in the 1960s. A competitor league, the American Football League (AFL), was formed in 1960 to challenge the NFL's dominance of the sport. While NFL leaders at first dismissed the AFL as an upstart, the AFL had substantial success in recruiting and signing top college talent. The two leagues announced they would merge in 1966, and in 1970 the modern NFL was created with two conferences, the National Football Conference (NFC) and the American Football Conference (AFC).

At the heart of the merger was a game that has become the linchpin of the NFL's global marketing efforts: the Super Bowl, billed—probably inaccurately—as the most-watched single sporting event in the world. (Soccer's World Cup draws far more viewers worldwide; however, the World Cup occurs only once every four years, while the Super Bowl is an annual event. The Super Bowl is the most-watched television event in the United States every year.) The Super Bowl began as a competition between the winners of the NFL and AFL championships. While the game started as a relatively small affair, almost an afterthought to each league's regular season, the Super Bowl is now an international marketing extravaganza. The NFL claimed that Super Bowl XLI (2007) was televised in 232 countries with a potential audience of 750 million to 1 billion, for example, although as a practical matter fewer than 100 million people outside the United States watched the game.[36] (Super Bowls are always listed by roman numerals in recognition of the game's supposed monumentality.) I can attest that the 2008 game, Super Bowl XLII, was the first Super Bowl broadcast live in the United Kingdom. Given the time difference between the United States and the United Kingdom, the game began at about 11:30 p.m. local time.

Marketing the Super Bowl as an international game has been only part of the NFL's global strategy. The league also created a subsidiary in Europe. NFL Europa went by several different names from 1991 to 2007. Most of its teams were based in Germany. The NFL shut the league down in 2007 in favor of more aggressive efforts to market its primary product, the NFL, to a global audience.

In 1986, the league started to literally take its product on the road. It began playing at least one preseason game internationally each year. Tokyo and London have seen the most games, but the league has sent teams to Berlin, Mexico City, Barcelona, Dublin, Osaka, and Sydney as well. Starting in 2007, the league sent two teams to London to play a regular season game at Wembley Stadium. This game has become a regular feature of the NFL's season. While this cost one team a home game and the home ticket sales associated with it, the NFL felt that it was an important part of increasing its international appeal.

There are significant barriers to the NFL's global spread, however. Among these is a marked lack of familiarity with football's rules and ethos worldwide. One small example can be found in the fact that kickers, an important but relatively small part of a football game, often receive the biggest cheers in arenas outside the United States. This makes perfect sense, of course: soccer players are by definition kickers, and superstar David Beckham's kicking skills are of such international acclaim that the 2002 cult hit movie *Bend It like Beckham* played off them to ground its soccer-based love-and-cultural-struggle story. But while points after touchdown, field goals, punts, and kick-offs can play a crucial, sometimes even determinative, role in the outcome of a football game, kickers and kicking occupy only a tiny amount of field time in football. The league emphasizes the aggressive, intense hitting and physicality of its players as the source of the game's energy and excitement, not the play of kickers—who usually avoid the most intense action unless they are compelled to join in during an emergency. Put another way, NFL superstars are usually quarterbacks, linebackers, and wide receivers. Kickers are specialists without broad appeal.

Football is also a team sport whose stars' faces are obscured by masks and helmets. Thus, the very equipment required to play the game in relative safety guarantees that as the players engage in their acts of courage and athleticism and strength, they will not be seen except through the slotted gaps of a face mask or by the numbers they wear on their backs. This stands in stark contrast to soccer, basketball, and baseball: the crowd could actually see Brazilian soccer hall of fame legend Pelé kick his remarkable bicycle kick into the net; they now watch stars like Ronaldo and Ronaldinho and Becks (David Beckham) who are so globally famous they only need one name for everyone everywhere to know who they are. (Outside the United States, of course.) Similarly, the National Basketball Association (NBA) has made Chinese star Yao Ming a central part of its global outreach efforts, making him the face of the NBA in Asia. The NBA rode the shoulders of stars like Michael Jordan and Magic Johnson to global prominence in the 1980s (although it should be noted that even at his height of popularity,

Michael Jordan would not have had anything close to the global following of a modern soccer superstar). It is simply harder for football to duplicate the personality-based global marketing efforts that other sports have been able to utilize.

Football is also quite complex and expensive to organize. Soccer, after all, requires nothing more than some players, something that can be kicked, and a place that is mutually agreed on as a goal in order to be enjoyed. As the monks of *The Cup* proved, a Coke can is sufficient. Basketball, too, requires little more than a ball, a couple of players, a flat space free of obstructions, and a hoop of some sort ten feet above the ground. Even shoes are optional. Moreover, the skills developed in these casual games can translate into national and international success: many stars of professional basketball learned the game in the rough-and-tumble world of pickup ball in an inner-city playground, for example. Indeed, it is possible to become a superstar in basketball through dint of hard work, as NBA Hall of Fame player Larry Bird did through endless hours of practice in the barn next to his childhood home regardless of the weather or the temperature.

None of this is true for football. In part this is the result of things like insurance, uniform costs, and travel expenses. Organized football teams require a substantial amount of money to support players as they practice and play. NFL teams have forty-five active players on their rosters, for example, all of whom need to be transported to games, fed, insured, cared for when they get hurt, and of course paid. Some college teams have more than one hundred players with the same needs—other than getting paid. But even unorganized football is much harder to develop than is either soccer or basketball. A football field is 120 yards long and 53½ yards wide—both of which, of course, are uncommon measurements in a world that has largely adopted the metric system. It takes eleven players on both offense and defense to play the game, and while it is possible to play both offense and defense, players usually need to specialize in one or the other (or a separate specialty like kicking) to have a chance to advance. And while it is possible to play a version of football with less than a full complement of eleven players, a player usually needs to compete on a full-sized field against a full roster of talented opponents to really have a chance to become a professional. These limitations make it harder for football to spread globally than for most other international sports.

Of course, the forces that limit the global spread of football are unlikely to deter the league's efforts to build a world of football fans. As suggested by the global success of franchises like Coca-Cola and McDonald's, as well as the spread of American styles like blue jeans, American manufacturers, franchisers, and marketers have demonstrated repeated success in taking their products to the world. The NFL today is in the same position as McDonald's, Coca-Cola, and countless other global American businesses have been in the past. Football may or may not become a global sport: the failure of NFL Europa points to the difficulties the league may have in spreading its product across the planet. That said, the track record of American goods and services, whether those discussed in this chapter or the movies, music, and television programs discussed in chapter 3, suggests that it is likely that American football will become at least a much bigger sport around the world.

## SOCIAL NETWORKING AMERICA

The newest and arguably the most important force promoting the globalization of American popular culture is social networking. Originally conceived of as a way for friends—mostly college students at a few elite schools—to identify and interact with one another online, social networks have exploded into platforms for commerce, brand identification and loyalty, and even political revolutions.

To say that social networking has been a growing phenomenon is like saying Mount Everest is sort of tall or the Pacific Ocean is kind of large. As hard as it is to imagine today, the notion that large numbers of people would want to connect with people they rarely see, friends they had from many years ago, strangers they have never met except online, and businesses and products that they declare they "like" digitally was unimaginable even fifteen years ago. To anyone older than about twenty years of age, social networking is a remarkable innovation. Of course, to increasing numbers of younger people, social networking is just the way things are. This fact is likely to have a profound effect on the globalization of American popular culture, as will be addressed at the end of this section as well as in chapter 6.

Facebook stands at the center of the social networking revolution. While it was not the first social network, Facebook is today far and away the most expansive, popular social network in the world. At least 800 million  people worldwide are members, meaning that if Facebook were a country it would be the third most populous country in the world. Notably, however, there are significant regional gaps in Facebook's membership: the site has few members in China, for example, where the government seeks to control online access and has created competitor services like Renren, Youku, and Weibo. (China's efforts to control its citizens' access to things like American popular culture and Facebook will be addressed in more detail in chapter 5.) Similarly, Facebook has little penetration in Portuguese-speaking Brazil or in poorer regions of the world like Saharan and Central Africa. These limitations admitted, however, it is nonetheless the case that Facebook has the broadest reach of membership of any social networking service in the world.

Facebook was created in 2004. It was derived from a programming exercise in which Harvard student Mark Zuckerberg hacked into the databases of each of Harvard's residence halls to create a database in which fellow students could rate the relative attractiveness of Harvard's female students. The Facebook, as it was originally titled, was intended to provide an online alternative to a hard copy text in which Harvard University pictured all of its students. Users had to have a Harvard e-mail address to join the site. Soon thereafter, however, access to The Facebook was broadened to include students at other universities— most notably Stanford University in Palo Alto, California. Opening membership to Stanford students brought The Facebook to the attention of the technology professionals in Silicon Valley, which is centered in nearby San Jose, California. The company moved operations to California to be among the technology-savvy companies and programmers there; Facebook, as it was now renamed, opened to everyone with a valid e-mail address in 2006.

Whatever Facebook's charms are as a place for people to maintain or rekindle their friendships with high school friends or distant family, for the purposes of this book what matters is the profound role Facebook and sites like it play in bringing American popular culture to a global audience. Facebook has provided marketers, sellers, producers, and proponents of American popular culture with multiple, reinforcing ways to push their goods and services to a worldwide audience. A movie producer can, for example, create a fan page for a film he or she is making. Facebook subscribers can "like" the page to receive updates about the movie, comments from stars, and to participate in interactive games or other activities related to the picture. Such fan pages can be created in multiple languages, or members can "like" a page in a language like English should they wish to. In other words, the producer can build an audience for the movie by constructing an online community of support for the film—a community that can be global because it is virtual. And what is true for a film can, of course, be just as true for music, for television programs, or for consumer goods like blue jeans, fast food, and sporting events. Facebook empowers the making of new kinds of interconnections among consumers and producers in digital relationships that could not exist otherwise.

Of course, much of Facebook's role in spreading American popular culture globally is not quite so marketed or directly transactional. That is, it is not necessary that a producer create a page that someone "like" in order to connect a user to American popular culture content. Rather, Facebook has large numbers of fan pages constructed by ordinary users unconnected to the project at hand. Facebook hosts *Star Trek* fan pages and clothing style fan pages and pages celebrating cultural events that are made and administered by persons-at-large, Facebook members who care about the issue/work/artifact and simply chose to express themselves on the matter, letting other users find them along the way. This user-driven content is if anything more authentic and meaningful to the member than producer-driven content; it exists as an expression of the fantasies and desires of people who have no financial incentive to promote the topic at hand. They engage the issue because they want to, finding a connection that is meaningful to them to sustain their interest in the topic.

Much of the content posted on Facebook by fans or producers is, importantly, exactly the kind of digitally extracted material that so concerns movie, music, and television producers, as was discussed in chapter 3. Content, perhaps embedded from sites like YouTube (owned by Internet search giant Google) or ripped from other sources, can be uploaded into Facebook's servers for display and advertising. Indeed, as was discussed in chapter 3, some opponents of restricting downloads, legal or not, point out that all such activity is a form of advertising for a given product: the person may not have paid for the rights to the song they post on Facebook, but when others hear it, they may well pay to download the album, movie, or television program. In either case, of course, American popular culture products end up being promoted.

Facebook, it should be noted, works hard to promote connections between users and content like that created by producers or fans. The company mines the data that users provide to it to try to refine both the advertisements users see and the messages the site sends to them. Facebook tracks users' connections with other users, assessing who a given member spends more time with and who receives less attention. Facebook also charts how much time its users spend on various sites and embeds cookies in the user's browser that report the member's "likes" of various persons, products, and services. Further, the company tracks what a member's friends "like" and how a member's friends interact with Facebook, on the theory that one's friends are similar to you in interests and experiences and so can serve as a proxy for your goals and desires. All of this information, in turn, informs Facebook's ad placements and other "pushed" material like recommended pages that it presents to users. Facebook even shapes the e-mail its users see (or don't) according to the algorithms it employs to control the user's experience.

Facebook also works hard to keep its users online and connected to the site. Facebook wants to be its members' primary Internet portal and hopes its users move from Facebook-driven link to Facebook-posted advertisement in an endless cycle of Facebook-promoted content. Moreover, it offers a platform for users to play online games like FarmVille, Mafia Wars, and Angry Birds that seek to keep users coming back to the site to win bonus points, connect with others playing the game, and fill members' entertainment wants and needs. As of February 7, 2012, for example, the official Facebook Angry Birds "like" page had more than fourteen million members; FarmVille's had very nearly as many. Notably, many people spend remarkable amounts of time playing these games, thus living in a Facebook-constructed artificial environment. (All, of course, while Facebook examines users' behaviors, seeking ways to better deliver particular types of users to specific advertisers.) Indeed, if anything, Facebook might do even more to connect its users to its interface than it actually chooses to do: one former student of mine suggested that Facebook could alter a nation's sleep patterns and likely undermine its economic productivity simply by requiring that anyone playing FarmVille had to water their farm for at least ten minutes every three hours or their crops would die.[37]

To the degree that Facebook is successful in keeping its users connected to its servers and to each other, it can also be seen to promote something that can be termed a Facebook culture. The service encourages people to make numerous connections with other people, as well as products and services. It also promotes a kind of easy, casual conversational exchange among persons that may challenge established social conventions in many communities. (Take the rise of "text speak" as one example: people no longer spell out whole words, but instead communicate in an array of symbols and consonants that get the message across without taking the time to type out a full word.) This is, notably, easier to do in a language like English than it is in, say, a pictographic language like Chinese, and so may promote English as an international language. This is a recognizably American style of interpersonal exchange that, like learning to queue at McDonald's or to eat with one's hands, might reshape various cultural norms in "connected" societies.

Taken as a whole, Facebook can be seen as an engine for developing, curating, and promoting a vast array of cultural products to the broader world. Users from almost everywhere there is enough political freedom and electric infrastructure can engage with whatever material is posted on the site. And, of course, Facebook is not the only social networking platform; others, like Twitter, are popular, and blogging platforms like Tumblr, WordPress, and Blogger have proliferated. The ten or so years in which the world has grown increasingly wired together have brought with them the exponential growth of connections and linkages through which American cultural products can enter global use.

Inevitably, however, social networking has its critics. Facebook, in particular, has come under repeated criticism for its casual attitude toward users' privacy. Facebook is premised on the notion that members desire to share their information, and so it has regularly changed or otherwise created privacy settings for its users that allow the maximum number of people to know what a given member is doing or sharing at a particular time. Notoriously, for example, Facebook at one point planned to announce its members' purchases on its feed if the members logged in to a company through Facebook's site. Concerns that users might be buying presents or other things they wished to keep private led Facebook to withdraw that function. Even today, however, users of the online music service Spotify must log in to the site with their

Facebook IDs—a requirement that allows both companies to gather private information about users and potentially to share it with others.

There are additional concerns about social networking's role in what might be termed "creeping Americanism" globally. Social networks empower technology-comfortable people with access to basic infrastructure like cell phones and electricity to connect in new and sometimes surprising ways, both locally and internationally. As a practical matter, therefore, social networks are places where younger people tend to congregate—virtually. In other words, it is precisely those people who cultures typically fear will be corrupted by external influences (children and the relatively young, as was discussed in chapter 1) who are most active in engaging in global cultural exchanges through social networks. Likewise, it is precisely those people who are most worried about the cultural corruption of their children by alien and external forces—parents and social elders—who are most disconnected from social networking. The tension is obvious. And notably, as parents and grandparents move to join Facebook in particular, younger people have moved to services like Twitter to escape parental oversight. The groundwork has been laid for a generational gap of unprecedented scope, as will be discussed in chapter 6.

As will be discussed in more detail in chapter 5, social network services like Facebook and Twitter have also faced criticism for being tools of political rebellion and revolution as well as of straightforward thuggery. The "Arab Spring" protests of 2010–2011 were organized through sites like Facebook and Twitter. So too were the "Occupy" protests that began on Wall Street but rapidly spread around the world in the summer and fall of 2011. However, it is also clear that criminal activities like the London riots of August 2011 were abetted by social networking services. Notably, each of these events did not just cause social and political controversy. They also prompted government efforts to crack down and limit users' access to social networking services. The technology may be neutral, but its use never is.

## EVERYTHING, EVERYWHERE, ALL THE TIME

The five artifacts examined in detail in this chapter—Coca-Cola, McDonald's, blue jeans, the NFL, and social networks—represent only a small slice of American popular culture beyond movies, music, and television programs. Many other companies, products, and practices might have been discussed to illustrate the global spread of American popular culture. Moreover, as the tie-in between McDonald's and Coca-Cola described earlier in this chapter suggests, the forces, products, ideals, values, rituals, and business practices embedded in American popular culture can work in intersecting and mutually supportive ways. American pop culture is a global behemoth.

The global ubiquity and interconnectedness of American popular culture can perhaps best be illustrated in a vignette offered by Robert J. Foster in the introduction to his book *Coca-Globalization*. Foster describes a night of entertainment he enjoyed in Papua New Guinea (PNG), arguably as far away from the bright lights and high-tech world of modern consumer culture as it is still possible to get today. As he puts it in this extended quote:

> On the last night of my brief visit in 2000, I did witness something that I had never before seen in these islands: a Pepsi commercial. As a fundraising event for the local community school, a video night had been organized. Dozens of school age children and a smaller contingent of adults of all ages poured into a gated enclosure on a perfect moonlit evening to watch a motley assortment of offerings—*Space Hunter, Jeremiah Johnson*, Moses and Michael Jackson's *Greatest Hits* (deliberately shown late in the program, after the younger children had fallen asleep). The worn cassettes were played on a television monitor hooked to a VCR and powered by a noisy diesel generator. The dusk to dawn marathon began with a compilation of music videos by Papua New Guinean pop bands, a stream of highly stylized song and dance routines almost invariably staged on a beach. Just before the tape ended, a brief promo for Pepsi-Cola, a sponsor of the recording company that produced the music, filled the monitor. Attractive young Papua New Guinean men and women cavorted together on screen in a speeding motorboat. In the audience, the adults clucked and the teenagers whistled at the spectacle. As the commercial's upbeat jingle finished, the warm night air moved to the hissed sounds of children enunciating the word "Pepsi" or practicing their English by reading aloud the mellifluous slogan, "It's Pepsi in PNG."[38]

It's all there—absent, perhaps, a Facebook page announcing the event, which couldn't have been made because Facebook did not yet exist when this party occurred. American movies and music are tied to American products in a seamless whole. The PNG artists' work probably would be recognized as pop anywhere in the world because it flowed from forms generated in American pop culture. Advertising promoted not just a brand and lifestyle identity but English as well. There was even a brief glimpse of Frankfurt School–like concern about the moral content of the programming on the docket: Michael Jackson's hits had to be played after the youngest children went to sleep, not before.

In some ways, what is remarkable about Foster's story is not the fact that Papua New Guinean children were learning English from a Pepsi commercial, but the fact that Foster was surprised by it at all. Papua New Guinea is, admittedly, on the fringes of world trade and world politics, but the world is rapidly becoming smaller, and fewer and fewer places retain the kind of cultural isolation that would be needed to avoid exposure to the various components of American popular culture. People worldwide report learning English from American movies, music, and television; there is no inherent reason why the people of Papua New Guinea should be any different. Foster's many travels to the region sensitized him to the changes that led to a small group of New Guinean fund-raisers watching American programming with a Pepsi commercial, but it is unlikely that anyone without such long experience would have been as surprised. One more or less expects to see products, styles, and values of American popular culture across the world, at least most of the time.

This expectation is enhanced when the diversity of pop culture is accounted for. Movies show characters driving cars; these can be and often are obviously American. They show styles of dress, modes of behavior, and attitudes toward authority, religion, tradition, and sexuality that often manifest recognizably American perspectives on these contentious issues. In some cases, explicit placements of music or products are added to a film or television program, and numerous websites push Internet users to download ringtones, purchase items, or participate in social networks dedicated to various products and programming. Fast-food restaurants offer tie-ins with movies and music; the purchase of consumer items can bring coupons to some store or film. Social networks tighten these linkages by having consumers "like" products and establish brand and personal affiliations online. And consumers consume it all, in vast quantities across the world in more and more markets.

## CONCLUSION

As has been suggested throughout this chapter and in chapter 3, anything as globally pervasive, appealing, and potentially culturally transformative as American popular culture tends to generate concern, fear, opposition, and even anger. People worry that their children are adopting alien values shaped by a distant power they have no influence over. Local producers worry that international conglomerates will drive them out of business. Local artisans, performers, critics, and artists worry that native, domestic cultural forms of music, art, and performance will be abandoned in favor of the whiz-bang wizardry of Hollywood productions. Yet others, both in the local community and elsewhere, worry that environmental degradation will destroy traditional ways of life and the natural environments that sustained them. In the end, all fear that unique, important, and distinctive ways of life may be crushed and replaced by a washed-out, generic culture that political theorist Benjamin Barber once referred to as "McDisneySoft." Perhaps today that term should be expanded to "McDisneySoftBook."

Such concerns are not surprising. Nor are they irrational or panicked. As was discussed in chapter 1, people usually respond in these ways when they perceive that their culture is under assault. This reaction is inevitably more intense when the agent of cultural change is distant and apparently untouchable. It is to be expected, then, that various communities worldwide have acted to protect or otherwise shield their cultures from the apparent onslaught of American popular culture. As is discussed in detail in chapter 5, such reactions have been common worldwide. However, even as some communities have sought to limit the influence or power of American popular culture in their societies, most of the world's major economic powers have been working to lower trade barriers and enhance contacts among the world's communities. Popular culture has been a contentious and significant part of these efforts. It is to the question of how American popular culture intersects with the world of global trade policy that chapter 5 turns.

## NOTES

1. The following discussion of the development of the franchise in the United States is derived from Carrie Shook and Robert L. Shook, *Franchising: The Business Strategy That Changed the World* (Englewood Cliffs, N.J.: Prentice Hall, 1993), 139–66; John A. Jackle and Keith A. Sculle, *Fast Food: Roadside Restaurants in the Automobile Age* (Baltimore: Johns Hopkins University Press, 1999), 139–62; and Thomas S. Dicke, *Franchising in America: The Development of a Business Method, 1840–1980* (Chapel Hill: University of North Carolina Press, 1992).

2. "World Motor Vehicle Production," http://oica.net/wp-content/uploads/ford-2010.pdf (accessed 27 January 2012).

3. "World Motor Vehicle Production."

4. Orville Schell, "How Walmart Is Changing China (and Vice Versa)," *The Atlantic* (December 2011): 80–98.

5. Starbucks Company Profile, http://news.starbucks.com/images/10041/AboutUs-CompanyProfile-Q4-2011-12_14_11-FINAL.pdf (accessed 27 January 2012).

6. "2010 Ranking of the Top 100 Brands," http://www.interbrand.com/en/best-global-brands/best-global-brands-2008/best-global-brands-2010.aspx (accessed 31 January 2012).

7. This history is adapted from http://www.thecoca-colacompany.com/heritage/pdf/Coca-Cola_125_years_booklet.pdf (accessed 31 January 2012); "The Chronicle of Coca-Cola," http://www.thecoca-colacompany.com/heritage/chronicle_birth_refreshing_idea.html (accessed 31 January 2012); and Mark Pendergast, *For God, Country, and Coca-Cola: The Unauthorized History of the Great American Soft Drink and the Company That Makes It* (New York: Scribner, 1993).

8. Pendergast, *For God, Country, and Coca-Cola*, 354–71; quote on 365.

9. See Cecil Munsey, *The Illustrated Guide to the Collectibles of Coca-Cola* (New York: Hawthorn Books, 1972) for a guide on such matters.

10. See http://www.killercoke.org (accessed 31 January 2012).

11. Except where otherwise noted, the history of McDonald's presented here is derived from numerous sources, including Shook and Shook, *Franchising*, 139–66; Jackle and Sculle, *Fast Food*, 139–62; http://www.mcdonalds.com/us/en/our_story/our_history.html (accessed 31 January 2012); http://www.mcdonalds.com/corp/about.html (accessed 4 February 2009); and Funding Universe, "McDonald's Corporation," http://www.fundinguniverse.com/company-histories/McDonalds-Corporation-Company-History.html (accessed 2 March 2011).

12. Jackle and Sculle, *Fast Food*, 135–36.

13. "2010 Ranking of the Top 100 Brands."

14. Francis Fukuyama, *The End of History and the Last Man* (New York: Free Press, 1992).

15. Jonathan Steele, "Muscovites Find Perestroika in a Restructured Cow," *The Guardian*, 1 February 1990.

16. James L. Watson, ed., *Golden Arches East: McDonald's in East Asia* (Stanford, Calif.: Stanford University Press, 1997).

17. "McDonald's to Open a Restaurant a Day in China in Four Years," http://www.bloomberg.com/news/2011-07-29/mcdonald-s-franchises-to -account-for-up-to-20-of-china-business.html (accessed 31 January 2012).

18. Watson, *Golden Arches East*, 1–38.

19. Watson, *Golden Arches East*, 1–38.

20. Watson, *Golden Arches East*, 1–38.

21. Watson, *Golden Arches East*, 1–38.

22. Eric Schlosser, *Fast Food Nation: The Dark Side of the American Meal* (New York: Houghton Mifflin Harcourt, 2001).

23. "Financial Highlights," http://www.aboutmcdonalds.com/mcd/investors/ financial_highlights.html (accessed 31 January 2012).

24. This history is derived from Jeans and Accessories, "The History of Blue Jeans," http://www.jeans-and-accessories.com/history-of-blue-jeans.html (accessed 31 January 2012); and The Great Idea Finder, "Blue Jeans History," http://www.ideafinder.com/history/inventions/bluejeans.htm (accessed 31 January 2012).

25. Beverly Gordon, "American Denim: Blue Jeans and Their Multiple Layers of Meaning," in *Dress and Popular Culture*, ed. Patricia A. Cunningham and Susan Voso Lab (Bowling Green, Ohio: Bowling Green State University Popular Press, 1991), 34.

26. Gordon, "American Denim," 36.

27. Gordon, "American Denim," 37.

28. Virginia Wallace-Whitaker, "Awareness of American Brand Names in the Soviet Union," paper presented at the annual meeting of the Association for Education in Journalism and Mass Communication, 10–13 August 1989.

29. "How Many Pairs of Denim Jeans Do Consumers Own?," http://lifestyle monitor.cottoninc.com/LSM-Fast-Facts/001-How-many-pairs-denim-jeans -do-consumers-own/?category=denim&sort=viewall&mainSection=fastFacts &currentRow=3 (accessed 31 January 2012).

30. "How Many Pairs of Denim Jeans Do Men Own?," http://lifestyle monitor.cottoninc.com/LSM-Fast-Facts/002-How-many-pairs-denim-jeans -do-men-own/?category=denim&sort=viewall&mainSection=fastFacts& currentRow=11 (accessed 31 January 2012); and "How Many Pairs of Denim Jeans Do Women Own?," http://lifestylemonitor.cottoninc.com/LSM-Fast

-Facts/003-How-many-pairs-denim-jeans-do-women-own/?category=denim&
sort=viewall&mainSection=fastFacts&currentRow=12 (accessed 31 January
2012).

31. "Percent of Consumers Who Love or Enjoy Wearing Denim," http://
lifestylemonitor.cottoninc.com/LSM-Fast-Facts/004-Percent-consumers-wear
ing-denim/?category=denim&sort=viewall&mainSection=fastFacts&current
Row=13 (accessed 31 January 2012); and "Do Men and Women Prefer to
Wear Denim Jeans or Causal Slacks?," http://lifestylemonitor.cottoninc.com/
LSM-Fast-Facts/009-Men-Women-Prefer-Denim-Jeans-Casual-Slacks/?category
=denim&sort=viewall&mainSection=fastFacts&currentRow=17 (accessed 31
January 2012).

32. Scott Robert Olson, "Hollywood Planet: Global Media and the Competitive Advantage of Narrative Transparency," in *The Television Studies
Reader,* ed. Robert C. Allen and Annette Hill (New York: Routledge, 2004),
114.

33. Except where otherwise noted, the following history is adapted from
"A Brief History of the Game," http://www.hornetfootball.org/documents/
football-history.htm (accessed 31 January 2012); http://www.sportsknowhow
.com/football/history/football-history.shtml, pp. 1–4 (accessed 31 January
2012); "The History of American Football," http://www.talkamericanfootball
.co.uk/guides/history_of_american_football.html (accessed 31 January 2012);
and "History of American Football," http://en.wikipedia.org/wiki/History_of
_American_football (accessed 31 January 2012).

34. Tim Layden, "Embarrassing Moments," http://sportsillustrated.cnn
.com/2006/writers/tim_layden/07/14/moments/index.html (accessed 31 January 2012).

35. Chicago Bears, "Tradition: History by Decades," http://www.chicago
bears.com/tradition/HistorybyDecades.html (accessed 31 January 2012).

36. Bill Briggs, "Super Bull!," http://www.msnbc.msn.com/id/16877331/
ns/business-us_business/t/super-bull/#.Tyg-0uOXQhw (accessed 31 January
2012).

37. Justin Thomson, personal communication, April 2011.

38. Robert J. Foster, *Coca-Globalization: Following Soft Drinks from New
York to New Guinea* (New York: Palgrave Macmillan, 2008), x–xi.

# CHAPTER 5

## GLOBAL TRADE AND THE FEAR OF AMERICAN POPULAR CULTURE

This chapter explores the legal context of international trade in popular culture—a trade that is tightly linked to global fears of the power of American popular culture to corrupt societies and overwhelm competitors. It begins with an extended discussion of two competing schools of thought regarding trade in culture. One, advocated by the United States, holds that cultural products are like any other goods and should be traded freely in order to guarantee everyone across the globe the chance to enjoy entertaining programming at low cost. The other school, advanced by most of the rest of the world's nations but led by Canada and France, insists that cultural products are different from other goods and services and should not be subject to the free trade rules that have increasing influence over the global economy. These two schools of thought can be seen to have shaped, and to continue to shape, many international agreements in the post–World War II period.

This chapter analyzes the cultural features of these trade agreements and then offers a series of case studies of the ways several different countries have attempted to limit the influence and power of American popular culture in their countries. To the degree that people link American values with globalization as such, they tend to resist and reject those forces that promote globalization worldwide.

It should be noted here that the trade agreements examined in this chapter focus on measurable trade in products like movies, music, and television. The audiovisual industries are recognized around the world as having a profound and powerful ability to shape and define a culture. Accordingly, nations and communities tend to both jealously guard their domestic culture-producing institutions and to react to perceived threats to their local cultures from foreign sources. However, as was discussed in chapter 4, culture operates at levels and in ways not always directly expressed in the kinds of tangible, measurable ways that can be regulated by trade agreements. As a consequence of this immeasurable dimension, the impact and fear of American popular culture is greater than a narrow focus on television programs, music, and movies might suggest. Discussions of global trade in culture matter for reasons beyond, or in addition to, those that can be calculated in the flow of audiovisual products around the planet. Thus, this chapter uses regulation of the global trade in movies, music, and television as a proxy for greater concerns about the ways in which American popular culture affects the global community. As will be seen, while people around the world enjoy the goods and services created by American pop culture makers, they and their governments fear these artifacts as well. This fact has shaped the way globalization has developed.

## TRADING AMERICAN POPULAR CULTURE

As was addressed in chapter 1, the process of globalization has been tightly bound up with a series of decisions made by a number of countries, led by the United States, to open their borders to (relatively) open markets, the easy exchange of capital, and to new economic, political, and cultural systems. As will be seen, concerns that popular culture and other forms of mass communication may harm or destroy local cultures have been central to these agreements from their inception. Accordingly, restrictions have been built into international trade in cultural products since the very first General Agreement on Tariffs and Trade (GATT) was passed to promote freer trade in the Western world in 1947. In fact, it is the case today that other than enforcing restrictions on population migration and requiring their residents to register with the state, some of the strictest state regulations on global trade focus on cultural goods and services. Cultural matters have been both contentious and important from the very beginning of the modern era of globalization.

At the core of concerns about trade in culture lies a deceptively simple question: is popular culture a commodity like rice or computers or automobiles, or is it an agent of socialization that shapes culture? If popular culture is a commodity, the logic of the free market suggests that few, if any, restrictions ought to be placed on its global exchange. If people like American popular culture products, and those products can be created in the United States more cheaply than they can be produced anywhere else, then people ought to be allowed to enjoy as many American popular culture products as they like without regulation. Anything less will guarantee that people will have access to fewer audiovisual entertainments or other goods, at higher prices, than they would have in a world of global free trade in culture.

By contrast, if popular culture is a meaning-bearing entity, if its products both manifest and shape culture, then diverse states and communities have an interest in limiting the access and influence of a popular culture alien to their own. That is, if American popular culture is, in fact, American, and it does, in fact, produce changed values and attitudes in its consumers, then local communities have reason to fear American popular culture. American popular culture might be invited in through the front door but then throw local culture out the window.

### THE AMERICAN ARGUMENT

Unsurprisingly, the United States has been at the forefront of efforts to reduce barriers to the trade in cultural products since the beginning of the era of contemporary globalization in the 1940s. The U.S. position has been and remains that popular culture products are no different from any other commodity and so no special rules or exemptions ought to govern cultural product trading worldwide. In part, this position is grounded on simple economic interests. As has been clear throughout this book, the United States holds a unique, globally dominant position in trade in popular culture. This does not mean that all popular culture produced and enjoyed around the world is American; rather, it means that in global pop culture matters, the United States is the nation most likely to benefit from free or relatively free trade. Its products already have a worldwide audience, and its makers have various competitive advantages in producing popular culture that make it likely that American popular culture would succeed in global trade. Moreover, the corporations that shape American popular culture are likely to be able to use their power and influence and wealth to compete against foreign producers, perhaps even purchasing their rivals or driving them out of business. Finally, while much of the rest of the world consumes American popular culture, the reverse is much less true: Americans watch few foreign movies or television programs and do not listen to significant amounts of foreign-produced music. This means that even as American producers might out-compete global popular culture producers in their home countries, those foreign producers are unlikely to out-compete American makers in the United States. This ensures a regular and profitable stream of income for U.S. producers that foreign producers lack. On purely economic grounds, then, free trade in culture makes sense to American policymakers and business leaders.

Yet the economic explanation is not the whole of the reason Americans advocate free trade in culture. U.S. policymakers and citizens alike tend to believe that free trade is a cultural necessity. Free trade combines cultural values like individualism, capitalism, optimism, and entrepreneurialism in ways that reinforce American popular support for things like democracy, freedom, and human rights. As was discussed in chapter 1, Americans might not always live up to the commitments their belief in free trade suggests they ought, but the underlying cultural norms are there nonetheless. Free trade is generally seen to be a component of the notion of freedom as such. Limits on trade in culture, for those who believe in such linkages, can feel like limits on freedom itself. For many American advocates of free trade, then, open trade in cultural products is a passionately held cultural belief, not only an economically advantageous one.

American trade negotiators and business leaders have adopted both economic and cultural explanations of their advocacy of free trade in culture. Speaking of efforts to liberalize the trade in movies in the late

1980s and early 1990s, for example, Peter Morici, who served as director of the U.S. International Trade Commission during the period, noted: "When we're talking about cinema, I think it's largely a commercial issue and not a cultural issue. Globally there's a preference for what Hollywood puts out. We have a very competitive industry, and that is certainly evidenced by the amount of film we sell worldwide." Similarly, a spokesman for the California Trade and Commerce Agency, Mike Marando, insisted: "Making movies is a market-driven product. We don't see it as cultural imperialism. We see it as a marketplace issue."[1]

Others have defended free trade in culture on the grounds that it enhances global culture rather than undermining it. Economist Tyler Cowen, who represented the United States at the United Nations Educational, Scientific and Cultural Organization (UNESCO), agreed that globalization was bringing cultures closer together and shaping common cultural experiences for many of the world's peoples. "You can see a poster of [basketball star] Michael Jordan in Bali, Indonesia, in South America, in Scandinavia, and of course in Chicago in the United States," Cowen acknowledges. But he argues that this common global experience does not necessarily lead to the destruction of local and distinctive cultures. Instead, he offers a broader understanding of diversity, one grounded on the choices people have available to them as they go about their lives: "Another notion of diversity is what I call 'diversity within society.' Diversity within society refers to the menu of choice. What do we have to choose from? What options do we have? What kinds of opportunities do we have with our lives? When we ask ourselves, 'Does globalization bring more of this kind of diversity?,' we find that the answer is usually yes."[2] Individual choice, then, is seen as an ultimate good. It enhances the quality and range of human freedom. To limit trade in culture is to limit the opportunities all people might have for self-expression and individual fulfillment.

## THE COUNTER-AMERICAN ARGUMENT

The countries generally insisting on exceptions for culture in free trade agreements make a series of linked arguments that, cumulatively, expose their collective fears that American popular culture products may lead to cultural corruption, cultural imperialism, and/or cultural homogenization. For them, the restrictions decried by the United States are seen as essential to their economic and cultural survival. Each may have a different basis for opposing unfettered trade in cultural artifacts, but they combine in alliances that seek to limit cultural globalization's potentially negative effects. Notably, many of these countries have agreed to free trade in other goods and services. They have generally agreed to accept the consequences of free trade in most aspects of international economic life in exchange for the economic benefits it brings. They simply exempt culture from such rules.

The first type of opposition to free trade in culture made by nations and communities opposing free trade in cultural artifacts can be termed the *culture exception*. Advocates of the culture exception insist that cultural trade is different from trade in any other good or service. Their argument is that cultures stay lost once they are lost. Languages, religions, styles of life, and orientations toward the shared community can die. Thus, free trade in culture is inherently more dangerous than free trade in other products. After all, while free trade in other products may cause one country's people to lose jobs in industries that produce goods that another country's people can produce more cheaply, those jobs can usually be replaced. Workers can be retrained into fields in which the nation has a comparative advantage—at least in theory. Moreover, free trade tends to make goods and services cheaper, thereby making it easier for people around the world, including the country that lost jobs in a particular field, to acquire goods and services at reduced cost. (Again, at least in theory.) In contrast, free trade in culture threatens cultural death, and so is to be avoided.

In 1993, for example, French president François Mitterrand revealed his fears of American cultural destruction when he claimed that "creations of the spirit are not just commodities; the elements of culture are not pure business. What is at stake is the cultural identity of all our nations—it is the freedom to create and choose our own images. A society which abandons the means of depicting itself would soon be an enslaved society."[3] Similarly, in 2002, a Canadian government group, the Cultural Industries Sectoral Advisory Group on International Trade, opposed free trade in cultural products on grounds that such trade would tend to create cultural homogeneity:

The underlying principle and overall objective of the instrument is to ensure that cultural diversity is preserved in the face of the challenge posed by globalization, trade liberalization and rapid technological changes. Although new information technologies, globalization and evolving multilateral trade policies offer indisputable possibilities for the expression of cultural diversity, they may also be detrimental to ensuring cultural diversity. This is particularly the case when, for example, domestic cultural content is not accorded reasonable shelf space in its own domestic market, when the over-concentration of production and distribution of cultural content contributes to the standardization of cultural expression, or when developing countries, because of lack of resources, run the risk of being excluded from the international cultural space as it is currently being constructed with new information and communications technologies. There is an urgent need to address these new developments to ensure that cultural diversity, as a factor of social cohesion and economic development, is preserved and enhanced.[4]

Likewise, in commenting on a proposed free trade agreement between the United States and Australia, the Music Council of Australia, in a report to the Australian government's Department of Foreign Affairs and Trade's Office of Trade Negotiations, insisted: "The larger context for this discussion is the need to maintain and foster cultural diversity. The rationale for trade liberalization depends upon the doctrine of comparative advantage which, in the cultural sphere, leads to cultural homogeneity. The two objectives are basically opposed. But in the cultural sphere, cultural diversity is more important than economic efficiency."[5]

The European Commission has likewise argued:

Cinematographic and televisual programmes are goods unlike any other: as privileged vectors of culture, they retain their specific nature amid the new types of audiovisual product which are currently multiplying; as living witnesses to the traditions and of the identity of each country, they merit encouragement; only a strong European industry will be able to guarantee both the diversity of programmes and an increase in the international influence of European cultures. Given the position of the image in our society, much is at stake in cultural terms.[6]

Culture, the argument goes, must be exempted from free trade.

Opponents of free trade in culture also make a business case for their position. Advocates of the business case for regulating free trade in culture focus on issues like jobs, their nation's balance of trade with other nations, and even national security in insisting that there are reasons to maintain limits on trade in certain industries, including audiovisual ones. For example, as is discussed later in this chapter, when the new Western bloc negotiated the 1947 GATT in the aftermath of World War II, the United States specifically exempted the European film industry from free trade demands. The United States agreed that the nations of Western Europe, which had been devastated in the war, needed time to recover before they would be able to compete with American products. In other words, the United States agreed that the shattered nations of Western Europe had an economic interest in protecting their domestic audiovisual culture industries from American competition so that the European industries could rebuild their facilities, hire new employees, and try to level the global playing field before facing competition from the international American popular culture powerhouse.

Since 1947 other nations have claimed that their nascent, infant industries needed time to grow before allowing them to face American competition—including, notably, the prospect of being bought on the open market by the global corporations centered in the United States. Yet others insisted that the jobs created by workers in the AV industries are important and required protection—even, it should be noted, when these same nations adopted free trade policies in other industries. In other words, even countries that basically accept the logic of free trade, and have consequently adopted policies that put some of their citizens' jobs at risk from international competition, nonetheless consider culture different and necessary to protect.[7]

Whether for business or cultural reasons, then, trade in culture and cultural artifacts is very controversial and contentious. This is true even for nations that otherwise seem to embrace free trade. Culture is different, at least for most of the nations of the world.

## POPULAR CULTURE IN
## INTERNATIONAL AGREEMENTS

This section explores the ways in which international efforts to create free trade among at least some of the world's nations have been affected by issues associated with trade in culture. While globalization is not driven only by free trade policies, global laws regarding how goods and services should be traded have been central to the ways in which globalization has unfolded at least since the end of World War II. As will be seen, the controversy about whether culture should be subject to free trade rules has been manifest in many of the global trade agreements passed since 1947. Indeed, some of the most contentious issues that free traders have had to address have been those centered on trade in cultural artifacts.

## GATT/WTO 1947–2012

Concerns and questions about trade in culture date from the first agreement that promoted free trade in the modern era, the General Agreement on Tariffs and Trade (GATT) adopted in 1947. Written for both economic and political reasons, GATT was conceived of as a way to build a strong and productive international economy among the world's major industrial powers. It was also viewed as a tool for building new, cooperative political relationships among countries that had recently been at war with one another. Policymakers expected that creating patterns of mutual trade and dependency on various partners for important goods and services would reduce the chances that the nations that had just unleashed the horrors of World War II on each other, and indeed that had suffered through World War I in the living memory of many people at the time, would go to war again. They sought to cement an alliance of Western, democratic powers against the newly emerged threat represented by the Soviet Union and the growing Communist bloc. GATT was expected to provide both economic benefits and political legitimacy for the new Western alliance.

GATT, notably, created a special exemption for cultural artifacts. Article 4 addressed European fears of American cultural imperialism in that it allowed European countries still recovering from the devastation of World War II to impose quotas on the number of foreign films—usually American—that could be distributed and shown in their countries. This was intended to give the European film industry time to rebuild itself with the revenues generated from domestic audiences without competition from American movies. In addition, it allowed European countries to provide subsidies to their film industries. These subsidies served to supplement the costs associated with producing and distributing movies, meaning that the filmmakers did not need to generate enough money from ticket sales in theaters to produce movies. Finally, Article 20 allowed nations to protect their "national treasures," however defined.[8] Thus, concerns about the protection of cultural products and culture-producing industries were enshrined in international law even as the era of modern globalization began.

The 1947 GATT agreement protected culture industries for other reasons as well. In particular, France insisted that culture be exempted from free trade in order to protect French culture as such. French policymakers believed (and continue to believe) that American films and other audiovisual programs have a unique capacity to shape and undermine French culture. American policymakers actually agreed, but they believed that the cultural changes that might follow from free trade in culture would be good for the Western alliance as a whole. As Irwin Wall puts it:

> One of the more curious aspects of the postwar period is the enormous amount of acrimony expended by both Americans and French over ostensibly superficial questions. Films and Coca-Cola . . . are a case in point. . . . At a time when basic essentials of food and coal were lacking, and the Americans were lending and then giving the French billions, both these nonessential items were pressed upon the French as exports for which they were expected to pay with their very scarce dollars. . . . Both items carried a symbolic importance as manifestations of the American "way of life," which magnified their importance far beyond the few millions they were expected to earn. Fitting symbols of the consumer society, both were symbols of anti-Communism as well.[9]

Little changed in matters of cultural trade after the original GATT was adopted in 1947. European nations consistently maintained their right to protect their culture industries through quotas and subsidies. Additionally, in an effort to avoid cultural homogenization, they also regularly declared their domestic movie, music, and television production companies and facilities to be national treasures not subject to purchase by international corporations. The United States has generally opposed this position and insisted, during what was called the Uruguay Round of GATT talks, which began in 1986, that cultural industries needed to be brought into the arena of free trade.

In the General Agreement on Trade in Services (GATS), negotiated during the Uruguay Round, signatories agreed to develop schedules on which their service and telecommunication industries were to be integrated into a global economy. As had happened in 1947, however, France continued to insist that audiovisual industries be exempt from free trade rules. This demand was a central sticking point in what turned out to be seven years of negotiations during the Uruguay Round and very nearly led to the collapse of the GATT negotiations as their December 15, 1993, deadline approached. In the end, the United States relented and agreed to pursue the question at a later date. Culture, again, was treated separately from other forms of trade as fears of American imperial or homogenizing culture became front and center in the talks.[10]

While cultural issues served as a point of contention in the Uruguay Round, they also stimulated new areas of international agreement. GATS took a necessary first step toward creating a truly global marketplace of ideas by strengthening international copyright laws governing creative works (including television programs, movies, and music). Without copyright protections, individuals and organizations have little incentive to publish their ideas for the world to use, develop, and implement. (It is precisely these copyright protections that digital pirates violate when they illegally copy or download movies, music, and television programming.) Second, GATS made it easier for international corporations to buy and own telecommunications companies around the world. Ownership of such facilities had previously been more restricted.[11] This change set the legal conditions under which it became possible for telecommunications companies to become transnational corporations. It was thus a key step in encouraging the kind of corporate centralization of the entertainment industry that was described in chapter 3.

The World Trade Organization (WTO) supplanted GATT in 1995. In 2001, the WTO initiated the Doha Round of trade talks to try to come to further agreements about international trade in agricultural products and services—including popular culture products.

Notably, the Doha Round has never produced an agreement. Indeed, negotiations have been essentially frozen since 2008. The global economic crisis has sent numerous nations into severe economic crises, and as a practical matter it has made nations far less open to free trade policies.

The biggest sticking point is trade in agriculture. As was noted earlier in this book, nations like the United States have tried to protect their domestic agriculture industries from competition from cheaper international sources, which has had the effect of reducing those nations' abilities to translate their agricultural and resource wealth into growth and development projects at home. The United States, in particular, has sought to protect its domestic agriculture industry from precisely the kinds of international free trade rules it generally seeks to achieve in most other areas of world politics.

However, this contradiction in logic has not prevented the United States from continuing to insist that culture and cultural products should be traded largely without barriers. Instead, U.S. negotiators have pursued the logic of free trade into new areas like the development of computer software and other virtual reality products. Unsurprisingly, those nations opposed to free trade in culture have resisted U.S. efforts in these newly emerging fields. These issues are likely to remain unresolved for the foreseeable future, as the Doha Round is completely stalled.

## POPULAR CULTURE AND THE UNITED NATIONS

At least one reason questions of trade in culture have become less prominent at GATT/WTO is that the venue for discussions about these issues has changed. As globalization progressed, its effects were felt in more and more countries, whether or not they were signatories to the GATT and WTO agreements. Increased trade and other contacts placed continuing and intensifying pressures on cultures around the world. Indeed, in the early part of the twenty-first century, UNESCO found that 50 percent of the world's languages were in danger of extinction and that 90 percent had no Internet presence. Only five countries monopolized the world's culture industries, while eighty-eight others had never had their own domestic film production facilities.[12]

The changed nature of the issue encouraged a changed response to it. Rather than focusing on the narrow confines of international trade agreements to which they might not have been privy anyway, many of the nations that were worried about the potentially negative effects of globalization on culture used their membership in the United Nations to push for a new way to address trade in culture around the world. In particular, they worked through the auspices of UNESCO to develop and ultimately adopt a new treaty that seeks to protect culture from most free trade rules.

In 2001, UNESCO passed a Universal Declaration on Cultural Diversity. In that document, the United Nations and the declaration's signatories insisted that cultural diversity is a "common heritage of humanity." They then called for the development of a treaty to promote and protect cultural diversity on a global scale.[13]

A draft treaty followed in 2005. This treaty clearly illustrates the tension between the integrating and fragmenting forces of globalization as it relates to fears of American popular culture corruption, imperialism, and homogenization. Passed on October 20, 2005, the draft was intended to empower states to protect their interests in their cultural industries. As the specific language states, the objectives of the Convention on the Protection and Promotion of the Diversity of Cultural Expressions are:

> (a) to protect and promote the diversity of cultural expressions;
>
> (b) to create the conditions for cultures to flourish and to freely interact in a mutually beneficial manner;
>
> (c) to encourage dialogue among cultures with a view to ensuring wider and balanced cultural exchanges in the world in favour of intercultural respect and a culture of peace;
>
> (d) to foster interculturality in order to develop cultural interaction in the spirit of building bridges among peoples;
>
> (e) to promote respect for the diversity of cultural expressions and raise awareness of its value at the local, national and international levels;
>
> (f) to reaffirm the importance of the link between culture and development for all countries, particularly for developing countries, and to support actions undertaken nationally and internationally to secure recognition of the true value of this link;
>
> (g) to give recognition to the distinctive nature of cultural activities, goods and services as vehicles of identity, values and meaning;
>
> (h) to reaffirm the sovereign rights of States to maintain, adopt and implement policies and measures that they deem appropriate for the protection and promotion of the diversity of cultural expressions on their territory;
>
> (i) to strengthen international cooperation and solidarity in a spirit of partnership with a view, in particular, to enhancing the capacities of developing countries in order to protect and promote the diversity of cultural expressions.

These goals, in turn, were to be met according to principles 2 through 8 of the convention:

2. Principle of sovereignty

States have, in accordance with the Charter of the United Nations and the principles of international law, the sovereign right to adopt measures and policies to protect and promote the diversity of cultural expressions within their territory.

3. Principle of equal dignity of and respect for all cultures

The protection and promotion of the diversity of cultural expressions presuppose the recognition of equal dignity of and respect for all cultures, including the cultures of persons belonging to minorities and indigenous peoples.

4. Principle of international solidarity and cooperation

International cooperation and solidarity should be aimed at enabling countries, especially developing countries, to create and strengthen their means of cultural expression, including their cultural industries, whether nascent or established, at the local, national and international levels.

5. Principle of the complementarity of economic and cultural aspects of development

Since culture is one of the mainsprings of development, the cultural aspects of development are as important as its economic aspects, which individuals and peoples have the fundamental right to participate in and enjoy.

6. Principle of sustainable development

Cultural diversity is a rich asset for individuals and societies. The protection, promotion and maintenance of cultural diversity are an essential requirement for sustainable development for the benefit of present and future generations.

Yet even as protectionism was to be allowed—and even promoted—in given communities, freedom in cultural exchanges was also to be promoted:

7. Principle of equitable access

Equitable access to a rich and diversified range of cultural expressions from all over the world and access of cultures to the means of expressions and dissemination constitute important elements for enhancing cultural diversity and encouraging mutual understanding.

8. Principle of openness and balance

When States adopt measures to support the diversity of cultural expressions, they should seek to promote, in an appropriate manner, openness to other cultures of the world and to ensure that these measures are geared to the objectives pursued under the present Convention.[14]

Notably, the vote on the convention was 148 for, 2 against, with 4 abstentions. Only the United States and Israel voted no.

Once drafted, the treaty went to UN member states for approval. It would go into effect once thirty nations adopted it. In a sign of international skepticism about and fear of the power of the international, American-driven industries that dominate global trade in culture, the treaty was ratified by December 2006. UNESCO Director General Kōichirō Matsuura noted that the "rapidity of the adoption process is unprecedented. . . . None of UNESCO's other cultural conventions has been adopted by so many States in so little time."[15] It went into international effect in March 2007.

It should be noted here that it is not at all clear how much effect, if any, this treaty will have either in protecting existing cultures from the apparent threats they face from global culture and cultural trade or in limiting the further expansion of globally dominant cultures. There is, after all, no jail to which UNESCO officials can send treaty violators, and as is the case with much of its work, the UN lacks meaningful enforcement authority over this treaty. The treaty even lacks the kind of legalized retaliation mechanisms that are embedded in GATT and WTO agreements: in those, signatories agree that if they violate the terms of the treaty, other parties can penalize trade items from the violating country with barriers like quotas and tariffs. Such language is not present in the UNESCO treaty, nor could the UN do much about regulating such terms in any case. But even more importantly, the global appeal of American popular culture (as one significant part of the overall global trade in culture) continues to expand. People across the world listen to American music (and, for that matter, watch American movies) and other cultural forms on their iPods; they wear American clothes; they eat at American restaurants. American culture has continued to spread regardless of the UNESCO treaty.

Rather than thinking of the UNESCO treaty as a credible limitation on the trade of American popular culture, it is probably more useful to see UNESCO's efforts as a symptom of a global skepticism about the cultural trading that is central to contemporary globalization. Regardless of the positions taken by U.S. trade negotiators in these matters, most people around the world both enjoy the products produced by the American popular culture industry *and* are fearful that these products are so suffused by the values, ideals, norms, rituals, behaviors, and styles of American life that they will overwhelm local, non-U.S. cultures. These fears are only intensified when economic livelihoods are put on the line, as happens when American goods and services compete with locally produced ones. Moreover, as is clear from chapter 4, American popular culture can influence social and political life in many ways beyond those detailed in this chapter. Cultural fears are thus likely to remain one of the central issues policymakers must contend with as globalization continues. They are also likely to generate some of the most intense reactions from people around the world who fear their ways of life are passing, only to be replaced by some new, essentially American, way of life.

## NAFTA

Tensions between desire for free trade and its general economic goods and fear of cultural competition can be examined in detail in the context of Canada-U.S.-Mexico relations as defined in the North American Free Trade Agreement (NAFTA). This trio of relationships is among the most important in the world. The United States and Canada share the world's longest undefended border, for example, and each is the other's biggest trading partner. The two countries have a virtually unmatched history of cooperation and peace. Similarly, Mexico provides the United States with much of its oil, and the complex dynamics of South and Latin American immigration (legal and illegal) into the United States have provided the source for great controversy, in the United States especially. Mexico is also a producer of large amounts of Spanish-language popular culture products sold and used in the United States.

Of course, for all the closeness of their relationships with the United States, both Canada and Mexico share certain problems in trade and cultural influence in their dealings with the United States. These are particularly acute for Canada. Canada, after all, is comparatively small in terms of population, having something over 34 million people (compared to the 312 million in the United States); it is predominantly English speaking (with the important exception of the province of Quebec); and it has its own domestic popular culture industry. In addition, Canadian policymakers believe that protecting its domestic popular culture industry is a crucial component of establishing and maintaining a Canadian national identity—a process made all the more difficult by the close relationship Canada has with the cultural behemoth that is the United States.[16]

Mexico, of course, is larger in population than Canada: it has a population of at least 113 million. Moreover, the fact that it is a Spanish-speaking nation insulates it somewhat from the power of American audiovisual culture artifacts, since these are usually produced in English. However, the economic power of the United States, combined with the global appeal of so much of American popular culture (both audiovisual and otherwise), works to make it harder for Mexico to maintain a cultural identity than it would have been were it not on the U.S. physical border.

Issues involving cultural trade were highlighted when the United States and Canada, along with Mexico, pursued and passed NAFTA in the 1990s. NAFTA lowered an array of trade barriers across North America. As is the case in trade negotiations across the world, during the NAFTA talks the United States sought to reduce restrictions both on international ownership of culture-producing institutions like movie studios and radio stations and on the exchange of goods and services traded across international borders. It also sought to reduce subsidies and other forms of government support for culture industries so that all nations would have to compete for market share on purely business grounds.

Canada and Mexico reacted to these American demands in ways that reflected their cultural vulnerability to the United States. Canadian negotiators, for example, resisted the American goals on much the same grounds as their European counterparts had. The Canadian Trade Negotiator's Office, for example, insisted, "It is critical to realize that open competition in a North American marketplace would threaten the ability (as well as the incentives) of our culture/communications industries to provide Canadian content to Canadian audiences. In this sense it would also threaten what gives us reason to call ourselves a sovereign nation."[17] Prime Minister Brian Mulroney likewise noted that

> Canadian cultural products are emphatically not the same as American cultural products. Cultural products express cultural identity, something individual to a given nation. Therefore, you cannot simply let American cultural products substitute freely for Canadian, unless you are willing to put open competition for its own sake ahead of maintaining our cultural heritage.[18]

Mexico took a starkly different position regarding trade in culture during the NAFTA talks. Mexico has a popular culture industry that serves a much larger market than does Canada's. Moreover, Mexico's movie, music, and television industries produce works in Spanish. This accords Mexican cultural products a degree of autonomy from American products not shared by Canadian works. Indeed, Mexican television shows, music, and movies have a substantial presence in Spanish-speaking populations in the United States itself—something that is not true of Canadian products created in English. American products are simply less competitive across this cultural gap. As a practical matter, the Canadian popular culture industry is far more vulnerable to American products than is Mexico's.

NAFTA reflects these cultural concerns. Canada enjoys special privileges when it comes to cultural trade that Mexico did not seek. For example, Annex 2106 exempts Canadian audiovisual industries from the free trade requirements embedded in the treaty. It also empowers the Canadian government to review and limit any U.S. investments in what the annex calls Canada's "cultural heritage or national identity"— clauses that generally refer to television stations, film production facilities, and the like.[19] Canada has thus been able to maintain its subsidies for film production and its ownership requirements for radio stations. As happened with other international trade negotiations, the United States consented to the culture exception in order to enhance the rest of the agreement on its terms.

In contrast, Mexican negotiators generally accepted the logic of free trade in their cultural exchanges with the United States. The major exceptions were that foreign ownership of Mexican audiovisual production companies was limited to 49 percent, and a quota of 30 percent was established for Mexican movies on theater screens. This quota, it should be noted, has never been enforced. As a consequence, the percentage of Mexican movies shown in Mexican theaters decreased to 10 percent by 1997.[20] Otherwise, trade in cultural products between the United States and Mexico is more in accord with the American vision of free trade than that of those nations, like Canada, that advocate for a cultural exception.

Notably, the Mexican case may ultimately undermine Canadian resistance to free cultural trade as regulated in NAFTA. American popular culture providers continue to pressure the U.S. government to reject protectionist cultural trade clauses in trade treaties. Among other threats, major American popular culture corporations have urged the U.S. government to place import tariffs on other Canadian products, such as lumber, to force the Canadian government to eliminate barriers to the free exchange of cultural artifacts. Mexican authorities, too, have recognized a large and growing market of Spanish speakers in Canada for whom Mexican-produced television programs and music might be particularly attractive. As a consequence, Mexican negotiators are also pushing Canada to reduce its trade restrictions on popular culture products.[21]

The likely outcome of these pressures is not immediately clear. However, the desire to protect culture and culture-producing enterprises from alien values and norms is clearly central to contemporary globalization, as is the desire to eliminate such barriers in favor of a truly free market. These competing goals are likely to continue to clash in the future. If anything, conflicts among those who wish to leverage the cultural and economic power of American popular culture products and those who wish to defend or protect local communities against what they see as threats to their continued existence are likely to intensify as more and more people around the world find American popular culture on the Internet, in their restaurants, in their towns and villages, and on their bodies as clothing. The future is therefore likely to bring a continuing cycle of claims from those who insist that free trade promotes freedom and from those who insist that trade in culture threatens national and cultural identity. Cultural cleavages can be expected to remain central forces in shaping contemporary globalization.

## AMERICAN POPULAR CULTURE AND
## FRAGMEGRATION IN FOUR COUNTRIES

The rest of this chapter explores the ways four countries—France, Iran, Venezuela, and Hong Kong—have responded to the challenges to their national identity and cohesion they assert are posed by American popular culture. It also explores state efforts to control social networking as part of a broader campaign to retain sovereignty in a global age.

Notably, the four countries under study here have little in common. France, like the United States, is an advanced industrial democracy. France and the United States have a long, deeply interconnected history: France helped the United States win its freedom and was, in turn, liberated by the United States and its allies in World War II. It has maintained an uneasy alliance with the United States in the years since. Regardless of their policy differences, however, the two nations share a common political and economic tradition.

Iran, by contrast, is a theocracy run by Islamic mullahs. Prior to 1979, Iran and the United States were close allies; however, after the Islamic Revolution of 1979, Iran's leaders declared the United States the "Great Satan" and became one of the most active enemies of the United States—in cultural as well as political affairs. Its current progress in enriching nuclear fuel has heightened tensions with the United States and other nations in the world as concerns grow that it is seeking to build nuclear weapons. Iran is, accordingly, an isolated nation overtly hostile to U.S. politics and culture.

Venezuela is a South American country that has had a mixed relationship with the United States throughout its history. Venezuela-U.S. relations have been volatile, as various American and Venezuelan leaders have tried to promote each nation's interests against the other. Today, the relationship between the United States and Venezuela is particularly tense because Venezuela's president, Hugo Chávez, has taken the lead in resisting U.S. economic and political authority in the Western Hemisphere.

Hong Kong was, for most of the twentieth century, a colony of Great Britain, and so a haven for American ideas and people. It was also a center of production of the associated products of American political culture—for example, T-shirts and other clothing, the actual videocassettes consumers purchased once a movie was released to video, and the like. In 1997, however, Hong Kong was returned to China's control, putting one of the world's economic powerhouses under the control of the world's largest avowedly Communist country.

The lack of a common political history or cultural tradition among these four countries is quite useful for this study. After all, it would not be all that surprising if groups and countries that share values and ideals reacted similarly to what might be seen as alien concepts or demands. However, to the degree that disparate systems react in similar ways, the influence of the independent force can be assessed. As will be seen, American popular culture is a source of controversy in each of the four countries examined here. In addition, its effects play along the three dimensions of globalization described in chapter 1: economic, political, and cultural.

## FRANCE

As was noted earlier, France was and remains one of the closest U.S. allies in world affairs. While relations between the United States and France are often tense, theirs are the differences of family members: they disagree about how best to achieve their otherwise shared goals of democracy, human rights, and capitalism. Hence even as U.S.-France relations wax and wane from tight alliance (the American Revolution, World War I, and World War II) to skeptical and even wary distance (the Napoleonic years, France's post–World War II rejection of NATO membership, and its refusal to support the United States in its wars with Iraq and Afghanistan), the relationship endures for social, political, economic, and ideological reasons.

However, France is in a relatively difficult position today in terms of its cultural identity. Indeed, much of the explanation for France's position as a leader of the opposition to globalization in cultural products derives from its status as a proud nation that has been a global leader for much of its history but that now worries that its language and its culture are slowly being lost. Comparatively few people worldwide now speak French, after all, particularly in comparison with the growth of English as a global language. Likewise, many French people believe that deeply embedded traditions of secularism and nationalism are under challenge as religiously active Muslims move to the country. In this context, French policymakers worry that American and other cultural products will push historically French products out of the marketplace and will remake French culture at the same time.

Such concerns seem credible when the dominance of American products in the French market is recognized. As recently as 1980, 50 percent of movies shown in France were French while only 31 percent were American. By 1990, the percentages were more than reversed: only 31 percent of movies shown in France were French in origin while 59 percent were American. The 39 percent market share that French movies attained in France in 2001 was the highest it had been in many years. In 1990, France exported only 35 million francs' worth of television programming to North America (which includes Canada's French-speaking province, Quebec), while importing 600 million francs' worth.[22]

French leaders have responded to these concerns with an array of rules and regulations that seek to protect France's distinctive culture. To protect the linguistic and cultural status of French, for example, France has passed a series of laws mandating use of the language. The most important of these has been a series of laws requiring the use of proper French in commercials, advertisements, and popular culture programming. Law 94-665, passed in August 1994, is typical. Article 1 notes the key position of the French language in French culture and goes on to state that French "shall be the language of instruction, work, trade and exchanges and of public services." Article 2 extends this requirement into the commercial sphere, requiring: "The use of French shall be mandatory for the designation, offer, presentation, instructions for use, and descriptions of the scope and conditions of a warranty of goods, products and services, as well as bills and receipts. The same provisions apply to any written, spoken, radio and television advertisement."[23]

French authorities have used this law to cite and fine companies, individuals, and even websites for violating the requirement for the public use of French. For example, just between January and April 1996, French language advocate groups brought 1,926 allegations of violations of Law 94-665 to the attention of French authorities; thirty-three convictions resulted from these efforts. A French linguistic society sued the Walt Disney Company for violating Law 94-665 at one of its Disney stores in Paris. While Disney initially fought the case, it conceded in time and removed the offending merchandise from the store's shelves. Another group sued the British cosmetics company The Body Shop for failing to translate the labels on products like pineapple face wash into

French, and yet another linguistic society sued the Georgia Institute of Technology—usually known as Georgia Tech—for failing to advertise its programs in French in online ads it offered there.[24]

Concerns about the erosion of French culture extend to the realm of social networking. In May 2011 France banned radio and television stations from urging audience members to go to the stations' Twitter feeds and Facebook pages for more information or to "like" the station. French authorities argue that such requests violate a 1992 law that bans "secret" promotion of non-French cultural artifacts. Thus even the use of social networking platforms is problematic in France's cultural space.[25]

The success of France's efforts to protect its culture is hard to assess. For example, English has hardly disappeared from daily use in France regardless of what French laws might say, and while subsidies to the French film industry (which in the early 1990s ran over $350 million per year) have allowed the nation to maintain an active role in movie production, American movies dominate French screens.[26] (French-made movies have virtually no presence in the United States, of course.) Similarly, while the French government can ban radio and television stations from explicitly referencing Facebook and Twitter, such social networking platforms are pervasive in France—and thus French people, especially younger people, have extraordinary access to American popular culture. Moreover, in light of French birthrates and the rate of immigration into France, it seems hard to believe that any restrictions on popular culture will ensure the survival of French culture as a majority of French people think of it today. However, the fact that the French are so fixated on protecting their culture is itself indicative of the importance of culture to contemporary globalization. France's restrictions may well be misaimed and ineffective, but they are passionately held. For the French, concerns about creeping Americanism are central to their relationships with the world at large.

## IRAN

Iran provides an interesting test case for the perceived influence of American popular culture on national and cultural identity for a number of reasons. From the mid-1950s through the end of the 1970s, Iran was one of the closest allies of the United States in the Middle East.

However, in 1979, the shah of Iran was overthrown and replaced by an Islamist government that rejected the Western-oriented social and economic programs of the shah's regime. Where the shah had offered his people, including women, the opportunity to get an education and enjoy the benefits of a consumerist society (while savagely repressing any movement for political or social equality or democracy), the theocratic state imposed by Muslim mullahs led by the Ayatollah Ruhollah Khomeini sought to enforce what it believed were true Muslim values like requiring women to cover their bodies and faces before going out in public and mandating that men should grow beards. Political control was centralized in Islamic councils that determined who could or could not become part of the government.

Tensions exploded between the United States and the new, theocratic Iranian government as soon as it came to power. Some of the reasons for this were immediate: a group of radical Iranian students occupied the U.S. embassy in Tehran starting in November 1979, for example, which is technically an act of war. They and a series of government supporters held more than fifty Americans hostage for the next 444 days, releasing them only after Ronald Reagan was inaugurated president of the United States on January 20, 1981. More broadly, Iran sponsored an embargo of oil shipments to the United States that sent the U.S. economy into a deep recession. Iran also sponsored the growth of other Islamist political movements like Hezbollah and Hamas in an effort to export its revolution and its anti-American sentiments. The United States considers these groups to be terrorist organizations. More recently, President Mahmoud Ahmadinejad of Iran has put his nation on a path that could lead it to build a nuclear weapon, a goal the United States opposes.

This international political struggle has continued in domestic and cultural affairs. Iranian policymakers have tried to insulate their citizens, particularly younger people, from what they consider to be the corrupting influence of American popular culture on what Iranian youths see, think, and want. Iran passed laws outlawing satellite dishes, Western music, and Western movies. It further established standards of dress that forbade women in particular from wearing Western clothing or makeup. Perhaps most famously, in 1989 Ayatollah Khomeini issued a fatwa, or religious order, that authorized any Muslim to kill the author of *The Satanic Verses*, an Indian-born ex-Muslim named Salman

Rushdie. In many ways, then, Iran can be seen to have attempted to isolate itself from the effects of Western ideas and experiences, including those associated with American popular culture.

These efforts to isolate Iran from American and Western culture have found supporters in Iran. More conservative members of Iranian society clearly link Westernization and Americanization as the forces they are fighting to resist. One, a woman named Khaki, notes: "You as a person should never forget your country. Iranian people prefer to go out of the country and show themselves as American." Similarly, she notes, "My uncle has been in the U.S. for 25 years. I can never accept his ideas. Too much democracy."[27] Other social conservatives have come to believe that encroaching American popular culture is a dangerous consequence of globalization, one that threatens the stability and cultural integrity of Iran. As Ayatollah Jannati put it, "The biggest vice facing us is the cultural offensive. . . . What are those seeking the opening of the way for the U.S. thinking about? Why are you betraying Islam?"[28]

It is not particularly surprising, of course, that social conservatives resist change—such resistance is a useful working definition of what it means to be a social conservative, regardless of one's country or community. However, many nonconservatives have also expressed worry at the threat of an American cultural invasion in Iran. Even people who have largely accepted the goods and benefits associated with Western life and American culture—*Titanic* and Nike, Levi's and rock and roll—are concerned that American popular culture will destroy Iranian culture. As a particular example, Iranian filmmakers—even reform-oriented, progressive ones—have worried that the unleashing of restrictions on American movies will lead to American cultural imperialism and the destruction of the native film industry.[29] Thus, like French and other policymakers who are otherwise supportive of globalization, some Iranian progressives worry that American corporate power may undermine the economic environment in which some Iranians make their living.

It is not clear that Iran's efforts to isolate itself from the feared consequences of exposure to American popular culture are working, however. Younger women have begun insisting on the right to wear something other than the *hijab* and have spent years slowly amending the published dress code to allow more hair and more skin to be exposed in what has been called the "pink revolution."[30] In addition, many young people are teaching themselves English through the Internet, as well as with imported Western music and satellite television; they are, at the same time, exposed to and drawn to Western fashion and programming and social styles. (While satellites are banned in Iran, the ban is flouted openly and satellite dishes are common there.) Movies like *Titanic, Face/Off,* and *Air Force One* have been widely available through satellite services and bootleg videotapes for many years.[31] American popular culture has undoubtedly led many Iranians to desire closer contacts with the rest of the world.

Notably, in response to this period of liberalization, Iran's religious leadership exercised its constitutional authority to strike the names of candidates it deemed unacceptable for election to the national assembly and a wide range of regional offices. Many reform leaders were excluded from elections both in 2004 and in 2005. As a consequence, a new, more conservative leadership came into power in Iran without the legitimacy of having won a truly representative election.

The cultural and political tensions between traditionalists and progressive forces within Iran were violently exposed in the summer of 2009. That year, protests broke out in the aftermath of what were widely believed to be fraudulent elections in Iran. Protestors, who were disproportionately young people, took to the streets to express their frustration that their hopes for greater political and social freedom had been thwarted by the regime.

These protests, it should be noted, occurred only a few months after Facebook had been unlocked to Iranian members. The Iranian government began to allow its citizens to join Facebook in February 2009; a month later, it was the twelfth most popular website in Iran. Young Iranians joined to share their political and social views in a relatively free way.[32]

Facebook became a central tool of the Iranian rebellion. In particular, video footage shot on a cell phone of a young Iranian woman, Neda Soltani, lying dead on the street, a victim of Iranian security forces, went viral and served as a rallying cry for anti-regime activists. Like-minded people and groups used Facebook to organize their efforts to bring down the Iranian government. While their efforts were ultimately unsuccessful—the regime violently crushed the uprising—their actions served as a training tool for a later round of rebellions: the Arab Spring revolts of 2010–2012 (discussed later in this chapter).

American popular culture is thus at the heart of political and social tension in Iran. Whether it is the demand for access to American movies, music, and television programs or the demand for the kinds of personal and political freedoms implicit in social networking, American popular culture stands in conflict with the traditionalist, authoritarian ambitions of the Iranian political leadership. Moreover, the leadership seems to understand this, and it takes active steps to try to lessen or avoid what it sees as the negative effects of American popular culture in Iranian society. The globalization of American popular culture is central to contemporary political and social life in Iran.

### VENEZUELA

Like Iran, Venezuela has had a varyingly open and/or tense relationship with the United States. It is an important producer of oil, much of which is exported to the United States. The United States is Venezuela's biggest trade partner and the single largest recipient of Venezuelan oil exports. Venezuela is also the fifth-largest export market for U.S.-produced goods and services in Latin and South America. In addition, Venezuela shares a border with Colombia. The United States provides substantial support to the government of Venezuela to assist the United States in interdicting illegal drugs being transported from Colombia for consumption in the United States.[33] Political values also encourage close relations between the two nations: legally, Venezuela has been a stable, democratic government since the late 1950s. (As will be discussed below, the long rule of Venezuelan President Hugo Chávez has led some to question the authenticity of Venezuela's commitment to democracy.)

Relations between the two nations have not always been amicable. Venezuela, for example, fell within the zone of influence of the so-called Monroe Doctrine, in which the United States claimed the right to intervene in the political affairs of any country in the Western Hemisphere in order to protect U.S. interests. This bald assertion of U.S. power left many Venezuelans with the sense that the United States was an exploiter rather than a partner. More recently, Hugo Chávez has become an international hero to the anti-globalization movement worldwide for his efforts to extricate Venezuela from the globalization process shaping the world today. In turn, the United States has accused Chávez of creating an authoritarian dictatorship with only the facade of democracy, as constitutional changes have allowed Chávez to remain in office longer than he otherwise could have, and have allowed him to concentrate political power in his office. The United States is likewise displeased with Chávez's close ties with Cuba, a nation with which the United States has had a dispute for more than fifty years.

At the core of Chávez's objections to contemporary globalization—objections shared by many of his supporters both inside and outside Venezuela—are the inequities that often emerge as free trade and other aspects of globalization expand in various societies. As was noted in chapter 1, globalization is often accompanied by significant disruption in people's jobs and lives as new, often foreign, companies enter local markets and provide goods and services more cheaply than the community can. (Walmart's "Always Low Prices" slogan serves as a useful example here: their prices are low because of high volumes of international sales and the corporation's concomitant ability to negotiate cheap prices from suppliers. Local stores lack such sales and negotiating power and so cannot offer the cheap prices available at Walmart. Many therefore go out of business. Moreover, these jobs are often replaced by lower-paying jobs if they are replaced at all: a job at Walmart is likely to pay less, and have fewer or no benefits, compared with a person's pre-Walmart job.) Many people find their lives devastated as a consequence.

Notably, such disruptions are not always economic. As has been clear throughout this book, new cultural forms and products also enter globalized societies. These can undermine existing rites and practices and devastate local forms. These new forms are, of course, particularly attractive to younger, technologically savvy, and connected people, thus opening the prospect that a particular culture will die out as the young opt to enter the global—perhaps American—world order. Cultural disruption can be at least as traumatic as economic disruption, if not more so.

Of course, many others benefit from globalization. Investors do, at least most of the time, as do those who supply the new transnational companies with services and goods the companies cannot acquire elsewhere. In some cases, they benefit by becoming extraordinarily wealthy. Others benefit from the corruption that often follows the infusion of large amounts of foreign currency. This, in turn, makes it easy for some to acquire good educations for their children, good homes for their families, and good health insurance for their loved ones, even as others struggle to feed themselves. Children and families who learn English and grow comfortable in the new global community can succeed in ways their parents and grandparents never imagined.

Hugo Chávez has become a populist hero, both in Venezuela and among anti-globalization groups worldwide, by using Venezuela's status and wealth as a major oil exporter to limit the power of transnational corporations in favor of lessening inequities in Venezuelan society. (In so doing, of course, he made himself an enemy to those people and groups who had benefited from globalization, including many inside Venezuela itself.) For example, in 2001 Chávez promoted a hydrocarbons law that limited foreign ownership of Venezuelan oil companies. The law nationalized the production and distribution of oil, making profits earned from the sale of oil a part of the state's budget rather than a corporation's. It further limited the degree to which foreign companies could own other aspects of the oil production industry.[34]

Chávez has used the new revenue derived from oil production to increase social programs aimed at the poor and disadvantaged across Venezuela. The money has been used to build schools and health clinics across the country. Against the claims of the globalizers, Chávez insists that the state can still play an important role in limiting the worst effects of globalization in its home country—at least when the nation in question controls a large amount of a significant resource like oil.

Chávez has gone further in his anti-globalization rhetoric and policies than simply redistributing revenue within Venezuela. He has opposed U.S. efforts to push for lower oil prices and has established close ties to the Cuban government against U.S. wishes. He has opposed U.S. policy in Iraq and is the region's leading opponent of establishing a free trade agreement among the United States and the countries of Latin and South America. In November 2005, he successfully opposed the creation of CAFTA, the Central America Free Trade Agreement, at a conference of hemispheric leaders in Argentina. Chávez has consequently become a symbol of the rejection of Western-style American globalization. He has also become a major thorn in the side of U.S.

policymakers. In perhaps the most extreme example of the kind of intense anger Chávez has generated among American leaders, one conservative American activist, the Christian evangelical leader Pat Robertson, once used his television religious/news show, *The 700 Club*, to call for Chávez's assassination by U.S. Special Forces.

Notably, there has been a popular culture component to Chávez's anti-globalization challenge. In the summer of 2005, in an effort to oppose the threat of American cultural imperialism and to guarantee the diversity of Venezuelan music against American cultural homogenization, Venezuela passed a law requiring that 50 percent of all music played on its radio stations be Venezuelan in origin. The effect of the law, in turn, was to challenge the globalizers' assertions that American popular culture was providing a market for the products people truly wanted to enjoy: in the aftermath of the law's passage, sales of traditional Venezuelan music skyrocketed, while sales of American acts declined. One record store manager in Caracas put it: "We've always had traditional Venezuelan records in stock, but before a few months ago we never sold any—not one. It was all Britney Spears, Backstreet Boys and that sort of thing. But now I'd say one-third of our business comes from Venezuelan artists, which is absolutely incredible." Similarly, a nineteen-year-old Venezuelan music fan noted, "It's kind of fashion now to listen to traditional music. It has just taken off in three months."[35]

The United States insists Venezuela has other restrictions on trade in popular culture as well. Foreign musical performers giving concerts in Venezuela have to give equal stage time to national entertainers. Venezuelan movie theaters have to comply with annual quota requirements that dictate the distribution and exhibition of Venezuelan films. At least half of the nation's television programming must be produced in Venezuela.[36]

While popular culture is only a small component of Venezuela's challenge to the integrationist forces at the core of the globalization process, it plays an important role in generating national pride and identity. Given the hostility of the United States to the Chávez regime, this reservoir of nationalism may prove to be an important resource as Venezuela attempts to chart a course of trade with, but not domination by, the United States, economically, politically, and culturally. American popular culture is clearly not as controversial in Venezuela as it is in both France and Iran, but it remains a continuing point of contention between the two countries.

## HONG KONG

The case of Hong Kong offers another, but very different, example of the way American popular culture shapes contemporary globalization. Through much of the twentieth century, Hong Kong had one of the world's most powerful capitalist economies. Its status as a British colony with a unique combination of a large population of well-educated people, one of the world's most accessible and strategic ports, and very loose regulations on business encouraged many companies to set up operations there. So successful was this combination of forces that in the latter half of the twentieth century Hong Kong became one of the so-called Asian Tigers, the Asian economic superpowers like Japan, South Korea, and Singapore (another small island nation with a global economic presence far larger than its geographic position would predict). Hong Kong was a central hub in the emerging globalist capitalist order from at least the 1950s on.

Given Hong Kong's status as a British colony, English became the common language there. The colony also enjoyed relative political and social freedoms, including access to and widespread enjoyment of an array of popular culture entertainments from the United States, Thailand, Korea, Japan, and China.[37] As a consequence, Hong Kong's citizens were broadly integrated into the West's economic, political, and cultural systems throughout the twentieth century.

This integration was challenged in 1997, when, as required by treaty, Hong Kong reverted to Chinese rule. While this event would have always been significant, it was actually momentous for one reason more than any other: mainland China's government became Communist in 1949, meaning that once transferred, one of the world's most capitalist communities would come under control of the world's largest Communist country. Accordingly, the reversion of Hong Kong to Chinese rule meant that one of the most productive, integrated capitalist economies in the world was to be administered by a nation whose formal political doctrine was anticapitalist. Moreover, China does not practice Western legal and political principles like democracy and human rights. Many people wondered how—or whether—Hong Kong could survive the transition.

At one level, the concerns of those who doubted China could effectively manage a capitalist Hong Kong were misbegotten. By 1997, China had begun a large-scale process of turning significant areas of its countryside into havens for capitalist production and development. Shanghai, in particular, has grown into an enormous city in a region in which capitalist business practices are encouraged both for international corporations wishing to trade with or manufacture products in China and for Chinese people who wish to engage in entrepreneurial capitalist business ventures themselves. China promised to allow Hong Kong to continue to play its central role in international capitalist trade on a similar basis and has largely done so in the years since it assumed political management of the former British colony.

At another level, however, concerns about Chinese rule seem appropriate. To return to the arguments described earlier in this chapter, it is worth remembering that many advocates of globalization insist that capitalism and democracy are inextricably intertwined. The argument goes that nations would have to allow their people to be as creative and innovative as possible in order to compete in a global economy. This, in turn, would require democracy and other forms of respect for human rights. Chinese policy, by contrast, is grounded on the assertion that capitalist economic growth can be separated from democracy and demands for human rights. As a consequence, Shanghai remains under strong control of the state, and individual rights are not protected there. When China took over administration of Hong Kong, it assumed control of an area that had not only been capitalist for a long time but had been relatively integrated into Western norms of democracy and human rights as well. While China promised to promote democracy in Hong Kong, it has not, in fact, done so. This is a profound challenge.

Given the linkages among capitalism, globalization, and American popular culture, there is inevitably a connection between American popular culture and the way China manages Hong Kong. For example, large numbers of the actual consumer goods people enjoy that are based on popular American movies, music, and television programs (e.g., action figurines, CDs, DVDs, clothes, T-shirts, bags, dolls, and everything in between) are manufactured in Hong Kong. Hong Kong is also one of the world's largest producers of illegal bootleg copies of American popular culture products, many of which are bought and sold across mainland China. This fact poses a problem for Chinese authorities, who want their citizens to participate in a capitalist system but also wish to avoid the political and social ideas embedded in the items they produce: if American popular culture tends to corrupt or replace indigenous values, Chinese policymakers have to figure out how to make people capitalist without also making them democratic or even American.

One particularly interesting example of Chinese efforts to limit the potentially pernicious threat of American popular culture can be seen in the relationship the Chinese government has established with The Walt Disney Company. Disney has built a theme park in China, Disneyland Hong Kong. However, the Hong Kong government invested almost 80 percent of the cost of building the park and owns 57 percent control of it. As a consequence, the government can control what does or does not go into the park.

Of course it does not follow that, to adapt a marketing slogan from Las Vegas, "What happens in Hong Kong stays in Hong Kong." From the perspective of the Chinese government, Hong Kong was "special"— a community already integrated into the politics and economics of the wider world. This does not mean, however, that China would support bringing American popular culture products to the mainland. And, indeed, China later resisted the Disney company's request to build a theme park in Shanghai. Notably, this resistance resulted from Disney's insistence that it would need to broadcast the Disney Channel in China to introduce its characters to the nation's population. China's leaders were unwilling to have such blatantly American programming on their airwaves.[38] Disney has subsequently announced plans to open a theme park in Shanghai by 2016. A Chinese company has taken majority ownership of the park, with Disney retaining a 43% ownership share.[39]

The Internet provides a particularly challenging environment for the Chinese government to act to limit the effects of Western ideas or entertainments in Chinese life. The rise of Facebook and other social networking services, along with Google's seemingly inescapable grasp of Internet searches, offers a strong challenge to any government that seeks to control its citizens access to information the government does not want them to see. This is particularly true for a nation like China, which is deeply embedded in the global economy and has a rapidly growing class of wealthy, technologically engaged citizens. For example, as was noted in chapter 4, China has embraced American fast food.

It seems to desire the commercial aspects of American popular culture while fearing the political and social implications of an open society. So how does a nation promote McDonald's and KFC but not allow its citizens to explore news and audiovisual programming as well?

China regulates Internet content quite heavily, banning many sites related to democracy, human rights, or religious groups and ideas that are forbidden to operate in China. Indeed, its efforts are so extensive that critics refer to it as the "Great Firewall of China." In seeking to control the kinds of information its citizens have access to, China runs its own social networking sites. These are monitored by government officials. Likewise, Internet searches and download traffic are routed through government-controlled servers so that authorities can enforce their rules with state-managed content filters. They have also compelled international corporations to agree to filter their search responses in China: both Microsoft and Google have at times agreed to comply with Chinese law and limit various banned search terms. (Google has now withdrawn from its agreement and no longer legally operates in China.) In another, quite disturbing case, the Internet search and content firm Yahoo! gave the Chinese government the name of a Chinese dissident journalist who had posted information embarrassing to the Chinese government on one of its sites in Hong Kong. Notably, this provision of information occurred without a court order, as Hong Kong law requires. (The dissident journalist was sentenced to ten years in jail.[40])

It should be noted that it is not clear that China's efforts to restrict its citizens' Internet access are entirely successful. For example, anyone with access to a VPN client can log directly in to computers based outside China and access the Internet openly and freely. Additionally, Chinese Internet users have become skilled at using code words to avoid censors. For example, the phrase "empty chair" has no inherent offensive meaning. However, Chinese users know that it refers to Nobel Prize–winning dissident Liu Xiaobo, who was not allowed to travel to Oslo, Norway, to receive his Peace Prize—and whose absence from the ceremony was symbolized by an empty chair on the central dais. Other code words and phrases exist. To be "harmonized" is to be censored, since "harmony" is one of the goals of official Chinese policy that is used to justify censorship in the first place. Chinese Internet users have even found a way to swear online: the words for "grass mud horse" sound, when spoken together, like a Chinese swear word. Websites marked with this word are advertising their status as sites opposing China's censorship practices.[41]

In sum, like France, Iran, and Venezuela, even a nation as powerful and prominent as China shapes its policies and actions in tension with American popular culture. China is open to, and indeed is a significant participant in making and distributing many of the products that shape the global market in culture artifacts. Yet it shies away from embracing the political and social values embedded in much of American popular culture and seeks to prevent its people from experiencing these ideas and attitudes. It is, like much of the rest of the world, both attracted to and wary of the American popular culture juggernaut.

## SOCIAL NETWORKS, POLITICAL REVOLUTIONS? THE CASE OF THE ARAB SPRING

One reason nations like Iran and China might be particularly worried about the political and social content of American popular culture can be seen in the way American cultural artifacts like social network services played a central role in the so-called Arab Spring, the series of political uprisings that swept across much of the Arab world from Tunisia to Syria from the winter of 2010 through the spring of 2012. Starting with a wave of protests in Tunisia that led to the ouster of the longtime dictator of that country, Zine El Abidine Ben Ali, and continuing through violent uprisings in Syria in winter 2012, numerous countries—Egypt, Libya, Yemen, Bahrain, Saudi Arabia, Jordan, Kuwait, and Algeria among them—have faced revolutions and rebellions that led to the end of the dominant regime (Tunisia and Egypt); a civil war that led to the death of one of the world's longest-ruling leaders (Libya); a coup that replaced another authoritarian ruler (Yemen); and political violence that has been viciously suppressed (Bahrain, Algeria) or is ongoing (Syria). Change is happening across a wide swath of regimes that have been notable mostly for their stability and their cruel repression of their citizens' freedoms.

For the purposes of this book, what matters about these rebellions and revolutions is that they were for the most part organized through social networking services like Facebook and Twitter. (Obviously the revolutions are more important than the means by which they were undertaken. However, this is not a book on the Arab Spring.) The

Tunisian revolution, for example, is now recognized to have started when a young Tunisian street vendor, Mohamed Bouazizi, set himself on fire after being abused by a Tunisian government official. As horrible as this act of self-immolation was, in and of itself it was unlikely to set off a political revolution: terrible things happen all over the world all the time, and for the most part life continues as usual. In this case, however, antiregime activists in Tunisia used Bouazizi's plight as a symbol of political protest. They turned to Twitter and Facebook to both publicize the abuses that led to Bouazizi's suicide and to recruit and organize new activists to protest the authoritarian Tunisian regime. Essentially, tech-savvy protestors mobilized a resource they understood but the state didn't to draw in large numbers of Facebook and Twitter users to work to overthrow the Tunisian regime. And, notably, this strategy worked: Bouazizi burned himself in mid-December 2010; President Ben Ali fled the country after the Tunisian Army abandoned him just a month later.

The tactics that worked in Tunisia were tried elsewhere, most notably in Egypt through spring 2011. While the Egyptian Revolution took longer and was much bloodier than the Tunisian Revolution, the outcome was the same: a dictator of long standing was deposed in favor of a regime the people hoped would take steps to build a democracy in their country.

Notably, Egypt attempted to stop the use of social networks as a tool of political revolution by quite literally pulling the plug on the nation's Internet service. The idea was to sever the link between the revolution's leaders and the users of social network services, and thereby to quell the growing protests. After all, regardless of the protestors' desires for democracy, human rights, and economic opportunities, the regime wished to survive in its privileged, authoritarian position. However, organizers and activists were able to cobble together landline telephones, fax machines, and access to Internet servers outside Egypt to continue their protest planning activities. In the end, the ubiquity and decentralized nature of the digital world defeated the regime's efforts to quash online organizing.

The success of these two revolutions, along with the ousters of autocrats in Yemen and Libya, led some commentators to suggest that these were "Facebook revolutions." The notion was that Facebook was the key to the revolution—that without it, or perhaps Twitter as well, the revolutions in Tunisia and Egypt would not have been possible. Indeed, Egypt's revolution was undoubtedly facilitated when Wael Ghonim, an Egyptian-born Google executive living in Dubai, set up a Facebook page to commemorate the death of an Egyptian man named Khaled Said at the hands of Egyptian government officials. As happened in Tunisia, this act of commemoration inspired passion among those angry with the regime; Ghonim reported that just two minutes after he created his tribute page to Khaled Said, three hundred people had joined it.[42] Social networks certainly provided platforms on which revolutions could be built.

That said, calling such revolutions "Facebook" revolutions seems profoundly blind to the sacrifices and risks taken by the peoples of Tunisia and Egypt and Syria and Bahrain and elsewhere as they sought political and economic freedom. They, not Facebook, deserve credit for the risks they took and the goals they achieved. Social networking platforms provided a readily accessible tool that protestors could use to organize challenges to regimes that were well established and seemed quite stable, but they did not undermine the regimes themselves.

Whether or not the Arab Spring was made up of "Facebook" revolutions is not, of course, really the issue here. Instead, the prominence of Facebook and Twitter in these revolutions serves to highlight the profound role that American popular cultural artifacts can play in social and political affairs. Put another way, while it is wrong to assert that Facebook *caused* the Arab Spring, it is also hard to imagine how the revolutions and rebellions that have swept the Arab world would have happened *without* such social networks. As such, they can be seen to have played an important role in world affairs, albeit one never anticipated by their creators.

## CONCLUSION

The relative success that antigovernment forces had in using Facebook, Twitter, and similar services to manage their revolutions highlights the reasons that governments like those of Iran and China seek to control and manage such platforms. After all, whether or not you or I approve of the ways a particular government abuses its citizens' rights and dignities, the governments themselves wish to retain power. Accordingly, whether it is fear that a social network will be used to organize a revolution, or that the Internet (and even Disney) will expose its people to values and ideals the government thinks will challenge the regime's authority, governments all over the world seek to control and limit the effects of American popular culture.

In addition, whether in individual cases or as a matter of international law, American popular culture has been and remains one of the most divisive, most limiting forces in the process of globalization. Fears of both the economic and the cultural power of American popular culture are central to international efforts to restrain its effects on people's lives around the world. While this chapter has explored these tensions only in the arenas of the global audiovisual industry, the scope of popular culture is broad and deep. American pressures to make the trade in cultural artifacts mere commodities of exchange as part of the larger process of globalization may well be encouraging the fragmentation that globalization seems inevitably to stimulate. It is, in any case, central both to the way globalization has developed and to its likely future.

## NOTES

1. Quoted in Simona Fuma Shapiro, "The Culture Thief," *New Rules*, Fall 2000, 10, http://www.newrules.org/publications/new-rules-journal-fall-2000.

2. Quoted in Patricia M. Goff, *Limits to Liberalization: Local Culture in a Global Marketplace* (Ithaca, N.Y.: Cornell University Press, 2007), 142–43.

3. Quoted in Shapiro, "Culture Thief."

4. Cultural Industries Sectoral Advisory Group on International Trade, *An International Agreement on Cultural Diversity: A Model for Discussion*, September 2002, 4–5.

5. Music Council of Australia, *Submission to the Department of Foreign Affairs and Trade's Office of Trade Negotiations*, 28 January 2003.

6. Goff, *Limits to Liberalization*, 90.

7. Goff, *Limits to Liberalization*, 24–35.

8. Hernan Galperin, "Cultural Industries in the Age of Free-Trade Agreements," *Canadian Journal of Communications* 24, no. 1 (1999): 49–77.

9. Quoted in Goff, *Limits to Liberalization*, 120.

10. Galperin, "Cultural Industries."

11. Galperin, "Cultural Industries."

12. UN News Centre, "New UN Treaty to Preserve World's Rich Cultural Diversity to Come into Force in March," 19 December 2006, http://www.un.org/apps/news/story.asp?NewsID=21046&Cr=UNESCO&Cr1 (accessed 21 February 2012).

13. UNESCO, "Convention on the Protection and Promotion of the Diversity of Cultural Expressions," 20 October 2005, http://portal.unesco.org/en/ev.php-URL_ID=31038&URL_DO=DO_TOPIC&URL_SECTION=201.html (accessed 2 March 2012).

14. UNESCO, "Convention."

15. UN News Centre, "New UN Treaty."

16. See Goff, *Limits to Liberalization*, 36–56, for an extended discussion of the issues facing Canada in relation to the United States.

17. Quoted in Goff, *Limits to Liberalization*, 44.

18. Quoted in Goff, *Limits to Liberalization*, 55.

19. Galperin, "Cultural Industries."

20. Galperin, "Cultural Industries."

21. Galperin, "Cultural Industries."

22. Goff, *Limits to Liberalization*, 85.

23. http://www.dglf.culture.gouv.fr/droit/loi-gb.htm (accessed 21 February 2012).

24. Christine Vanston, "In Search of the *Mot Juste*: The Toubon Law and the European Union," *Boston College International and Comparative Law Review* 22, no. 1 (1999): 175–93, http://lawdigitalcommons.bc.edu/cgi/viewcontent.cgi?article=1217&context=iclr (accessed 21 February 2012).

25. "France Bans Facebook and Twitter Promotion on TV," http://www.france24.com/en/20110606-business-technology-france-regulators-ban-facebook-twitter-promotion-on-tv (accessed 21 February 2012).

26. Benjamin Barber, *Jihad vs. McWorld: How Globalism and Tribalism Are Reshaping the World* (New York: Ballantine Books, 1996), 92.

27. "Iranian Youth Divided on Future," *Toronto Star Newspapers*, 8 June 2003.

28. John Lancaster, "Barbie, 'Titanic' Show Good Side of U.S.," *Washington Post*, 27 October 1998, http://www.washingtonpost.com/wp-srv/inatl/longterm/mia/part3.htm (accessed 2 March 2012).

29. Lancaster, "Barbie."

30. Barbara Slavin, "New Attitudes Color Iranian Society, Culture," *USA Today*, 28 February 2005, http://www.usatoday.com/news/world/2005-02-28-iran-pink_x.htm (accessed 21 February 2012).

31. Lancaster, "Barbie."

32. Maryam Sinalee, "Iran's Youth Sign Up to Facebook," http://www.thenational.ae/news/world/middle-east/irans-youth-sign-up-to-facebook (accessed 21 February 2012).

33. U.S. Department of State, "Background Note: Venezuela," http://www.state.gov/r/pa/ei/bgn/35766.htm (accessed 21 February 2012).

34. U.S. Department of State, "Venezuela."

35. SFGate.com, "Venezuela Imposes National Music Quotas, Law Limits Airplay for Foreign Tunes," 19 July 2005, http://www.sfgate.com/cgi-bin/article .cgi?f=/c/a/2005/07/19/MNG5FDQ2NI1.DTL (accessed 21 February 2012).

36. Shapiro, "Culture Thief."

37. For a fuller discussion, see Wai-Chung Ho, "A Cross-Cultural Study of Preferences for Popular Music among Hong Kong and Thailand Youths," *Journal of Intercultural Communication* 7 (September 2004).

38. Keith Bradsher, "Disney Takes Exception to China's Media Rules," *New York Times,* 12 September 2005, http://www.nytimes.com/2005/09/12/ business/worldbusiness/12disney.html (accessed 2 March 2012).

39. "Fact Sheet," http://en.shanghaidisneyresort.com.cn/en/press/company -information/fact-sheet (accessed 23 February 2012).

40. BBC News, "Yahoo 'Helped Jail China Writer,'" 7 September 2005, http://news.bbc.co.uk/go/pr/fr/-/2/hi/asia-pacific/4221538.stm (accessed 2 March 2012).

41. Maria Shao, "Chinese Take Creative Approach to Internet Censorship," http://sprie.gsb.stanford.edu/news/3225 (accessed 23 February 2012).

42. Jose Antonio Vargas, "Spring Awakening," *New York Times Book Review*, 19 February 2012, 12.

# CHAPTER 6

## AMERICAN POPULAR CULTURE AND THE FUTURE OF GLOBALIZATION

As has been seen throughout this book, there is something different about the products of American popular culture. The early transnational corporations that produced movies, music, and television programs took advantage of permissive laws, an open culture, a diverse audience, and ideal filmmaking weather to build global empires of audiovisual entertainment—empires that gave American producers an advantage in competing for the mass international entertainment audience that exists today. As a consequence, American movies, music, and television programming, whether produced in the United States or derived from forms of entertainment created by Americans, largely dominate world trade in popular audiovisual culture.

American influence in popular culture goes beyond the audiovisual industry, of course. People around the world wear American styles of clothing, eat at American restaurants, drink American concoctions, and even enjoy distinctively American forms of sport. They connect through social networking services that are grounded on American styles of social interaction and serve as access points to multiple components of American popular culture—and can serve as platforms on which to build political and social revolutions. Chapters 3 and 4 chronicled a small number of these American cultural products, but it is worth remembering here that Coca-Cola spawned countless competitors, as did McDonald's and blue jeans—and Facebook, for that matter. Football is only the most recent American sport to go global: baseball and basketball have had audiences around the world for decades. These forms of popular culture, along with the audiovisual industries and many others, have spread American business styles, American cultural practices, and even American English as a mode of what sometimes seems to be universal communication across the planet. American popular culture is a global juggernaut.

The popularity of American cultural products derives, at least in part, from the transparency and flexibility they embody. In creating works to satisfy an American audience, U.S. producers learned to appeal to a broad audience. They also grew into powerful companies that could take advantage of global economic and political changes to build a worldwide market for their goods. This business synergy made American products attractive around the world. American products and styles emerged from a U.S. context into a global community that was remarkably open to integrating American goods and services into their cultures.

Yet the transparent appeal and corporate power that gave American producers of popular culture a comparative advantage in world trade have brought fear to the hearts of many people and communities worldwide. Some groups fear that members of their communities will abandon their traditional, local cultures in favor of an Americanized, global one. Others fear that American companies will use their power and wealth to drive local producers out of the market. Yet others fear both. Ways of life, after all, are found both in cultural products and in the means of making them in the first place. American popular culture can challenge both.

The history of the twentieth and early twenty-first centuries, at least in terms of popular culture, has seen the global spread of American popular culture go hand in hand with international efforts to restrict

its influence. Global trade agreements have sought to both protect local culture producers and cultural forms and to allow large numbers of
people worldwide to seek American movies, music, television, clothes,
food, sports, and other cultural artifacts. If nothing else, globalization
has made American popular culture a flashpoint across the world.

This chapter assesses the likely future of American popular culture
as an agent of globalization. It argues that those who fear the global
trade in American popular culture have reified and sanctified current
cultural orders into eternal "cultures" that need protection from the
prevarications of cultural "others." This chapter challenges this frozen
vision of cultures in conflict. Culture is a more flexible concept than
is generally recognized, a fact that will shape the future ways in which
the globalization of American popular culture occurs. However, fears
of corruption, imperialism, and homogenization will likely continue as
long as human beings seek to train their children to share their values
and to live in communities of like-minded people—in other words, as
long as there are cultures. But the nature and terms of the debate will
shift over time as both the products of American popular culture and
the audiences that enjoy them change. This change will subsequently
alter the way American popular culture affects globalization as a process toward globality. While it is likely that true globality will never
be achieved, it is also the case that American popular culture cannot
and will not utterly corrupt, overwhelm, or wash away all diversity in
cultures across the globe.

## CULTURAL CHANGE, HYBRIDITY, AND AMERICAN POPULAR CULTURE

The discussions of Canada, France, Iran, Venezuela, Hong Kong, and
the Arab Spring offered in chapter 5 showed that policymakers across
these countries and regions feared that American popular culture could
remake the local one. French and Canadian leaders both worry that
American culture would replace a distinctively French or Canadian
culture and fear that American corporations will drive domestic companies out of business as well. Iran seeks to keep its people free from the
temptations of American popular culture, albeit incompletely, while
Venezuela considers its internal popular culture industry both a source
of national pride and an important contributor to the national identity.

While China favors Disney's operations in Hong Kong, it worries that Disney might undermine local values elsewhere in the country—even in Shanghai, one of the most globalized cities on earth. And, of course, Arab rulers now overthrown or facing rebellion did not want to face such upheavals—even if those of us outside the region might think the Arab Spring is a politically good thing.

These reactions are grounded in a common concern that transcends even the obvious economic reasons some nations oppose free trade American products. They are grounded on the sense that American popular culture can transform local cultures into something different. American popular culture is seen as an agent of change in the local culture that robs what is distinctive and unique at home and replaces it with a globalized, American social and political order.

## TYPES OF CULTURAL CHANGE

The fear that American popular culture can remake local cultures rests on the belief that cultures are basically fixed and immutable and so do not change easily over time. In this view, "culture" exists as a whole of integrated values, practices, and rituals, and if cultural change occurs, it is usually coerced and illegitimate. Change is seen to result from the imposition of one set of cultural values on another people, such that the weaker culture loses its identity and is effectively wiped out.

The sense that cultural change is inevitably coercive derives in part from culture's basic stability. After all, cultures can be said to exist as definable and recognizable things only if they persist long enough for some group or community to develop a set of ideals, attitudes, rituals, norms, and behaviors that distinguish them from some other group or community. Since cultures are relatively stable, changes, particularly dramatic changes, are generally seen to be unlikely.

The sense that cultural change is the result of hostile takeovers also rests on a streak of xenophobia common to all cultures. Every culture, after all, defines itself both in terms of what its members believe/feel/ do and in terms of what those members do not believe/feel/do. By definition, aliens and strangers stand in some degree of tension with the local culture. If cultural changes occur while the local group is in contact with some stranger or strangers, it is common for native people to assume that the changes are the result of the work of the alien group.

Moreover, if members of the local community believe that the changes are harmful or negative for their way of life, it is normal for them to blame, fear, resent, and even scapegoat the outsiders. Any changes are believed to result from some external, alien force imposing a new order on a particular community.

Notably, this fear of a cultural other that imposes unwanted and dangerous changes on the local community exists in tension with the ways that change actually occurs in cultures. As will be seen, cultural change is ongoing, and while change might happen because one culture destroys another, that is not the only reason cultures change. Instead, at least three types of cultural change can be expected over time. Two of these—pattern-maintaining change and change toward flexibility—generally reinforce existing cultural patterns, beliefs, institutions, and behaviors. Only the third—cultural disruption—tends to undermine established structures.[1] Each type of change must be analyzed in order to understand if the kinds of changes feared by those opposed to cultural globalization are likely to happen.

Culturally disruptive change occurs when the existing institutions, values, norms, and practices of a society are overwhelmed in the face of some challenge. Existing patterns of life are profoundly disrupted when changes come too quickly to be assimilated effectively. An obvious example would be the changes that may follow when a society is conquered in a war. The winning group has the opportunity, if it wishes, to try to remake the culture of the loser by reorganizing schools, retraining teachers, barring local religions, and numerous other acts. Similarly, mass disease or a severe environmental crisis may make it impossible for a society to maintain its beliefs and practices. In such conditions, ordinary life cannot sustain itself, and unanticipated cultural consequences are likely to follow. Change in such circumstances is likely to be both painful and destructive.

Those groups and individuals who fear the spread of American popular culture typically associate its effects with this kind of sudden, shocking change. Old values are expected to give way to new ones as people, especially young people, adopt the cultural styles found in American products. Established industries seem likely to be swept away and to be replaced by global corporate titans. Entire ways of life might be destroyed quickly. The only option is to resist and work to prevent the end of one's own culture.

Pattern-maintaining change is actually more common than disruptive change, but it is much less controversial. Indeed, after the fact it hardly seems like change at all. Pattern-maintaining change happens when new technologies, ideas, attitudes, norms, and values enter a culture and are integrated into it in ways that strengthen or reflect established forms of social organization. An obvious example is the way that Americans adopted the automobile. The car transformed America in numerous ways: it moved people off farms and out of cities into suburbs, for example, even as it sped up the pace of American life by making trade and travel across large distances convenient for most people. It also destroyed numerous existing industries like stable/livery services and profoundly undermined the blacksmith trade. Moreover, cars were not popular when they first hit America's roads; in fact, many towns and villages passed laws restricting their use. Farmland was replaced by tarmac and pollution spread, as more and more people took their cars on the road. All of this, and much more, changed American culture dramatically. Whatever the modern consensus about the innate Americanness of the automobile, the gap between what America was like pre-automobile and what it grew into once it adopted the automobile is profound.

Despite the changes the car caused in America, in time most Americans came to see owning a car as core to American identity. Automobiles came to represent freedom and independence, and they allowed Americans to express their innate individualism. The car changed America, but it is generally seen to have reinforced American culture rather than shattering it.

The story of the integration of the automobile into American life offers useful insights into the question of how any changes caused by American popular culture might be experienced around the world. After all, car ownership only seems pattern maintaining in retrospect. It took many years before a consensus developed that automobile ownership was an important indicator of American identity: the modern American car culture of most adults owning cars they use regularly is largely a product of the post–World War II period. By extension, while the use and integration of American popular culture products may be disruptive in many cultures across the world, it does not follow that these disruptions will ultimately destroy local communities. Instead, they may be recognized as promoting local cultural values and opportunities. The Internet, for example, flows both ways: it is possible for people around the world to download American music and other products, but it is also possible for Americans to download materials from other cultures. Any analysis of the cultural future of globalized trade in American popular culture needs to recognize this fact.

Similar analysis can be offered of the third type of cultural change that can be seen ongoing around us: change that enhances a culture's flexibility. Change toward flexibility occurs as societies grow more complex, or what sociologists refer to as "differentiated." Agrarian societies, for example, are relatively nondifferentiated: almost everyone in a given community grows his or her own food with the intent of feeding his or her own family, and while political, religious, military, or other leaderships usually exist, their sizes are typically constrained by the amount of food the community can grow. The culture of such societies is usually quite simple. Roles are well defined, taboos are clear, and social practices are typically tightly controlled. As societies differentiate, however, their cultures grow more flexible. For example, if some people are trained and supported as full-time health-care workers (whether medical doctors or medicine people), society needs to have a role and a place for such people to have an identity and a place. It also needs to develop systems through which such people can be provided with food and other needs that they did not themselves create. A similar process of cultural adaptation needs to occur if an industrial revolution takes place, science expands the realm of the known, or previously repressed groups are integrated into the workforce. The more functions, ideas, institutions, and values a society admits, the more flexible it can be said to be.

Changes toward flexibility, it should be noted, can be quite disruptive. New ways of life replace old ones. To return to the example offered above, now that cars predominate in America's transportation system, there are virtually no blacksmiths and livery stables in America anymore. What were once crucial elements of life in the United States have slipped away in time. Yet these changes are generally recognized to have been necessary, at least in retrospect. To take a more extreme example, if one community organizes its military around horse-riding armored knights and another buys fighter jets and tanks, the first group is virtually certain to be destroyed in a war with the second. It is probably best for a society that wishes to survive to give up using armored knights for defense and to buy jet fighters and tanks—or to ally themselves with powerful nations that have such weapons. Differentiation and complexity are important to cultural survival, even if the new order is strikingly different than the old one.

On its face, change toward flexibility is the least probable type of change likely to be caused by American pop culture products. After all, differentiation is a long-term process. However, it is likely that people living in communities that are much less differentiated than the United States will be exposed to American pop culture products in this modern era of globalization. To the degree that American movies, music, television, clothes, food, sports, and other artifacts carry American values and styles to the world, they may challenge the norms and values of cultures that are much less complex than that of the United States. Such exposure may, in turn, promote cultural change in those societies that may induce cultural differentiation. Such changes may seem like cultural disruption to cultural traditionalists, but may, instead, be first moves to building more complex societies that are capable of surviving in the new, global era. It simply does not follow that any cultural change at all constitutes the profound disruption of a particular culture.

Take, for example, the case of an all-woman rock band now active in Saudi Arabia.[2] Saudi Arabia is one of the most closed, theocratic, restrictive regimes on Earth. Its restrictions are particularly harsh for women: women cannot drive cars, nor can they walk safely through most cities and towns while unescorted or with their faces uncovered in public. Religious police have beaten women who have violated these taboos. While some of these restrictions have been loosened in recent years, Saudi Arabia remains one of the most repressive regimes on the planet. Thus, many commentators were stunned when the government recently named a woman to the position of deputy minister.

While many people, even inside Saudi Arabia itself, decry the country's cruel suppression of human rights and the government's utter unwillingness to create a democracy there, it should be noted that many Saudis favor this regime. Many people see restrictions on women's freedoms as a natural part of Arab, Saudi, Muslim culture. Challenges to this way of life are therefore sometimes seen as attacks on Arab and/or Muslim culture as such. Moreover, as might be expected given Saudi Arabia's policies, even the idea of rock and roll itself is troubling. Rock music is, as was discussed in chapter 3, associated with rebellion, nonconformity, and opposition to authority. Its grounding ethos suggests it cannot easily abide the kinds of restrictions common in Saudi Arabia today. Add to this basic skepticism of rock and roll music the fact that there is now an all-female band performing in underground sessions to avoid police response, and you have the makings of a major cultural clash in that intensely conservative nation.

What makes the existence of an all-female rock band in Saudi Arabia interesting, at least from the perspective of the discussion of cultural change offered in this chapter, is how it highlights the complexity of distinguishing "disruptive" changes from "pattern-maintaining" and "complexity-oriented" changes. It also forces attention to the question of whether or not an existing culture—if one can be said to exist in a meaningful way—necessarily deserves to continue in whatever shape it is in today.

The simple existence of a women's rock group in a country like Saudi Arabia might be seen to pose an existential disruptive threat to a cultural system grounded in the repression of women, of course. Yet it is possible to imagine the group singing about traditional values and the virtues of motherhood and life in the home. Were this the case, any emergence of a women's music scene in Saudi Arabia could eventually be seen to reinforce traditional ways of life there. Numerous examples of such transformations exist. Some groups perform Christian rock, for example, using a popular musical form that some Christian traditionalists insist is inherently ungodly to promote religious faith. It does not necessarily follow that rock must be disruptive. The rise of women's rock might lead to renewed commitment to historical Saudi lifestyles.

Alternatively, the emergence of a Saudi women's music scene might also portend growing cultural differentiation. Many of the world's societies have discovered that they need to promote and take advantage of women's skills in order to prosper. Women serve in an array of roles and responsibilities in large parts of the world, and it is not at all clear that societies that deny women rights and fail to acknowledge their talents can survive on a planet in which other communities empower women's success. The rise of women's rock in Saudi Arabia might be a harbinger of other, bigger changes that could make it possible for Saudi culture to evolve and survive in a globally interconnected world.

Last but not least, of course, Saudi women's rock may well augur a disruptive transformation of Saudi society. It may indeed indicate that traditional Saudi culture is on the way out, to be replaced by some other regime. But then again, were we to take this concern to its logical conclusion, it would be clear that no change since the time human beings first developed cultures has been legitimate. All cultural change since the beginning of culture itself has led to transformations in the lived experiences of peoples experiencing those changes. Yet in retrospect people do not usually believe that the lives they live today are somehow a betrayal of their cultural tradition. Instead, they commonly believe that their current practices are reflections and logical extensions of the cultural heritage they claim. Thus, if the existence of women's rock in Saudi Arabia actually exposes fractures in Saudi society and leads to the replacing of the old system by a new one, it does not follow that such a profound cultural disruption is something to be feared or opposed. The fact that a change is disruptive does not make it illegitimate.

Cultures simply are not fixed or immutable. Pressures to integrate new ideas, technologies, and institutions (pattern-maintaining change) tend to make societies more complex (change toward flexibility) at the cost of undermining various members' livelihoods, ideals, and cultural identities (cultural disruption). What is pattern-maintaining change for some is cultural disruption for others. Change toward cultural flexibility disrupts the cultural values preferred by traditionalists who wish to maintain an established way of life. Consequently, cultures change over time and yet usually retain a sufficiently distinctive character that members of particular communities still think of themselves as "American" or "French" or "Thai."

When discussing the likely future of the globalization of American popular culture, then, it is not particularly useful to complain that American culture changes local ones and stop there. Such change may occur, but what matters is what happens in the moment of cultural intersection. Points of cultural contact can bring both coercive and consensual types of change that, while disruptive, may sustain or transform cultures. The question in any given moment of change, then, is whether the processes are forced on a particular community or not. Those that are coercive are likely to be met with resistance and resentment and will take root only if the force promoting the change can sustain pressure on the community over time. Those that result from more voluntary patterns of adoption may disrupt established traditions, but are nonetheless more likely to be integrated into the local culture over time. For the purposes of this chapter, the central question is: which type of change is more likely as American popular culture intersects with cultures around the world?

## CULTURAL CHANGE AS CULTURAL HYBRIDITY

To anticipate the answer to this question, while it is certainly possible that most changes that occur in societies that integrate American popular culture products into their societies will be coercive, this is not likely. Instead, most cultural change is, in general, the result of integrative and evolutionary developments. Cultural change usually results in the creation of hybrid cultures, to return to a concept introduced in chapter 1. There is no reason to think that anything will be any different in matters of popular culture than they are in most other arenas of culture. Thus, while people across the world are likely to decry the changes to their culture that are occurring at any given moment, in time, most people will recognize the resulting hybrid as distinctively "their" culture.

In the discussion of the concept of hybridity in chapter 1, hybridity was roughly defined as "mixing," or "the ways in which forms become separated from existing practices and recombine with new forms and new practices."[3] Cultural communication and hybridization are two-way processes—Western societies may be as influenced by non-Western ones as non-Western communities are influenced by the West. While certain cultural forms may have predominance—Western values may supersede local ones because of their market advantages or the preponderance of American military power, for example—there is nonetheless variation within "Western" culture, and non-Western cultures have influenced and continue to influence one another as well as Western culture itself. The final product of these interactions is not necessarily corruption, imperialism, or homogenization, but can instead be something entirely new. As was noted in chapter 1, Jan Nederveen Pieterse has referred to this mixing of cultures as tending toward mélange—a system in which many hybridized cultures interact in a constantly evolving process.[4] Marwan M. Kraidy likewise noted that cultural hybridity was the likely endpoint or result of globalization.[5]

Why does cultural mixing occur? At least part of the answer lies in the historical pattern of population migrations that have led the world's peoples to be distributed across the planet as they are. As people move, they bring their cultures with them, making cultural contact, and perhaps mixing, inevitable. Contemporary population migrations are generally from what is termed (awkwardly) the Global South toward what is called (again somewhat awkwardly) the Global North. While this hemispheric labeling misses the fact that there are many underdeveloped areas in the North and, likewise, that there are developed areas in the South (e.g., Australia and Singapore), it does capture the essence of the contemporary flow: from less developed, less safe, less politically free areas toward safer, more developed, and more democratic regions. Such shifts can also occur within countries, as is happening in China: while China has a population living in its largest cities that exceeds the population of the United States (the world's largest economy), China still has hundreds of millions of peasants living in rural areas, many of whom earn less than two dollars a day. As rural people move to China's major cities they, too, are effectively moving from the Global South to the integrated, globalized North, even if they never leave their home nation. Finally, such shifts can occur both within and across nations, as is happening in India. Regardless of the physical direction of travel, these movements are toward globally integrated regions and away from rural, less connected ones.

Notably, as was discussed in chapter 1, it is at such points of contact that Samuel Huntington and Benjamin Barber see conflict of one form or another inevitably emerging. These authors predict cultural war will result as one group tries to impose its worldview on the other, while the latter resists. Contact is expected to cause conflict, not consensus.

The empirical record suggests that culture war is not the inevitable result of cultural contact, however. The interaction of the "other" and the known *might* lead to cultural conflict, but such contacts can also bring adaptation, learning, shading, and subtlety rather than brute force and the thoughtless imposition of another's values on a hapless, innocent population.

For example, the historical record suggests that what appears to be *the* culture of the United States today is the result of many changes over time. What seem to be core components of American culture are in fact hybrids of former forms. To offer a few examples, it is worth remembering that the American English in which this book is being written is an evolved combination of Anglo-Saxon and Norman French that began developing well over a thousand years ago and has continued to evolve with considerable influence and loaned words from classical Latin and Greek, as well as from modern French, Italian, Spanish, Arabic, Turkish, Persian, and numerous other language groups. In addition, it turns out that most Americans did not drink beer regularly until large numbers of Germans moved to the central United States in the latter half of the nineteenth century and established, among other breweries, what became the Anheuser-Busch brewery in St. Louis, Missouri. Likewise, it took the immigration of large numbers of Irish Catholics into the major cities of the American Northeast to change the anti-Catholic bias of traditional American culture in the late 1800s: in the early days of Irish and Catholic migration into the United States, American cultural traditionalists formed political organizations like the Know-Nothing Party to stop Catholic immigration. In time, however, cities like Boston, which had long been controlled by a Protestant aristocracy, eventually transformed into Irish Catholic–run communities. As a consequence of changes like these and many others, few people born in the United States in 1825 would recognize the way Americans live today.

What is true in the history of the United States is true globally as well. There are countless examples of the ways in which one set of cultural practices ultimately informed and shaped ideas and values that are later seen as intrinsic to the second culture. Judaism, Christianity, and Islam share a common ideological and theological tradition grounded in the teachings of Abraham. The profound political, economic, and social tensions that separate many adherents of these faiths today have resulted from the ways in which each has interpreted its heritage and its history, not because they emerged from different religious roots. Coffee is not native to Europe, even though Europeans arguably turned it into a global drink. Potatoes and tobacco came from the Western Hemisphere before being transplanted and adopted around the world. Horses did not exist in the Americas until Spanish conquistadors brought them in the 1500s; as a consequence, the iconic image many people have of the American Great Plains tribes galloping across the West chasing bison was made possible only when Spanish conquerors came to the Western Hemisphere and set about the literal destruction of many native cultures. Thus, something that seems intrinsic to an indigenous American culture—horses for the Plains tribes—was in fact an unintended consequence of colonialism and attempted genocide.

(It is worth noting that perhaps the most vivid and most beautiful presentation of this image appears in a Hollywood movie: Kevin Costner's 1990 Academy Award–winning global hit, *Dances with Wolves*.)

Even these few examples suggest that human beings have become exceptionally skilled at meeting groups and individuals of other cultures and learning from and adapting to their values. When we assess the impact of any cultural form on globalization, then, it is important to assess whether (and how) the particular ideas, images, values, and norms embedded in the cultural artifact are perceived and responded to by the societies and groups experiencing the "other" culture.

## GLOBAL CULTURAL HYBRIDITY
## AND AMERICAN POPULAR CULTURE

If nothing else, the global ubiquity of American popular culture suggests that it is an important source of the ideas, values, styles, behaviors, attitudes, and rituals that can promote cultural changes around the world. Indeed, as the discussions of the cultural changes caused by the introduction of McDonald's into Japan or the spread of blue jeans across the world showed in chapter 4, American popular culture has in fact caused changes in other cultures. Other brief examples can be offered. The long-running American television hit *The Simpsons* was adapted and shown in the Arab world as *Al Shamshoon*. Homer's name was changed to "Omar," while Bart was "Badr."[6] There is now a thriving global industry in Japanese rap, and indeed hip-hop music has spread worldwide, with local performers singing in indigenous languages. The last Mexican state without a McDonald's, Zacatecas, opened one in 2004.[7] Many of these changes have been highly controversial, of course: in Turkey I had a conversation with a student who acknowledged his own grandparents' deep skepticism of Turkish rap music, even though he insisted that many Turkish performers use it to shape and reinforce Turkish identity. But however popular or unpopular these cultural transitions have been, they are ongoing and important features of global politics today.

Cultural hybridity is not a one-way street, however. American pop culture products are dominant in global trade, but they do not emerge from a fixed cultural context any more than any cultural artifact of any other culture does. American popular culture has emerged and continues to develop as life and culture in the United States has grown and changed. American pop culture therefore may offer something of a model of what may happen as globalization moves forward. For example, consider the following:

- In 2010, salsa generated almost $300 million more in sales than did ketchup.[8]
- Large numbers of Asian, Indian, and Arab workers hired by American contractors to load trucks, staff military bases, and perform manual labor for American units sent to Operation Iraqi Freedom regularly came together to watch Bollywood movies; some American soldiers and contractors watched as well.[9]
- Cricket leagues have been formed in some areas of the United States, particularly areas with large Indian and Pakistani populations.
- The movie *Crouching Tiger, Hidden Dragon* was a breakaway hit in the United States despite the fact that it was in Chinese, starred Chinese actors, and was in the style of traditional Chinese martial arts films, not an established American genre. Westernized variants of Chinese martial arts films, like *The Matrix* trilogy and the two parts of *Kill Bill*, have become major hits as well.
- The American singer-songwriter Paul Simon used the music of Ladysmith Black Mambazo, a group that performs traditional South African music, in a collaboration that produced a worldwide hit.
- Caribbean reggae and Cuban musical forms enshrined in movies like *Buena Vista Social Club* have become popular across the United States.

At first glance this is a pretty unremarkable list. Various pop culture entertainments are popular both in the United States and across the world. Indeed the list seems little more than a reflection of realities of the entertainment industry in a globalized world. Yet the very unremarkableness of this list is in fact profoundly meaningful. In contrast with the predictions offered by Huntington or Barber, none of these essentially hybrid cultural artifacts have stimulated strong opposition, either in the United States or elsewhere.

For example, no American cultural or political leaders are currently engaged in a campaign to stamp out salsa eating as dangerous to American national pride or cultural integrity, even though salsa now outsells ketchup in America's grocery stores. This is actually quite remarkable given that salsa's rise as a condiment has been associated with the growing importance of Hispanic immigrants to the United States. Large and increasing populations of people from Latin and South America have been legally and illegally immigrating to the United States in the last several decades. This, in turn, has been linked to an expansion of Hispanic political influence in the United States: in the 1970s, the Frito-Lay company was forced by Hispanic economic and social action to eliminate its "Frito Bandito" character at about the same time Cesar Chavez was able to unionize itinerant Hispanic farm laborers under the auspices of the United Farm Workers. Subsequent political activism has brought one Latino politician, Bill Richardson, to several elected positions including governor of New Mexico. Every recent presidential election has seen major-party candidates go out of the way to speak Spanish at several points in the campaign. This political presence has been mirrored by an increasing Hispanic presence in American social and cultural consciousness. Many Americans now celebrate Cinco de Mayo (May 5) as an informal holiday (Mexican Independence Day), even though Mexican Independence Day is actually September 16. Spanish is now among the most sought-after language skills among employers and job seekers in the United States. Salsa did not cause these changes, of course, nor have all these changes occurred smoothly and without resistance. They have, however, largely occurred without the kind of violence and cultural warfare expected by pessimists about cultural globalization.

There is reason to think that similar changes can take place in other countries. Among other things, while people may protest rock music or Coca-Cola plants worldwide, these items remain popular. So far, at least, it does not appear that anyone has fought a war about an American movie. Likewise, when reporter Jake Silverstein asked his Mexican contacts if going to McDonald's instead of making their own lunch over a fire was not likely to undermine or corrupt Zacatecan culture, he found that "without exception . . . [they] seemed to think I was insane to suggest that it might be preferable to build a small wood fire and reheat a taco when there was a possibility of visiting McDonald's for a burger and fries. . . . After all, a man could still build a fire and reheat his wife's cooking if he wanted to."[10] American pop culture products do seem to penetrate global markets without always causing obvious cultural disruptions. Instead, hybrid forms emerge both overseas and in the United States itself.

## THE FUTURE OF AMERICAN POPULAR CULTURE AND GLOBALIZATION

Its global prominence places American popular culture in a unique position in world affairs. It is an agent of change in a world that is resistant to change, especially when that change is driven from far away and may well sweep away local cultures—and local jobs and businesses at the same time. It manifests values typically associated with American culture. These ideals are popular and appealing worldwide. They also induce fear and resentment at the same time.

There are powerful forces driving the globalization of American popular culture. Some, like the advantages American manufacturers enjoy in areas like marketing, distribution, and technology for their products, are asymmetrical. They are structural advantages that can make it relatively easy for the transnational corporations that produce American popular culture to impose their products on the rest of the world through free trade competition or the ruthless undercutting of local cultural products, while facing little counter competition from other culture makers. Others, such as the natural evolutionary flexibility of culture and the transparent appeal of American values and products, are social advantages that are shaped by time and context. Both have favored the spread of American pop culture products around the world.

The insight that most cultural change creates hybrid forms is particularly important in the context of the global spread of American popular culture. As was seen earlier in this chapter, American cultural products go out into the world at large and promote new cultural practices. It is also true that global artifacts come to the United States and reshape American culture. This reciprocal process leads to an obvious question: how will American movies, music, and television programs shape globalization in the future? While no complete answer to this question can be offered, several developments seem likely to emerge over time. The following section takes each in turn as it seeks to frame a final answer to the question of how American popular culture will affect globalization for years to come.

- *American audiovisual products will continue to be a major force in global trade and entertainment well into the future.*

As a consequence of both their established position and the increasing spread of communications technology, American movies, music, and television programming can be expected to retain their position as the most watched, most used, and most traded types of popular culture around the world. Indeed, the decline in numbers of restrictive authoritarian regimes that followed the end of the Cold War, combined with the movement of people from the less connected, underdeveloped Global South to the connected Global North, suggests that the market for American audiovisual entertainment and other cultural products is likely to expand at an escalating rate as new markets are identified and developed. Whereas the Global North has been largely saturated with American programming for nearly a century (at least in the case of films), the Global South and its billions of people are a relatively untouched market. As a consequence of their established production, financial, distribution, and marketing capacities, the transnational corporations that control the American audiovisual industries are well positioned to take advantage of these new markets as they open. American AV culture can therefore be expected to increase in global influence in the coming decades.

- *The global demand for other American products, like clothing styles and brands, restaurants and sports, is also likely to grow over time.*

The end of the Cold War brought many new opportunities for the expansion of American culture products. Corporations like McDonald's, Coca-Cola, and Starbucks have taken advantage of these opportunities to push their products all over the world. They have been able to do this both because they are large and wealthy companies that have the resources to pursue global expansion and because many of their products were well-established markers of American identity even before they entered foreign markets. These products were desired even before they were broadly available. The loosening of global trade restrictions has simply made it easier—or possible—for many American products to reach consumers who were well primed to accept them. Moreover,

American producers now have extensive experience taking their brands global, suggesting that even if they enter markets not really aware of American goods and services, American producers have the skills needed to introduce their products and create markets for them. These experiences suggest that American products will maintain and expand their presence across the world.

- *Social networking will continue to be a platform for the spread of information, products, cultural styles, and political and social change around the world.*

It does not take much imagination to estimate that Facebook will soon have over a billion members—or, put another way, that it will be used by one of every seven or so people on the planet. Even if Facebook is eventually replaced—given the pace of technological change, replacement seems inevitable—something else will rise in its place. But whether it is Facebook or successor platforms, social networking services make it possible to tie large parts of the world together around shared ideas, values, practices, and of course, cultural artifacts like movies, music, television programs or restaurants, sports events, and clothing styles (to name a few). Moreover, the creativity with which social networking services can be used to coordinate actions ranging from a marketing campaign to a revolution suggests that these sites are going to remain an integral part of the global community for the foreseeable future. They are, consequently, likely to be pivot points around which American popular culture engages the broader globe—and around which global cultural practices and artifacts enter the American cultural space.

- *The YouTube-ification of entertainment is likely to expand.*

Kevin Allocca, YouTube's trends manager, recently noted that at least forty-eight hours of video is uploaded to YouTube every *minute*.[11] Once "released" into YouTube's servers, videos can transmit images as mundane as a child playing with a ball or as intense as a political or military conflict around the world. Moreover, some of those videos can go viral, meaning that for some reason or another other people get excited by what they see, more and more people view it, and indeed whole cultures of copycats and parodies can be spawned from the original source—or from the copies themselves. This viral process offers some challenge to established content makers, as people find ways to entertain themselves without accessing traditional sources of audiovisual entertainment. However, there is no practical reason that television and movie studios as well as radio, music, and other culture makers cannot develop content that they can post to YouTube and use to promote their products. YouTube might become a platform for distributing movies, music, and television like Netflix is, and indeed Google is working to make the online site Hulu such an alternative. In either case, the traditional boundaries between "produced" and "amateur" content may erode in ways that make it easier for American cultural products to be integrated into local cultures as local people take American source material and adapt it for local audiences. Likewise, it may become easier for international material to penetrate the U.S. market as Americans take global artifacts and reconstitute them for American audiences.

- *American popular culture will continue to be a major source of controversy in global trade agreements.*

Given the economic, political, and cultural dimensions of the globalization of American popular culture, it is likely that while the United States will continue to push for free trade in cultural artifacts, most of the rest of the nations of the world will resist. American popular culture products generate enormous profits worldwide, and by extension, limit the number of dollars any community can spend on locally produced culture. This provides economic incentives for states and competitor companies to try to limit the local scope of American popular culture. In addition, constituted as it is by culture-bearing and culture-generating artifacts, American popular culture is likely to raise concerns from cultural traditionalists who fear that their way of life is under attack. As a consequence, whether as a result of economic or cultural pressures or for their own interests, political leaders around the world have made limiting American popular culture a central platform of their national and international agendas. Continued resistance to the globalization of culture is likely, as the passing of the UNESCO treaty on cultural diversity demonstrates.

- *Challenges to American movies, music, and television programs will arise for a variety of economic, political, and cultural reasons, leading to new alliances seeking to limit the effects of American popular culture within their communities.*

Given the multiple ways in which American popular culture intersects with and challenges cultures around the world, it is reasonable to assume that cultural groups, not just governments, will also work to limit its effects in their countries. New political alliances, such as the one between Iranian mullahs and filmmaking progressives against American films described in chapter 5, have formed among groups that otherwise share few interests. Similarly, some feminist groups in the United States have combined forces with evangelical Christian groups to fight the spread of pornography, whose makers have used new technologies like digital cameras and the Internet to create and distribute their products globally. Similar combinations can be expected to form as more and more places and people experience the political, economic, and cultural effects of American popular culture programming. The globalizing of American popular culture is thus likely to be a factor in creating resistance to it.

- *Increased exposure to American popular culture will encourage the development of hybrid forms that have value to local cultures.*

As was addressed earlier in this chapter, exposure to the ideas, forms of entertainment, values, and social practices of one culture does not necessarily breed resentment, anger, and rejection. Rather, people can learn from each other. This has certainly happened with American music. The band that many people consider the greatest rock group of all time, the Beatles, was British, after all, and rap music has become local in many cultures around the world. Similarly, many stars of American country music today are from Australia. Television programs, too, can sponsor copycat products: a Russian version of the American game show *Wheel of Fortune*, for example, is popular there. In addition, *The Simpsons* has spread across the world despite its inherent irreverence and anti-authority spirit. Blue jeans and fast food are popular not just because they are American but also because they have been integrated into local cultures as meaningful and important parts of the community's identity. There is no logical reason to presume that similar results will not follow when new people and new communities engage with American popular culture in the future.

- *Just as other cultures can adopt and integrate American programming, American culture can adapt and integrate entertainment forms originated elsewhere.*

As the example of Americans' acceptance of salsa suggests, Americans are no more likely to automatically reject everything from somewhere else as "alien" and "other" than are people around the world. Moreover, the megacorporations that produce American popular culture have an economic interest in surveying world markets in search of programming that might be popular in the United States. In fact, reality shows like *Big Brother*, *American Idol*, and *Whose Line Is It Anyway?* originated in Great Britain before coming to America. Humiliation TV—such as *Fear Factor* and similar American programs in which people engage in dangerous stunts or subject themselves to "gross-out" eating or endurance contests in pursuit of various prizes—was pioneered in Japan. As more pleasant examples, the success of the Colombian pop singer Shakira has occurred across language boundaries, and it is worth noting that many subscribers to Telemundo are not native Spanish speakers. The international hit television show *Who Wants to Be a Millionaire* originated in the UK before becoming the narrative frame around which the 2008 Academy Award–winning film *Slumdog Millionaire* was set. *Slumdog*, notably, was set in Mumbai (Bombay), India, and ended with a much-loved dance scene that evoked similar scenes common in Bollywood movies. Such cultural learning constitutes a two-way street, with each side informing the other.

- *Pop cultural interchanges can create economic and cultural bonds among people that may not be represented by political institutions.*

Whether as producers, consumers, or participants in shared entertainments that develop subcultures, it is likely that diverse people around the world will develop relationships of mutual interest around the products of American popular culture. An obvious example of such linkages has been the worldwide spread of fan clubs of the *Star Trek* series. *Star Trek* is literally a global phenomenon, and millions of people worldwide collect paraphernalia, attend conferences, and assert the IDIC (infinite diversity in infinite combinations) creed at home and abroad. Likewise, golfers can recognize each other globally by what they wear and what they carry; similar subcultures exist around the world covering "sk8ters," rappers, and coffee aficionados. Such common bonds may not be expressed in the political system, however, for a variety of reasons ranging from the rules of the system being written to advantage cultural conservatives (Iran) to sheer democratic inertia— both sk8ters and rappers lack either (or both) the numbers or the desire to challenge American policy toward specific countries. When we analyze the effects of American popular culture on globalization, then, it is important to look beyond the public statements of political leaders.

- *American popular culture may facilitate the emergence of a global culture, at least to a limited extent.*

As American popular culture reaches larger and larger audiences, as local cultures adapt and integrate American forms, and as American culture itself adapts to the ideas, norms, and values of other cultures for a variety of economic and pragmatic reasons, it is likely that relatively shared vocabularies, concepts, and frames of reference will emerge to serve to support the use of American movies, music, and television programming. The fact that most of American popular culture's products are presented in English, which is also a language of international global commerce, will only facilitate the rise of some kind of a common global culture. Moreover, the fact that American popular culture is substantially "American" suggests that the general form and character of any emergent global culture is likely to be based on principles of choice, freedom, and consumption, at least in commercial affairs. It is easy to image Internet slang as a nearly universal linguistic, for example. New vocabulary such as "btw," "u," "r," and other contractions can be deployed to get their meaning across by people with only limited understanding of English spelling or grammar. Likewise, common cultural phrases now exist across the world. "OK" is perhaps the first truly global word, while phrases like "I'll be back" (*The Terminator*) spread around the world. Given these examples, it seems likely that at least some version of a consumer-driven, product choice–filled culture will emerge, at least among the worldwide users and marketers of American popular culture.

- *Cultural integration is more likely within and among components of the Global North than it is within and among the Global South, thereby deepening the gap between north and south.*

The sharing of popular culture products is, by definition, more likely in areas that have markets that have both an interest in and the capacity to consume a given product. Put another way, it makes little economic sense for Disney or any other transnational corporation to market a global blockbuster in rural India or rural China, since a ticket might cost eight or more dollars and many people there make less than two dollars a day. Thus, global exchanges of dollars, ideas, experiences, values, images, and technologies are likely to be concentrated in the globalized parts of the world. This, in turn, can be expected to encourage global migration from south to north as the gap between how one *is* living and how one *might* live widens. Indeed, the appeal of American popular culture should add energy to this migration, as people literally move "off the farm" in order to experience the world of possibilities manifested in the products of American popular culture—including the wealth, freedom, and lifestyles embedded in American culture. Accordingly, concerns of nations in the Global North about immigration, cultural cohesion, and the identity of the nation's people can be expected to grow more intense for the foreseeable future.

- *Resistance to the spread of American popular culture, whether organized by states or by citizens, is likely to be hard.*

While numerous nations and social groups are attempting to limit the influence and power of American popular culture in their communities, three factors appear likely to limit the effectiveness of these efforts in the long run: (1) the spread of the technology through which American cultural artifacts can be accessed, (2) the global appeal of American culture in general, and (3) global population movements. As a practical matter, satellites and the Internet make gaining access to American popular culture relatively easy. Almost all national efforts to ban satellite dishes have failed for lack of enforcement, even in what are perceived to be fairly restrictive regimes like Iran and China. North Korea may be the world's only exception, and even it is now facing the problem of smuggled Internet content that both exposes the regime's practices and allows its citizens access to the wider world. In addition, the products created within American popular culture are desirable and sought after worldwide. This does not mean that local forms need disappear, as the experience of Venezuela demonstrates (chapter 5), but it does suggest that efforts to ban appealing programming wholesale are unlikely to succeed, especially given easy technological access to them. Finally, the contemporary worldwide population migration from the Global South to the Global North (however conceived) means that there will be increasing numbers of people in areas and communities in which American popular culture is already present and pervasive. Under such conditions, plans or hopes to ban American cultural products are doomed to failure.

- *Nothing is inevitable about globalization and American popular culture.*

Among other things, the analysis of the ways in which American popular culture has affected the process of globalization offered in this book ought to, at the least, provide an empirically based challenge to those scholars and pundits who insist that globalization is inevitable. As chapter 5 made clear, states still actively work to limit what are believed to be the pernicious economic, political, and cultural effects of American popular culture for their communities. Whatever the advocates of total globalization say about how people ought to behave in the marketplace, many peoples and governments are quite happy to accept less American programming, however enjoyable or inexpensive it might be, in favor of higher-priced, tax-subsidized local products. Nothing about globalization can be inevitable in such a world.

Resistance need not lead to culture war, however. As was addressed earlier in this chapter, cultures learn, change, and adapt. It is possible for cultures to integrate new ideas and experiences without necessarily experiencing corruption, imperialism, or homogenization. Accordingly, the interchange of American popular culture and cultures around the globe may encourage the emergence of new hybrid forms that accommodate new identities and opportunities for literally billions of people around the world. While this process will inevitably displace or distort some ideas and practices, the cumulative effect may be seen as beneficial rather than harmful. To the degree such change occurs, the world's movement toward globality will be enhanced.

## CONCLUSION

This book began by addressing the role American popular culture played in the Cold War. It has concluded with a consideration of how American cultural artifacts may influence the future of globalization. The evidence offered here shows that as one of the central components of contemporary global trade, American popular culture both encourages integration and promotes fragmentation as it shapes the way contemporary globalization is unfolding. The long-term course of globalization is, therefore, likely to emerge much as Manfred Steger has suggested: toward globality without ever actually achieving it.[12] American popular culture is one important component of this process, and it is likely to remain so for a long time to come. It is through popular culture that the rest of the world learns what "American" means, and any attempt to understand globalization without attention to the central role played by global interest in and fear of American popular culture is necessarily incomplete. In large measure it is through American popular culture that the rest of the world may decide whether to fear or favor the promise of a globalized planet.

## NOTES

1. The following discussion of the three types of cultural change is derived from Harry Eckstein, "A Culturalist Theory of Cultural Change," *American Political Science Review* 82, no. 3 (1988): 789–804.

2. Robert F. Wurth, "As Taboos Ease, Saudi Girl Group Dares to Rock," *New York Times*, 24 November 2008.

3. William Rowe and Vivian Schelling, *Memory and Modernity: Popular Culture in Latin America* (London: Verso, 1991), 231.

4. Jan Nederveen Pieterse, *Globalization and Culture: Global Mélange* (Lanham, Md.: Rowman & Littlefield, 2004), 69–71.

5. Marwan M. Kraidy, *Hybridity, or the Cultural Logic of Globalization* (Philadelphia: Temple University Press, 2005).

6. Jake Tapper, "'The Simpsons' Exported to Middle East," 18 October 2005, http://abcnews.go.com/WNT/story?id=1227362&page=1#.T05KLEprovo (accessed 29 February 2012).

7. Jake Silverstein, "Grand Opening: Ronald McDonald Conquers New Spain," *Harper's*, January 2005, 67–74.

8. Bloomberg Businessweek, "Best-Selling Condiments in the US," http://images.businessweek.com/ss/10/10/1007_bestselling_condiments/1.htm (accessed 28 February 2012).

9. Sgt. Tammy Johnson, 1244th Transportation Company, deployed to Kuwait and Iraq, April 2003–August 2004, personal communication.

10. Silverstein, "Grand Opening," 72.

11. Kevin Allocca, "Why Videos Go Viral," http://www.youtube.com/watch?feature=player_embedded&v=BpxVIwCbBK0 (accessed 27 February 2012).

12. Manfred B. Steger, *Globalization: A Very Short Introduction* (New York: Oxford University Press, 2003), 8.

# Recommended Readings

Adams, Francis, Satya Dev Gupta, and Kidane Mengisteab, eds. *Globalization and the Dilemmas of the State in the South*. London: St. Martin's, 1999.

Agee, Warren, Phillip Ault, and Edwin Emery. *Introduction to Mass Communication*, 10th ed. New York: HarperCollins, 1991.

Allen, Robert C., and Annette Hill, eds. *The Television Studies Reader*. New York: Routledge, 2004.

Almond, Gabriel. *A Discipline Divided: Schools and Sects in Political Science*. Newbury Park, Calif.: Sage, 1990.

Almond, Gabriel, and Sidney Verba, eds. *The Civic Culture*. Princeton, N.J.: Princeton University Press, 1963.

Anderson, Benedict. *Imagined Communities: Reflections on the Origin and Spread of Nationalism*. London: Verso, 1983.

Appadurai, Arjun, ed. *Globalization*. Durham, N.C.: Duke University Press, 2001.

———. *Modernity at Large: Cultural Dimensions of Globalization*. Minneapolis: University of Minnesota Press, 1996.

Axford, Barrie. *The Global System: Economics, Politics, and Culture.* Cambridge: Polity, 1995.

Banfield, Edward C. *The Moral Basis of a Backward Society.* New York: Free Press, 1958.

Baran, Stanley J., and Dennis K. Davis. *Mass Communication Theory: Foundations, Ferment, and Future.* Belmont, Calif.: Wadsworth, 1995.

Barber, Benjamin R. *Jihad vs. McWorld: How Globalism and Tribalism Are Reshaping the World.* New York: Ballantine Books, 1996.

Barker, Chris. *Global Television: An Introduction.* Malden, Mass.: Blackwell, 1997.

Barney, D. *The Network Society.* Malden, Mass.: Polity, 2004.

Barry Jones, R. J. *The World Turned Upside Down? Globalization and the Future of the State.* Manchester, UK: Manchester University Press, 2000.

Beck, Ulrich. *What Is Globalization?* Oxford: Blackwell, 2000.

Bellah, Robert N., et al. *The Good Society.* New York: Knopf, 1991.

———. *Habits of the Heart: Individualism and Commitment in American Life.* Berkeley and Los Angeles: University of California Press, 1985.

Benedict, Ruth. *Patterns of Culture.* Boston: Houghton Mifflin, 1934.

Bercovitch, Sacvan. *The American Jeremiad.* Madison: University of Wisconsin Press, 1978.

———. *The Puritan Origins of the American Self.* New Haven, Conn.: Yale University Press, 1975.

Berger, Peter L., and Samuel P. Huntington, eds. *Many Globalizations: Cultural Diversity in the Contemporary World.* New York: Oxford University Press, 2002.

Berlin, Isaiah. *Two Concepts of Liberty.* Oxford: Clarendon Press, 1958.

Bittner, John R. *Mass Communication: An Introduction.* 4th ed. Englewood Cliffs, N.J.: Prentice Hall, 1986.

Boorstin, Daniel J. *The Genius of American Politics.* Chicago: University of Chicago Press, 1953.

Bordo, Susan. *Unbearable Weight: Feminism, Western Culture, and the Body.* Berkeley and Los Angeles: University of California Press, 1993.

Brabee, Jeffrey, and Todd Brabee. *Music, Money, and Success: The Insider's Guide to the Music Industry.* New York: Schirmer Books, 1994.

Bryan, Lowell, and Diana Farrell. *Market Unbound: Unleashing Global Capitalism.* New York: Wiley, 1996.

Burnett, Robert. *The Global Jukebox: The International Music Industry.* New York: Routledge, 1996.

Carter, Erica, James Donald, and Judith Squires, eds. *Cultural Remix: Theories of Politics and the Popular.* London: Lawrence & Wishart, 1995.

Cerny, Philip G. *The Changing Architecture of Politics: Structure, Agency, and the Future of the State.* London: Sage, 1990.

Chalaby, Jean K. *Transnational Television Worldwide: Towards a New Media Order.* New York: I. B. Tauris, 2005.

Collins, Patricia Hill. *Black Sexual Politics.* New York: Routledge, 2004.

Combs, J. *Polpop: Politics and Culture in America.* Bowling Green, Ky.: Bowling Green State University Press, 1984.

Condry, Ian. "Japanese Hip-Hop and the Globalization of Political Culture." In *Urban Life: Readings in the Anthropology of the City*, edited by George Gmelch and Walter Zenner. Prospect Heights, Ill.: Waveland Press, 2001.

Connolly, William E. *Identity/Difference: Democratic Negotiations of Political Paradox.* Ithaca, N.Y.: Cornell University Press, 1991.

Connors, Michael. *The Race to the Intelligent State: Charting the Global Information Economy in the Twenty-first Century.* Oxford: Capstone, 1997.

Cornell, Grant H., and Eve Walsh Stoddard, eds. *Global Multiculturalism.* Lanham, Md.: Rowman & Littlefield, 2001.

Cox, Harvey. "The Market as God: Living in the New Dispensation." *The Atlantic Monthly*, March 1999, 18–23.

Crothers, Lane. *Rage on the Right: The American Militia Movement from Ruby Ridge to Homeland Security.* Lanham, Md.: Rowman & Littlefield, 2003.

Crothers, Lane, and Charles Lockhart, eds. *Culture and Politics: A Reader.* New York: St. Martin's, 2001.

Cunningham, Patricia A., and Susan Voso Lab, eds. *Dress and Popular Culture.* Bowling Green, Ohio: Bowling Green State University Popular Press, 1991.

Curtin, P. D. *Cross Cultural Trade in World History.* Cambridge: Cambridge University Press, 1984.

Dallmayr, Fred. *Achieving Our World: Toward a Global and Plural Democracy.* Lanham, Md.: Rowman & Littlefield, 2001.

Devine, Donald. *The Political Culture of the United States.* Boston: Little, Brown, 1972.

Diamond, Jared. *Guns, Germs, and Steel: The Fates of Human Societies.* New York: Norton, 1999.

Dicke, Thomas S. *Franchising in America: The Development of a Business Method, 1840–1980.* Chapel Hill: University of North Carolina Press, 1992.

Douglas, Mary, and Baron Isherwood. *The World of Goods.* New York: Basic Books, 1979.

Dowmunt, Tony, ed. *Channels of Resistance: Global Television and Local Empowerment.* London: BFI Publishing, 1993.

Eagleton, Terry. *The Idea of Culture.* Oxford: Blackwell, 2000.

———. *Ideology: An Introduction.* London: Verso, 1991.

Easton, David. *The Political System: An Inquiry into the State of Political Science.* 2nd ed. Chicago: University of Chicago Press, 1981.

Eckstein, Harry. "A Culturalist Theory of Political Change." *American Political Science Review* 82, no. 3 (1988): 789–804.

Edelman, Murray. *The Symbolic Uses of Politics.* Urbana: University of Illinois Press, 1964.

Eisenstadt, S. N. "Cultural Traditions and Political Dynamics: The Origins and Modes of Ideological Politics." *British Journal of Sociology* 32, no. 2 (1981): 155–81.

Ekachai, Daradirek, Mary Hinchliff-Pelias, and Rosechongporn Komolsevin. "Where Are Those Tall Buildings: The Impact of U.S. Media on Thais' Perceptions of Americans." In *Images of the U.S. around the World: A Multicultural Perspective*, edited by Yahya R. Kamalipour. Albany: SUNY Press, 1999.

Elazar, Daniel Judah. *American Federalism: A View from the States*. 3rd ed. New York: Harper & Row, 1984.

———. *The American Mosaic: The Impact of Space, Time, and Culture on American Politics*. Boulder, Colo.: Westview, 1994.

Ellis, Richard. *American Political Cultures*. New York: Oxford University Press, 1993.

Ellis, Richard, and Michael Thompson, eds. *Culture Matters: Essays in Honor of Aaron Wildavsky*. Boulder, Colo.: Westview, 1997.

Emmerson, Donald K. "Singapore and the 'Asian Values' Debate." *Journal of Democracy* 6, no. 4 (1995): 95–105.

Enloe, Cynthia. *Bananas and Bases: Making Feminist Sense of International Politics*. Berkeley and Los Angeles: University of California Press, 1989.

Falk, R. *Predatory Globalization*. Malden, Mass.: Polity, 1999.

Fanon, Franz. *The Wretched of the Earth*. Harmondsworth, UK: Penguin, 1967.

Farrar, Ronald T. *Mass Communication: An Introduction to the Field*. St. Paul, Minn.: West, 1988.

Featherstone, Mike, ed. *Global Culture: Nationalism, Globalization, and Modernity*. London: Sage, 1995.

Fink, Michael. *Inside the Music Business: Music in Contemporary Life*. New York: Schirmer Books, 1989.

Fischer, David Hackett. *Albion's Seed: Four British Folkways in America*. New York: Oxford University Press, 1984.

Foster, Robert J. *Coca-Globalization: Following Soft Drinks from New York to New Guinea*. New York: Palgrave Macmillan, 2008.

Frank, Andre Gunder. *Re-Orient: Global Economy in the Asian Age*. Berkeley and Los Angeles: University of California Press, 1998.

Freedman, Estelle B. *No Turning Back: The History of Feminism and the Future of Women*. New York: Random House, 2002.

Friedman, Jonathan. *Cultural Identity and Global Process*. London: Sage, 1994.

Fukuyama, Francis. *The End of History and the Last Man*. New York: Free Press, 1992.

Gabler, Neal. *An Empire of Their Own: How the Jews Invented Hollywood*. New York: Crown, 1988.

Galperin, Hernan. "Cultural Industries in the Age of Free-Trade Agreements." *Canadian Journal of Communications* 24, no. 1 (1999): 49–77.

Gamson, William. *Talking Politics*. Cambridge: Cambridge University Press, 1992.

Gans, Herbert. *Popular Culture and High Culture: An Analysis and Evaluation of Taste*. New York: Basic Books, 1974.

Gaventa, John. *Power and Powerlessness: Quiescence and Rebellion in an Appalachian Valley*. Urbana: University of Illinois Press, 1980.

Geertz, Clifford. *The Interpretation of Cultures*. New York: Basic Books, 1973.

Gellner, Ernest. *Encounters with Nationalism*. Cambridge, Mass.: Blackwell, 1994.

———. *Nations and Nationalism*. Ithaca, N.Y.: Cornell University Press, 1983.

Giddens, Anthony. *The Consequences of Modernity*. Stanford, Calif.: Stanford University Press, 1990.

Goff, Patricia M. *Limits to Liberalization: Local Culture in a Global Marketplace*. Ithaca, N.Y.: Cornell University Press, 2007.

Greenfield, Liah. *Nationalism: Five Roads to Modernity*. Cambridge, Mass.: Harvard University Press, 1992.

Gusfield, Joseph. *Symbolic Crusade: Status Politics and the American Temperance Movement*. Urbana: University of Illinois Press, 1966.

Hale, Cecil I. *The Music Industry: A Guidebook*. Dubuque, Iowa: Kendall/Hunt, 1990.

Hannerz, Ulf. *Cultural Complexity: Studies in the Social Organization of Meaning*. New York: Columbia University Press, 1992.

———. *Transnational Connections: Cultures, People, Places*. London: Routledge, 1996.

Harris, Nigel. *National Liberation*. London: I. B. Tauris, 1990.

Harrison, Lawrence E., and Samuel P. Huntington, eds. *Culture Matters: How Values Shape Human Progress*. New York: Basic Books, 2000.

Hartz, Louis. *The Liberal Tradition in America*. New York: Harcourt, Brace, 1955.

Havens, Timothy. "The Biggest Show in the World: Race and the Global Popularity of *The Cosby Show*." In *The Television Studies Reader*, edited by Robert C. Allen and Annette Hill. New York: Routledge, 2004.

Hayden, Patrick, and Chamsy el-Ojeili, eds. *Confronting Globalization: Humanity, Justice, and the Renewal of Politics*. New York: Palgrave Macmillan, 2005.

Hebidge, D. *Subculture: The Meaning of Style*. London: Methuen, 1979.

Held, David, Anthony McGrew, David Goldblatt, and J. Perraton. *Global Transformations*. Cambridge: Polity, 1999.

Hines, Colin. *Localization: A Global Manifesto*. London: Earthscan, 2001.

Hirst, Paul Q., and Grahame Thompson. *Globalization in Question*. Cambridge: Polity, 1996.

Hobsbawm, Eric. *Nations and Nationalism since 1780*. Cambridge: Cambridge University Press, 1992.

Hofstadter, Richard. *The American Political Tradition and the Men Who Made It*. New York: Vintage, 1974.

———. *The Paranoid Style in American Politics, and Other Essays*. New York: Knopf, 1965.

Holton, Robert J. *Globalization and the Nation-State*. New York: St. Martin's, 1988.

Hopper, Paul. *Understanding Cultural Globalization*. Malden, Mass.: Polity, 2007.

Hunt, Linda. *Politics, Culture, and Class in the French Revolution.* Berkeley and Los Angeles: University of California Press, 1984.

Hunter, James Davison. *Culture Wars: The Struggle to Define America.* New York: Basic Books, 1991.

Huntington, Samuel P. *American Politics: The Promise of Disharmony.* Cambridge, Mass.: Belknap, 1981.

———. *The Clash of Civilizations and the Remaking of World Order.* New York: Simon & Schuster, 1996.

———. *The Third Wave: Democratization in the Late Twentieth Century.* Norman: University of Oklahoma Press, 1991.

———. *Who Are We? The Challenges to America's National Identity.* New York: Simon & Schuster, 2004.

Inglehart, Ronald. *Modernization and Postmodernization: Cultural, Economic, and Political Change in Forty-three Societies.* Princeton, N.J.: Princeton University Press, 1997.

———. *The Silent Revolution: Changing Values and Political Life among Western Publics.* Princeton, N.J.: Princeton University Press, 1975.

Iriye, Akira. *Cultural Internationalism and World Order.* Baltimore: Johns Hopkins University Press, 1997.

Jackle, John A., and Keith A. Sculle. *Fast Food: Roadside Restaurants in the Automobile Age.* Baltimore: Johns Hopkins University Press, 1999.

Jameson, Frederick, and M. Miyoshi, eds. *The Cultures of Globalization.* Durham, N.C.: Duke University Press, 1998.

Johnson, Chalmers. *Blowback: The Costs and Consequences of American Empire.* New York: Henry Holt, 2000.

Katz, M. B. *The Undeserving Poor.* New York: Pantheon, 1989.

Keohane, Robert O. *After Hegemony.* Princeton, N.J.: Princeton University Press, 1984.

King, Anthony D., ed. *Culture, Globalization, and the World-System: Contemporary Conditions for the Representation of Identity.* Basingstoke, UK: Macmillan, 1991.

Kingdon, John W. *America the Unusual.* New York: Worth, 1999.

Kivisto, Peter. *Multiculturalism in a Global Society.* Malden, Mass.: Blackwell, 2002.

Klapp, Orrin. *Collective Search for Identity.* New York: Holt, Rinehart, and Winston, 1969.

Kluckhohn, Clyde. *Culture and Behavior.* New York: Free Press, 1962.

Kottak, Conrad Phillip. *Prime-Time Society: An Anthropological Analysis of Television and Culture.* Belmont, Calif.: Wadsworth, 1990.

Kraidy, Marwan M. *Hybridity, or the Cultural Logic of Globalization.* Philadelphia: Temple University Press, 2005.

Krasilovsky, M. William, and Sidney Shemel. *This Business of Music.* 7th ed. New York: Billboard Books, 1995.

Kuttner, Robert. *Everything for Sale: The Virtues and Limits of Markets.* New York: Knopf, 1997.

Lash, S., and C. Lury. *Global Culture Industry: The Mediation of Things*. Malden, MA: Polity, 2007.

Levine, Lawrence. *Highbrow/Lowbrow: The Emergence of Cultural Hierarchy in America*. Cambridge, Mass.: Harvard University Press, 1988.

Lewis, Bernard. *What Went Wrong? The Clash between Islam and Modernity in the Middle East*. New York: Oxford University Press, 2002.

Lipset, Seymour Martin. "American Exceptionalism Reaffirmed." In *Is America Different? A New Look at American Exceptionalism*, edited by B. Shafer. Oxford: Oxford University Press, 1991.

———. *American Exceptionalism: A Double-Edged Sword*. New York: Norton, 1996.

Lockhart, Charles. *The Roots of American Exceptionalism: Institutions, Culture, and Politics*. New York: Palgrave Macmillan, 2003.

Lull, James. *China Turned On: Television, Reform, and Resistance*. New York: Routledge, 1991.

Luttwak, Edward. *Turbo-Capitalism: Winners and Losers in the Global Economy*. New York: Harper & Row, 1999.

Macedo, Stephen. *Liberal Virtues: Citizenship, Virtue, and Community in Liberal Constitutionalism*. Oxford: Clarendon Press, 1990.

MacIntyre, Alastair. *After Virtue: A Study in Moral Theory*. Notre Dame, Ind.: University of Notre Dame Press, 1981.

Madsen, Deborah L. *American Exceptionalism*. Jackson: University of Mississippi Press, 1998.

Maltby, Richard. *Harmless Entertainment: Hollywood and the Ideology of Consensus*. Metuchen, N.J.: Scarecrow Press, 1983.

———. *Hollywood Cinema*. 2nd ed. Malden, Mass.: Blackwell, 2003.

McAdam, Doug, and D. Rucht. "The Cross-National Diffusion of Movement Ideas." *Annals of the American Academy of Political and Social Science* 528, no. 1 (1993): 56–74.

McAnany, Emile G., and Kenton T. Wilkinson, eds. *Mass Media and Free Trade: NAFTA and the Cultural Industries*. Austin: University of Texas Press, 1996.

McBride, Allen, and Robert K. Toburen. "Deep Structures: Polpop Culture on Primetime Television." *Journal of Popular Culture* 29, no. 4 (1996): 181–200.

McCrisken, Trevor B. *American Exceptionalism and the Legacy of Vietnam: U.S. Foreign Policy since 1974*. New York: Palgrave Macmillan, 2003.

Mead, Sidney E. *The Nation with the Soul of a Church*. New York: Harper & Row, 1975.

Merelman, Richard. "On Culture and Politics in America: A Perspective from Structural Anthropology." *British Journal of Political Science* 19 (1989): 465–93.

Miller, Daniel. *Worlds Apart: Modernity through the Prism of the Local*. London: Routledge, 1995.

Miller, Toby, Nitin Govil, John McMurra, and Richard Maxwell. *Global Hollywood*. London: BFI, 2001.

Mittelman, James H. *Globalization: Critical Reflections.* Boulder, Colo.: Lynne Rienner, 1996.

Moretti, Franco. "Planet Hollywood." *New Left Review* 9 (May–June 2001): 90–101.

Morris, Aldon. *The Origins of the Civil Rights Movement.* New York: Free Press, 1984.

Mukerji, Chandra, and Michael Schudson, eds. *Rethinking Popular Culture: Contemporary Perspectives in Cultural Studies.* Berkeley and Los Angeles: University of California Press, 1991.

Munsey, Cecil. *The Illustrated Guide to the Collectibles of Coca-Cola.* New York: Hawthorn Books, 1972.

Myrdal, Gunnar. *An American Dilemma.* New York: Harper & Row, 1944.

Neuhaus, Richard John. *The Naked Public Square: Religion and Democracy in America.* 2nd ed. Grand Rapids, Mich.: Eerdmans, 1984.

Nye, Joseph S. *Soft Power: The Means for Success in World Politics.* Cambridge, Mass.: Public Affairs, 2004.

Ohmae, Kenichi. *The Borderless World: Power and Strategy in the Interlinked World Economy.* New York: HarperBusiness, 1990.

———. *The End of the Nation-State: The Rise of Regional Economies.* New York: Free Press, 1995.

Olson, Scott R. "The Globalization of Hollywood." *International Journal on World Peace* 17 (December 2000): 3–18.

———. "Hollywood Planet: Global Media and the Competitive Advantage of Narrative Transparency." In *The Television Studies Reader*, edited by Robert C. Allen and Annette Hill. New York: Routledge, 2004.

Page, David, and William Crawley. *Satellites over South Asia: Broadcasting Culture and the Public Interest.* Thousand Oaks, Calif.: Sage, 2001.

Pendergast, Mark. *For God, Country, and Coca-Cola: The Unauthorized History of the Great American Soft Drink and the Company That Makes It.* New York: Scribner, 1993.

Pieterse, Jan Nederveen. *Globalization and Culture: Global Mélange.* Lanham, Md.: Rowman & Littlefield, 2004.

Putnam, Robert. *Bowling Alone.* New York: Simon & Schuster, 2000.

Pye, Lucien W. *Asian Power and Politics: The Cultural Dimensions of Authority.* Cambridge, Mass.: Belknap, 1985.

Ranney, Austin. *Channels of Power.* New York: Basic Books, 1983.

Reich, Robert. *The Work of Nations.* New York: Vintage, 1992.

Reiss, Timothy J. *Against Autonomy: Global Dialectics of Cultural Exchange.* Stanford, Calif.: Stanford University Press, 2002.

Riesman, David. *The Lonely Crowd.* New Haven, Conn.: Yale University Press, 1950.

Ritzer, George. *McDonaldization: The Reader.* Thousand Oaks, Calif.: Pine Forge Press, 2002.

———, ed. *The McDonaldization of Society: An Investigation into the Changing Character of Contemporary Social Life*. London: Sage, 1993.

Robertson, Roland. *Globalization: Social Theory and Global Culture*. London: Sage, 1992.

———. "Glocalization: Space, Time, and Social Theory." *Journal of International Communication* 1, no. 1 (1994).

Rosenau, James N. *Distant Proximities: Dynamics beyond Globalization*. Princeton, N.J.: Princeton University Press, 2003.

Ross, Marc Howard. "Culture and Identity in Comparative Political Analysis." In *Comparative Politics: Rationality, Culture, and Structure*, edited by Mark I. Lichbach and Alan S. Zuckerman. New York: Cambridge University Press, 1997.

Rowe, William, and Vivian Schelling. *Memory and Modernity: Popular Culture in Latin America*. London: Verso, 1991.

Rupert, Mark, and M. Scott Solomon. *Globalization and International Political Economy: The Politics of Alternative Futures*. Lanham, Md.: Rowman & Littlefield, 2006.

Said, Edward. *Culture and Imperialism*. New York: Knopf, 1993.

Sakr, Naomi. *Satellite Realms: Transnational Television, Globalization, and the Middle East*. New York: I. B. Tauris, 2001.

Sassen, Saskia. *Globalization and Its Discontents*. New York: Free Press, 1998.

Schiller, Herbert I. *Culture, Inc: The Corporate Takeover of Public Expression*. New York: Oxford University Press, 1989.

Schlosser, Eric. *Fast Food Nation: The Dark Side of the American Meal*. New York: Houghton Mifflin Harcourt, 2001.

Scholte, Jan Aart. *Globalization: A Critical Introduction*. London: Macmillan, 2000.

Seagrave, Kerry. *American Television Abroad: Hollywood's Attempt to Dominate World Television*. Jefferson, N.C.: McFarland, 1998.

Shook, Carrie, and Robert L. Shook. *Franchising: The Business Strategy That Changed the World*. Englewood Cliffs, N.J.: Prentice Hall, 1993.

Sklar, Robert. *Film: An International History of the Medium*. New York: Abrams, 1993.

Skocpol, Theda. *State and Social Revolutions*. New York: Cambridge University Press, 1979.

Smart, Barry, ed. *Resisting McDonaldization*. London: Sage, 1999.

Smith, R. M. *Liberalism and American Constitutional Law*. Cambridge, Mass.: Harvard University Press, 1985.

Soros, George. *The Crisis of Global Capitalism*. New York: Public Affairs, 1998.

———. *On Globalization*. New York: Public Affairs, 2002.

Sowell, Thomas. *Migrations and Culture*. New York: Basic Books, 1996.

Starr, Paul. *The Creation of the Media: Political Origins of Modern Communications*. New York: Basic Books, 2004.

Steger, Manfred B. *Globalism: Market Ideology Meets Terrorism.* 2nd ed. Lanham, Md.: Rowman & Littlefield, 2005.

———. *Globalization: A Very Short Introduction.* New York: Oxford University Press, 2003.

———, ed. *Rethinking Globalism.* Lanham, Md.: Rowman & Littlefield, 2004.

———. *The Rise of the Global Imaginary: Political Ideologies from the French Revolution to the Global War on Terror.* New York: Oxford University Press, 2008.

Steigerwald, David. *Culture's Vanities: The Paradox of Cultural Diversity in a Globalized World.* Lanham, Md.: Rowman & Littlefield, 2004.

Strange, Susan. *The Retreat of the State.* Cambridge: Cambridge University Press, 1996.

Straubhaar, Joseph D. *World Television: From Global to Local.* Los Angeles: Sage, 2007.

Sturmer, Corinna. "MTV's Europe: An Imaginary Continent." In *Channels of Resistance: Global Television and Local Empowerment,* edited by Tony Dowmunt. London: BFI Publishing, 1993.

Tapp, Robert B., ed. *Multiculturalism.* Amherst, N.Y.: Prometheus Books, 2000.

Tarrow, Sidney. *Power in Movement: Social Movements, Collective Action, and Mass Politics in the Modern State.* New York: Cambridge University Press, 1994.

Thompson, Michael, Richard Ellis, and Aaron Wildavsky. *Cultural Theory.* Boulder, Colo.: Westview, 1990.

Thurow, Lester. *The Future of Capitalism: How Today's Economic Forces Shape Tomorrow's World.* New York: Morrow, 1996.

Tilly, Charles. *From Mobilization to Revolution.* Reading, Mass.: Addison-Wesley, 1978.

Tocqueville, Alexis de. *Democracy in America.* New York: Knopf, 1945.

Toll, Robert C. *The Entertainment Machine: American Show Business in the Twentieth Century.* New York: Oxford University Press, 1982.

Tomlinson, John. *Cultural Imperialism.* Baltimore: Johns Hopkins University Press, 1991.

———. *Globalization and Culture.* Chicago: University of Chicago Press, 1999.

Turner, Frederick Jackson. *The Frontier in American History.* New York: Holt, Rinehart, and Winston, 1962.

Wallerstein, Immanuel. *Geopolitics and Geoculture.* Cambridge: Cambridge University Press, 1991.

Waters, Malcolm. *Globalization.* London: Routledge, 1995.

Watson, James L., ed. *Golden Arches East: McDonald's in East Asia.* Stanford, Calif.: Stanford University Press, 1997.

Weatherford, Jack. *Genghis Khan and the Making of the Modern World.* New York: Crown, 2004.

Weiss, Linda. *The Myth of the Powerless State.* Ithaca, N.Y.: Cornell University Press, 1998.

Whatmore, Sarah. *Hybrid Geographies: Natures, Cultures, Spaces*. London: Sage, 2002.

White, John Kenneth. *The Values Divide: American Politics and Culture in Transition*. New York: Chatham House, 2003.

Wildavsky, Aaron. "Choosing Preferences by Constructing Institutions: A Cultural Theory of Preference Formation." *American Political Science Review* 81, no. 1 (1987): 4–31.

———. *The Rise of Radical Egalitarianism*. Washington, D.C.: American University Press, 1991.

Wolf, Naomi. *The Beauty Myth: How Images of Beauty Are Used against Women*. New York: Morrow, 1991.

Wood, G. *The Creation of the American Republic*. New York: Norton, 1969.

Young, Robert C. *Colonial Desire: Hybridity in Theory, Culture, and Race*. London: Routledge, 1995.

# INDEX

*Note*: "t" following a page number indicates a table.

film in, 92, 96; and cultural trade, 179, 184, 188, 189; fragmegration in, 199–201; U.S. relations with, 198, 199
franchises: advantages of, 134–35; and brand identities, 136–37; defined, 134; history of, 137–40; NFL teams as, 162; top global, 139t
Frankfurt School, 27–28, 78, 80, 92, 99
freedom, 3–5. *See also* liberty
free trade: democracy associated with, 6; global role of, 6, 20–21; nation-state politics and, 23–24; obstacles to, 7; opposition to, 183–86; principles of, 20; problems with, 21–22; United States and, 22, 160, 181–83
Frito-Lay, 57, 234
Fukuyama, Francis, 152

gangsta rap, 56, 81
Gans, Herbert, 14
GATT. *See* General Agreement on Tariffs and Trade (GATT)
Gellner, Ernest, 38
gender, stereotypical roles, 49–50. *See also* men; women
General Agreement on Tariffs and Trade (GATT), 21, 181, 186–89
General Agreement on Trade in Services (GATS), 189
General Motors, 21, 140
Georgia Institute of Technology, 200
Germany: American movies in, 103; American television in, 121
Ghonim, Wael, 215
Gifford, Frank, 163
*Girls Gone Wild* (videos), 53
Gitlin, Todd, 2–3

Givenchy, 158
globalization: American popular culture and, 2–10, 19, 22–23; and anti-globalization, 206–8; AV entertainment production in context of, 85–86; characteristics of, 18; Coca-Cola and, 147; concept of, 17–19; cultural, 26–31, 206; economic, 19–23, 147, 206; Facebook and, 168–69; future of American popular culture and, 228–29, 235–44; and global culture, 241–42; McDonald's and, 151–55; nation-states and, 23–25, 207; opposition and resistance to, 25–26; opposition to, 18; politics and, 3–10, 23–26; *Star Trek* and, 70; two-way operation of, 30, 229, 232–33, 240; Venezuela and, 207
global mélange, 30
Global North, 230, 236, 242, 243
Global South, 230, 236, 242, 243
Global War on Terror (GWoT), 8–10
glocalization, 31
*Godfather* movies, 103
*The Gods Must Be Crazy* (movie), 146
Goldwater, Barry, 101
*Gone with the Wind* (movie), 46
"Goodbye Earl" (song), 48, 49
Google, 127, 169, 212, 238
Gore, Al, 111
Gore, Tipper, 111
*Grace under Fire* (television show), 47
*Grand Ole Opry* (radio show), 75
Grateful Dead, 78
Great Britain: and Hong Kong, 209; newspapers in, 95; television programming in, 240. *See also* United Kingdom, television in

# ABOUT THE AUTHOR

**Lane Crothers** is professor of politics and government at Illinois State University. He earned his Ph.D. in political science at Vanderbilt University and worked at both the University of Alabama in Huntsville and Eastern Washington University before coming to Illinois State University in 1994. His expertise is in the fields of political culture, political leadership, and U.S. foreign policy. He is author or co-author of four other books, including *Rage on the Right: The American Militia Movement from Ruby Ridge to Homeland Security* (with Rowman & Littlefield), *Street Level Leadership: Discretion and Legitimacy in Front-Line Public Service*, and *Culture and Politics: A Reader*, as well as several articles in the fields of political culture and political leadership.